Greg Perry

SAMS
Teach Yourself
Microsoft®
Windows XP
in 24 Hours

SAMS
201 West 103rd St., Indianapolis, Indiana, 46290 USA

Sams Teach Yourself Microsoft® Windows XP in 24 Hours

Copyright © 2002 by Sams Publishing

International Standard Book Number: 0-672-32217-X

Library of Congress Catalog Card Number: 2001089384

Printed in the United States of America

First Printing: September 2001

04   03   02   01   4   3   2   1

Trademarks

Warning and Disclaimer

ACQUISITIONS EDITOR
Betsy Brown

DEVELOPMENT EDITOR
Scott D. Meyers

MANAGING EDITOR
Charlotte Clapp

PROJECT EDITOR
Elizabeth Finney

COPY EDITOR
Karen Gill

PROOFREADER
Rowena Rappaport

INDEXER
Angie Bess

TECHNICAL EDITOR
Dallas Releford

TEAM COORDINATOR
Amy Patton

INTERIOR DESIGNER
Gary Adair

COVER DESIGNER
Aren Howell

Contents at a Glance

Contents

About the Author

GREG PERRY is a speaker and writer on both the programming and the application sides of computing. He is known for his skills at bringing advanced computer topics to the novice's level. Perry has been a programmer and trainer since the early 1980s. He received his first degree in computer science and then a master's degree in corporate finance. Perry's books have sold more than two million copies worldwide, with most of his titles being translated into several foreign languages. His works include *Sams Teach Yourself Office 2000 in 24 Hours*, *Absolute Beginner's Guide to Programming*, and *Sams Teach Yourself Visual Basic 6 in 21 Days*. He also writes about rental-property management, designs and produces Web pages, and travels as a hobby.

Dedication

This book is for a friend, Mark Seleznov in Scottsdale, a pro at financial education and the master in his field. You taught me exactly what I've needed for a long time, Mark. Thanks for all you do!

Acknowledgments

I have the opportunity to work with the best people in the publishing business. My sincere thanks go to the editors and staff at Sams Publishing who strive to produce computer books that teach all levels of computer users from beginners to experts. The people at Sams Publishing take their jobs seriously because they want readers to have only the best books possible.

During the production of this book, Betsy Brown did her usual: led this project to near-perfection in spite of all my mishandling along the way! Betsy has become the backbone of my projects and for that I'm grateful.

Elizabeth Finney continued her tradition of improving upon my raw writing until the writing actually became readable. I appreciate knowing Elizabeth and I thank her for the effort she puts into these books.

In addition to Betsy and Elizabeth, Dallas G. Releford found my mistakes and guided my accuracy. Scott Meyers helped develop this project and although he humbly doesn't admit to working hard, I know that he did. I appreciate everything, Scott.

I alone am responsible for any problems if there are any.

My lovely and gracious bride, Jayne, stands by my side day in and day out. Thank you, my dear Jayne. Thanks also to my Dad and Mom, Glen and Bettye Perry, who are my biggest fans. I love you all.

Tell Us What You Think!

As the reader of this book, *you* are our most important critic and commentator. We value your opinion and want to know what we're doing right, what we could do better, what areas you'd like to see us publish in, and any other words of wisdom you're willing to pass our way.

You can e-mail or write me directly to let me know what you did or didn't like about this book—as well as what we can do to make our books stronger.

Please note that I cannot help you with technical problems related to the topic of this book, and that due to the high volume of mail I receive, I might not be able to reply to every message.

When you write, please be sure to include this book's title and author as well as your name and phone or fax number. I will carefully review your comments and share them with the author and editors who worked on the book.

E-mail: consumer@samspublishing.com

Mail: Mark Taber
          Associate Publisher
          Sams Publishing
          201 West 103rd Street
          Indianapolis, IN 46290 USA

Introduction

You probably are anxious to get started with your 24-hour Windows XP tutorial. Windows XP is an exciting operating system by Microsoft, a completely revamped operating system from the Windows 9x and Windows Me operating systems that have been in use for many years. Windows XP uses the Windows 2000 code base as its foundation to provide a more stable and robust environment.

This book's goal is to get you up to speed as quickly as possible. Take just a few preliminary moments to acquaint yourself with the design of this book described in the next few sections.

What's New with Windows

Different, better, and still the same best describes how Windows XP compares to previous versions of Windows. Despite the similarities, Windows XP has some major differences that you should know about ahead of time so you can use it the way it is supposed to be used. Microsoft designed Windows XP so that you can concentrate on using your software and hardware rather than concentrate on using Windows XP.

Windows XP improves upon the Windows 9x interface that has become the standard. If you are new to the Windows environments—perhaps because you upgraded from a Mac operating system—consider yourself fortunate! You are about to be impressed. Following are some of the Windows XP key features:

- The Internet's online environment is more closely associated with the Windows desktop.

- Windows XP provides extensive support for multimedia and digital imaging.

- The Start menu is more operational and hides little-used programs until you're ready to access them. The items you need are always at your fingertips. You can make menu changes on-the-fly without messy dialog boxes.

- Advanced system tools, such as the automatic update of Windows system files when they become damaged and a rollback feature that enables you to return to a more stable point in time, help protect your computer files and monitor your hardware.

- Improved hardware support features enable you to attach new devices, such as FireWire cameras, into your computer without having to set hardware switches or determine appropriate interrupt settings.

- Windows XP continues the tradition of online support and provides firewall protection from unauthorized access into your computer.
- Windows XP does most of the setup work for you when you want to network another computer to yours.
- You can monitor newsgroups and make postings from Outlook Express's common interface.
- Your desktop now becomes an online access tool that lets you access Internet Web pages as easily as you access your own PC's files.

What This Book Will Do for You

Although this is not a reference book, you'll learn almost every aspect of Windows XP from the user's point of view. This book does not take up your time with those many advanced technical details that most of you will never need. I know that you want to get up to speed with Windows XP in 24 hours, and this book fulfills its goal.

Both the background and the theory that a new Windows XP user needs are presented. In addition to the background discussions, this book is practical and provides almost 100 useful step-by-step To Do tasks that you can work through to gain hands-on experience. The To Do tasks guide you through all the common Windows XP actions you'll need to make Windows XP work for you, instead of you working to use Windows XP.

Can This Book Really Teach Windows XP in 24 Hours?

Yes. You can master each chapter in one hour or less (by the way, chapters are referred to as "hours" in the rest of the book). Although some chapters are longer than others, the material is balanced. The longer chapters contain several tasks, and the shorter chapters contain background material. The balance provided by the tasks, background, and insightful explanations and tips make learning Windows XP fresh at every page.

Conventions Used in This Book

A question-and-answer section ends each chapter to reinforce ideas. This book also uses several common conventions to help teach the Windows XP topics. Following is a summary of the typographical conventions:

- The first time a new term appears, the term is *italicized*.
- Commands and computer output appear in a special `monospaced` computer font.
- Words you type appear in a **boldfaced** computer font.
- If a task requires you to select from a menu, the commands are separated with a comma. For example, this book uses File, Save As to select the Save As command from the File menu.

In addition to typographical conventions, the following special elements are included to set off different types of information to make them easily recognizable:

> Special notes augment the material you are reading in each hour. They clarify concepts and procedures.

> You'll find numerous tips that offer shortcuts and solutions to common problems.

> The Caution sections warn you about pitfalls. Reading them will save you time and trouble.

> Take some time out of your 24-hour tutorial to sit back and enjoy a more in-depth look at a particular feature. The coffee break sidebars are useful for exploring unusual Office XP features and uses and show you additional ways to utilize the hour's material.

Who Should Read This Book

Although this book is geared toward beginning computer and Windows users, advanced users will find it handy as well. Readers rarely believe that lofty claim for good reason, but the design of this book and the nature of Windows XP make it possible for this book to address such a wide audience. Here is why: Windows XP is a major improvement over the previous versions of Windows because of its secure, stable structure as well as its ease of integration into the networking, multimedia, and Internet's online technology. If you do not yet use the Internet, you'll pick up Internet skills faster with Windows XP due to the online efforts that Microsoft put into Windows XP.

Those of you unfamiliar with windowed environments will find plenty of introductory help to bring you up to speed quickly. This book teaches you how to start, exit, and manage almost every aspect of Windows XP. This book talks *to* beginners but does not talk *down* to beginners.

For those of you who presently use Windows 9x and Windows Me, this book also addresses you. Here is how: This book has several sidebars that explain how a specific Windows XP feature improves on or replaces a Windows 9x feature. With your fundamental base of Windows 9x understanding, you'll appreciate the new Windows XP features. Windows XP is similar to Windows 9x, so you will feel comfortable learning Windows XP. However, Windows XP has more than enough new features to keep Windows 95 and Windows 9x users interested and happy for a long time.

What to Do Now

What are you waiting for? Turn the page and get started on your 24-hour tutorial!

PART I
Wake Up with Windows XP

Hour

Hour 1

Taking a Bird's-Eye Look at Windows XP

Who says that a productive computer user cannot have fun being productive? Windows XP, often just called Windows, from the Microsoft Corporation, is colorful, fun, friendly, and powerful. This hour introduces you to Windows XP. You will see Windows XP's best features. Also, you will learn how Windows XP improves upon previous versions of Windows and provides much support for new media devices such as digital audio, cameras, and video.

In this hour, you will

- Learn why Windows XP is more robust than previous operating systems
- Read about the many versions of Windows XP
- See the minimum computing power required for Windows XP
- Learn how Windows XP greatly enhances the multimedia experience

Windows XP Simply Works Better

Microsoft redesigned the entire Windows interface to produce Windows XP. Windows XP is more colorful than previous editions. Windows XP's user interface is improved to allow you easier access to your programs and data. The *icons* (small pictures that represent options) and menus and windows have a more modern look to them. You'll enjoy working with Windows XP but if you really like the former Windows Me look, Windows XP enables you to easily change to the more traditional *Classic view* inside most windows.

As you become accustomed to Windows XP, you'll see that the entire operating system not only is more visual than previous Windows but XP has a similar feel to working on Web pages. With each version of Windows, Microsoft has attempted to tie the Internet more into the operating system's interface. The Internet will continue to play an important role in all computing and the Windows XP's graphical interface provides a Web-like feel.

As Figure 1.1 shows, when you point to a selection on the screen, Windows XP underlines the item not unlike a Web-page hyperlink; click once on the link and Windows XP takes you there.

FIGURE 1.1

Windows XP screens work as though they are pages on the Internet.

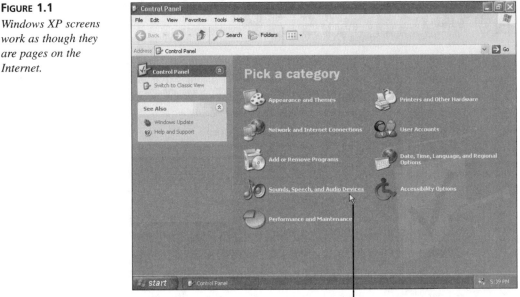

Mouse points to selection

1

More important than the interface, however, is Microsoft's completely redesigned operating system. If you're already using Windows 9x (including Windows 95 and Windows 98) or Windows Me, you know that, although those are decent operating systems, you still must reboot more often than you'd like. Things don't always act according to plan. This is because Microsoft designed these operating systems to take advantage of much older hardware than that which appears today, sacrificing some stability for maximum compatibility.

> The problems associated with those previous versions of Windows are not always the fault of Windows. Many third-party programs must consume some important system areas inside your computer. Earlier Windows versions tried their best to keep things straight but couldn't always compete with misbehaving applications.

Windows XP's entire foundation is rewritten and based on the Windows 2000 technology that provides a more stable and robust operating environment. Windows XP simply won't let those misbehaving programs get away with all they do inside other Windows versions. This means that not all your older applications (called *legacy applications* if they were written with an earlier Windows operating system in mind, generally pre-Windows 98) will work under Windows XP. XP offers a special *compatibility mode* that tricks XP into running many of those legacy applications that would not run under straight Windows XP. You'll learn more about the compatibility mode in Hour 8, "Installing Programs with Windows XP."

Windows XP Comes in Several Flavors

Windows XP comes in multiple editions:

- Windows XP Home Edition: The Home Edition is more consumer-focused, works well as an Internet-sharing operating systems, and provides the primary upgrade path for Windows 9x and Windows Me users.

- Windows XP Professional Edition: Upgrades Windows 2000 and provides tools needed for typical business-oriented processing such as support for advanced network configuration. Good for small businesses and corporate desktops.

- A Windows XP-based Server Edition: Used for systems that act as network and Internet servers that provide data and programs for large networks connected to the server.

- Windows XP-based Advanced Server Edition: An enterprise server system for massive networking server solutions.

 Special 64-bit editions of XP are available for advanced 64-bit Intel Itanium-based computer systems.

This 24-hour tutorial focuses on the Home Edition of Windows XP. Appendix A, "Differences Between the Windows Home and Professional Edition," explains the primary differences between Windows XP Home Edition and the Windows XP Professional Edition.

Do You Have the Necessary Hardware?

Microsoft admits that Windows XP is the next generation operating system. As mentioned in this lesson's first section, XP may not run legacy programs. Even worse, depending on your point of view, Windows XP won't run well on older hardware.

Table 1.1 lists the minimum hardware requirements for computers running Windows XP. More important than the minimum hardware is the recommended hardware (second column) for adequate performance. To bring your computer up to Windows XP's hungry hardware requirements, you might have to add more memory or disk space.

TABLE 1.1   Hardware Requirements for Windows XP

Component	Minimum Hardware	Recommended Hardware
Processor	Pentium III-233MHz	Pentium III-500MHz
Memory	64MB	128MB (64MB for each concurrent user is best)
Free Disk Space	1 Gigabyte	2 Gigabytes (one gig is required simply to install Windows XP)
Monitor	15-inch	17-inch

Getting a Feel for Windows XP

Most users like the look and simplicity of Windows XP and they appreciate the fact that Windows XP is also enjoyable to use. Although Windows XP is both fun and easy to master, it is also a computer interface system that offers tremendous power for anyone who uses PCs. With Windows XP you can manage your computer's hardware, data files, and online content easily, even if you are new to computers.

Windows XP contains a computer interface that attempts to please all groups of people, including novice computer users and advanced computer programmers. To achieve the lofty goal of pleasing a broad spectrum of users, Microsoft made Windows XP intuitive without being intrusive. In addition to a new interface, Windows XP blurs the distinction between your home or office PC and other computers around the world. XP's operating environment incorporates the online world because the information you want is not always on your hard disk. Windows XP helps you access the Internet as easily as you access the files on your own PC.

Figure 1.2 shows a typical Windows XP screen that Windows XP users might see. This Windows XP screen is often called a *desktop*, which you learn to manage just as you manage the desk at which you sit. Your screen might show a different set of icons, pictures, and text, and perhaps your desktop's background (called *wallpaper*) is different, but you'll see many of the same elements on your screen. In the Figure 1.2, the button labeled Start was clicked in the lower-left corner of the screen to produce the menu of options you see.

FIGURE 1.2

The Windows XP desktop is where you start programs and manage windows.

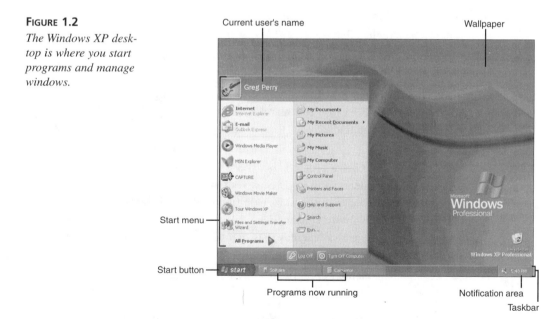

The Windows XP screen acts like a desktop from which to work on your computer. If you have a word processing program and you want to write letters, you would start the word processor program from the Windows XP environment. Windows XP is always there to help you interact with your programs and with the computer hardware.

Today you control computers through *graphical user interfaces* (*GUIs* pronounced *gooeys*), which provide visual interfaces that you control such as *icons* (pictures that represent programs), buttons, and scroll bars. Operating systems such as Windows XP no longer require the tedium of typed commands required by older computer environments. Windows XP is extremely graphical in nature. Instead of typing a command that directs the computer to start a program, you use the mouse or keyboard to point to an icon on the screen to activate the matching program.

If you are fairly new to computers, you might not understand why you would want to use Windows XP. Perhaps you've used a word processor or a spreadsheet but never have taken the time to find out what Windows is all about. Other newcomers to Windows XP might have migrated to the PC world from a Mac or from a big, mainframe computer. In a nutshell, Windows XP is all of the following:

- An operating system that manages your hardware and software operations. Windows XP provides uniform access to your system so that programs can better use your system's resources (such as disks and printers).

- A graphical user interface that enables you to start programs, go online, and control hardware graphically.

- Total Web integration that blurs the distinction between the PC on your desk and Internet pages.

- A platform from which you can listen to music, edit photographs, and watch DVDs. If you want help, you can search Windows XP help files or access the Internet to locate a help topic—all from within your desktop environment (see Figure 1.3).

- A secure system that helps protect against possible *virus programs* (programs that can destroy disk contents) and also keeps your system fine-tuned and running properly. With Internet access, you will be able to download the latest Windows updates as Microsoft releases future enhancements. A new *firewall* system, a program that monitors your online environment, exists that helps keep online intruders out of your computer's files as you surf the Web.

- A network management system that helps seamlessly integrate a *network* (a wired connection to other computers) and the Internet into your work environment.

Possibly the single greatest reason to use Windows XP is this: Microsoft designed Windows XP so that you can concentrate on using your software and hardware—not so that you have to concentrate on using Windows XP commands. As you'll see throughout these 24 lessons, the keyboard and mouse complement each other to give you easy control over every aspect of Windows XP.

FIGURE 1.3

The Windows Help and Support pages search both your PC and, optionally, the Internet to give you answers when you need assistance.

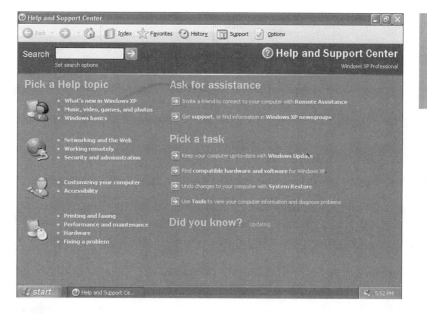

Mouse Around

The odds are good that you've used a mouse if you've used a computer before. Using the mouse involves following the *mouse pointer* arrow (also called the *mouse cursor*) around the screen. In Hour 4, you learn how to change the mouse pointer's shape from the arrow to something else.

Here's a quick review of the possible mouse actions you can perform:

- When you *move* the mouse, you physically move the mouse across your desk. (You might have a trackball, which remains stationary as you spin the trackball's sphere to move the pointer. Other mouse alternatives include touch pads that you point to and run your finger over to simulate mouse clicks and movements.) When you point to an object on the screen, you are moving the mouse to that object.

- When you click the mouse, you press and immediately release the left mouse button. To select graphical screen objects, you often click the left button. You use your right mouse button to display special pop-up menus. Hour 4 explains how to swap the left and right mouse button actions if you are left-handed.

- When you double-click, you press and immediately release the left mouse button twice in succession.

- When you drag screen objects with the mouse, you move the mouse pointer over an object that you want to move to another screen location. With the mouse pointer over the object, press and hold the left mouse button. The item under the mouse pointer is now temporarily welded to the mouse pointer. As you move the mouse (while still holding the mouse button), the screen object moves with the pointer. When you release the mouse button, Windows XP anchors the object in the mouse pointer's new position. In Windows terminology, *drag and drop* refers to the action of moving a screen object (such as an icon) to a different location. You can also use your right mouse button to drag items from one location to another in special cases explained throughout this text.

> Later hours will teach you additional ways to use the mouse. For example, the mouse can help you create special links, called *shortcuts*, to programs you use often. In addition, you can use the mouse to copy objects, such as files, from one location to another.

You can almost always use the keyboard instead of the mouse to perform many Windows XP operations. For many users, using the mouse is often easier than using the keyboard. If you are uncomfortable using a mouse, don't fret—mouse actions soon become second nature.

If you've used an earlier Windows version, you'll appreciate how Windows XP enables you to use a single-click to select screen objects instead of the double-click so common in previous versions. Microsoft wanted Windows items to respond as links just as Web pages connect to each other by links that you click.

Windows XP Knows Multimedia

More than any other operating system that came before it, Windows XP knows how to handle multimedia content. Windows XP includes operating system applications that can manipulate and play all kinds of digital information that comes in the form of audio or video.

Windows Media Player Grows Up

The *Windows Media Player*, an application that plays music and digital video, has
improved since version 1 and now, with version 8, which comes bundled with XP, Media
Player (see Figure 1.4) is a serious contender in the narrowing field of audio and video
players.

FIGURE 1.4

*Media Player plays
audio files, music CDs,
digital video, and
DVDs.*

> If you have Internet access, check out Microsoft's support site for the Media
> Player, http://www.WindowsMedia.com/, where you can get music, videos,
> news, weather, and much more content for Media Player.

If you have a CD writer, Media Player can create audio CDs by putting digital music
files that you drag together onto CDs. Media Player can locate music online. If you're
logged onto the Internet, Media Player automatically locates (in most cases) the CD's
song *playlist* (the CD's list of songs that you can organize into categorical playlists of
your own and name such as *My Jazz Collection*) and displays information about the
artist.

Data isn't just for numbers anymore

In the half a century or so that computers have been around, *data* has generally referred to facts and figures, stored in text and numeric formats that the computers processed. Numbers and text used to be the only kind of data that could be represented in the digital form that computers require to process and store.

Today, data is not limited to numbers and text. Given that so much audio, video, and photography is now digital, your computer processes virtually any kind of data imaginable.

The new forms of data require new kinds of programs to process and manipulate that data. That's why Windows XP comes packed full of programs that play audio and manage your music collection, provide video-editing tools, and capture and organize your photo collections.

Given the full-feature set of the Media Player, Microsoft added a moderately equipped video-editing program to Windows XP called the *Windows Movie Maker*. With Movie Maker, you can take clips from a video or from several videos, stored on your disk drive, and edit them into a single video feature that you then can play with Media Player.

Hour 23, "Making Movies with Windows XP," shows you how to use Movie Maker. Who knows, you might win an Oscar!

The My Music Folder Adds Functionality

Previous versions of Windows created a folder named My Music in which you could store all your music files. Windows XP goes one step further and adds a complete music search (in various ways, such as by title, artist, or music category) and can include cover art of your albums, which you can view while listening to your tunes.

Figure 1.5 shows the My Music folder. If you click a song or select multiple songs (such as holding Ctrl while clicking more than one song file), you then can click Play Selection to play the audio.

Your computer can store and process audio, such as that found on audio CDs, in several formats. Perhaps the most popular format is *MPEG-3*, a compact way to store music on disks and stored with the filename extension .mp3. The native Media Player format typically uses either the .asf or .wma filename extension. Other formats exist and Media Player can usually recognize and play most of them. You'll learn more about multimedia files and how to manage them in Hour 21, "Using Media Player."

FIGURE 1.5

The My Music folder is a complete repository for your music files.

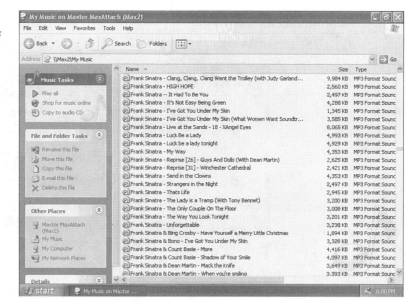

Of course, many people use Windows XP's audio features for background music while working. Simply select a few songs to play and then start your word processor or spreadsheet to begin your workday.

Your Windows XP Film Developer

The My Pictures folder is another way that Windows XP goes the extra step to help you manage your graphical data.

Figure 1.6 shows the My Pictures folder. Notice the options in the upper-left corner of the window. You can select multiple pictures and view them as a slide show, print pictures if you have an appropriate printer, and select a picture to use as your Windows XP desktop wallpaper.

Microsoft has teamed up with film development companies. When you select one or more prints and click Order prints from the Internet, the My Pictures folder automatically sends your selected photos to a developer and the prints soon arrive in your mail box (for a small charge, of course). The traditional film-to-store process is greatly streamlined and if you use a digital camera or scanner to store pictures on your computer, you will use the My Pictures window quite a bit.

FIGURE **1.6**

The My Pictures folder not only manages your pictures but helps you see slide shows and develop them into prints.

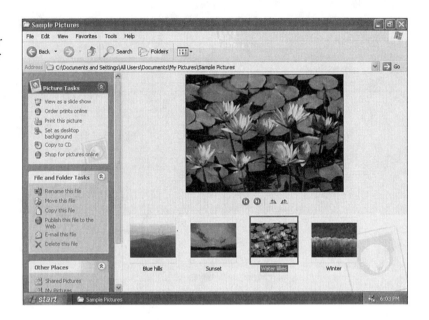

In addition to managing your stored photos, you'll be able to print your pictures directly from a digital camera or scanner. Select the paper type and photo layout and Windows XP does the rest. If you'd rather send your photos as e-mail, you may do so.

Make Sure You Understand Windows Controls

Before getting into specifics of Windows operations in the upcoming hourly lessons, make sure that you have a fundamental grasp of routine Windows operations. As you work with Windows XP, you'll see all kinds of windows appear and disappear.

A Window such as the one shown in Figure 1.7 is sometimes called a *dialog box*. Dialog boxes contain various *controls* with which to manage Windows XP. These controls can be *command buttons* that you click with your mouse to start or cancel a task; *check boxes* with a check mark, indicating an item you selected by clicking the mouse over the box; and *option buttons* that you select from a choice of options.

If a dialog box contains a *dropdown list*, you can click the list's down arrow to open the list and see the options that appear. Some dialog boxes contain multiple tabbed pages so that you can read and select from two or more pages of controls within the same dialog box.

FIGURE 1.7

Dialog boxes often contain several controls that select options and determine behavior.

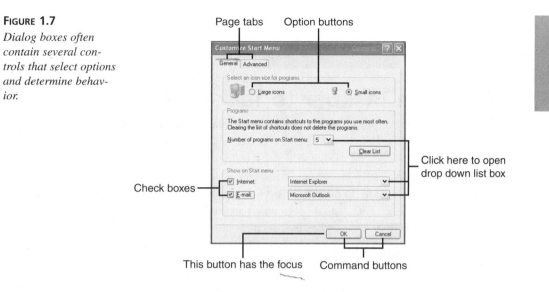

Page tabs   Option buttons

Check boxes

Click here to open drop down list box

This button has the focus   Command buttons

There are three ways to select an onscreen command button:

1. Click the button with the mouse.

2. Press Tab to highlight the buttons in succession. Shift+Tab moves backward. You will know that a button is highlighted by its darker outline around the button. Moving the highlight between onscreen controls is called *changing the focus*. As soon as the focus (the dotted highlight) appears on the button you want to select, press Enter to activate that button.

3. If a key's caption begins with an underlined letter, press Alt plus the underlined letter to trigger the button's action. This combined keystroke is called a *hotkey*. (Windows XP hides a dialog box's hotkeys until you press the Alt key on your keyboard.) Press Alt and, when the underlined hotkeys appear, you can press any button's underlined letter to trigger that button's action.

Certain windows use check boxes to indicate yes or no possibilities.

There are three ways to check (or uncheck) a check box:

1. Using the mouse, click either the check box or the message next to the check box.

2. Move the focus to the check box text (by pressing Tab or Shift+Tab) and press Enter.

3. Press Alt plus the hotkey of the check box's message.

In Hour 2, "Getting Started with Windows XP," you learn how to open and change to new windows without closing an existing window completely; it will be out of your way, but you will be able to return to it whenever you want.

Taking the Taskbar to Task

The area at the bottom of your Windows XP screen is known as the *taskbar*, and this primary button at the left is the *Start button*. The taskbar is perhaps the most important element in Windows XP because you'll use it to launch and switch between running programs. Windows XP *multitasks*, which means that you can run more than one program at the same time. In other words, you can download a file from another computer, print a spreadsheet, listen to an opera on an audio CD, and type with a word processor, all at the same time. The taskbar lists each program currently running. Figure 1.8 shows a taskbar that lists two programs and the My Computer window in memory at the same time.

FIGURE 1.8
The taskbar lists every open window.

Start button

Notification area

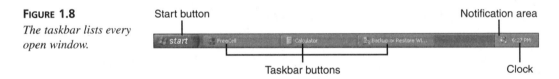

Taskbar buttons

Clock

Think of the taskbar as a television channel changer. On a television, there are several channels with programs going at the same time; you can switch between the channels by using the remote control. When you run more than one Windows XP program, you can switch among the programs by clicking the program buttons in the taskbar. The taskbar changes as you start and stop programs. Also, the taskbar's notification area changes so that only icons for commonly-used Windows elements appear at any one time.

Windows XP offers a tremendous number of ways to customize your desktop. You can often hide Windows XP elements that you don't use, including many items on the taskbar. Your taskbar might look slightly different from the ones shown in this book. Many screens in this book hide the taskbar intentionally so as to provide more space for the item being highlighted at the time.

The taskbar does more than list and manage running programs—it is the starting point for just about everything you do in Windows XP. If you want to rearrange files, start programs, change screen colors, modify the mouse, or view the contents of files, the taskbar contains the power to do all those things. The taskbar is your Windows XP launch pad.

The Start Menu: Your Windows Cockpit

At the left of your taskbar lies the *Start button*, a button that you click to display the *Start menu*. (You can press your keyboard's Windows key to display the Start menu also.) Figure 1.9 shows a typical Start menu. The Start menu gives you access to every part of your computer. Table 1.1 describes what each part of the Start menu does. From the Start menu, you can start programs, check disk space, manage files, and properly shut down the computer. You might also add additional programs at the top of the taskbar to launch those programs more quickly.

FIGURE 1.9

The Start menu is the command center for the rest of Windows XP.

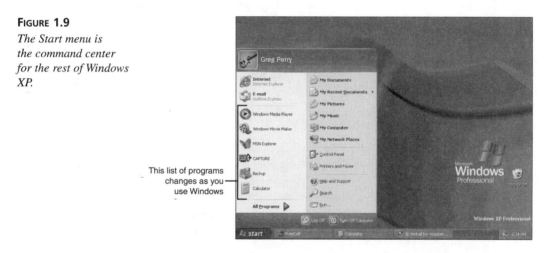

This list of programs changes as you use Windows

TABLE 1.1 Common Start Menu Commands

Section	Description
Program Names	Displays a list of the most recent programs you've used.
All Programs	Click to see a list of every program currently installed on your computer. Many are grouped together in folders that you can open by clicking that folder.
My Documents	Displays a window that contains the My Documents folder contents.
My Recent Documents	Displays a list of documents, or data files, that you've recently opened and might want to return to. Windows XP works from a data-driven viewpoint and enables you to work on your data without worrying about tedious program-starting details. Selecting a

TABLE 1.1 continued

Section	Description
	document, no matter which program created that document, launches the program and loads that data document into the program.
My Pictures	Opens your My Pictures window.
My Music	Opens your My Music window.
My Computer	Opens your My Computer window so that you can manage your computer's resources.
My Network Places	Opens your My Network Places window so that you can manage the network you might currently be connected to.
Control Panel	Enables you to change the configuration of Windows XP.
Printers and Faxes	Provides a list of installed printers and faxes inside your computer and enables you to add new ones.
Help and Support	Provides online help for the various tasks you can perform in Windows XP.
Search	Enables you to search your computer's and other computer's files for specific data.
Run	Gives you the ability to execute programs or open program group folders if you know the proper commands.
Log off	Enables you to release your computer's resources so that someone else can use your computer. If you work in a multiuser environment, you and others can log on to Windows XP, and Windows XP remembers your previous settings.
Turn off computer	Enables you to safely shut down your computer without losing data that you might otherwise lose if you did not shut down properly.

Place the mouse pointer over the Start button, but do not click the mouse button. After a brief pause, Windows XP displays a small *ToolTip* pop-up text box next to the mouse pointer that reads Click here to begin. If you are unsure what a Windows XP button does, move the mouse cursor over the button and wait a moment for the pop-up text box to appear.

1

Summary

You are off to a great start! It's time to push your own Start button, gear up your mind's memory chips, and begin exploring Windows XP to learn what it can do for you. Over the next 23 hours of study and tutorial, you will master the Windows XP environment and learn many shortcuts.

Keep in mind that Windows XP is not an end in itself. The application programs that you want to run are the most important parts of using your computer. It is Windows XP's job to help you work with your applications as painlessly as possible.

Q&A

Q How can Windows manage so many kinds of data?

A Actually, Windows can only manage digital data very well, but in today's world, many kinds of information, including pictures, video, and sound can easily be digitized.

Q What is the purpose of the taskbar?

A The taskbar shows you the programs and windows currently open as well as contains the Start button that produces the Start menu.

Workshop

The quiz and exercise questions are designed to test your knowledge of the material covered in this hour. The answers are in Appendix C, "Answers to Quizzes."

Quiz

1. Why is the Windows screen called the *desktop*?
2. *True or false*: Windows XP comes in several versions.
3. What is the difference between moving and dragging your mouse?
4. What is the artwork called on your Windows desktop?
5. What is a ToolTip?

Exercises

1. Start your computer, let Windows XP start (you may have to select an account at an opening screen to indicate who you are), and click the Start button once Windows XP loads.

2. Display the Windows help system by displaying your Start menu and selecting Help and Support. Look through the help screens to learn more about Windows XP. Hour 6, "Calling for Help," explains how you can use the Help and Support screen to locate specific information that helps you use Windows XP more effectively.

HOUR 2

Getting Started with Windows XP

When you first begin using Windows XP you will immediately notice the account screen that requires you to select an account before proceeding. Accounts enable different users to maintain different Windows XP settings. You'll learn all about accounts in this hour's lesson.

In addition, you will master the ins and outs of Windows management. In an hour from now, you'll know how to open, close, minimize, maximize, and do just about everything else. (But don't worry—you won't have to clean any windows.)

In this hour, you

- Learn what an account is
- Set up an account for yourself
- Assign a password to your account
- Manage your desktop's windows to maneuver better throughout Windows XP

First Things First

Windows XP automatically starts when you turn on your computer. Before you can use Windows XP you must tell XP who you are.

Logging On

At one time, only users networked to other computers had to worry with *logging on*, the process of telling the computer who you are by entering a name and password to gain access to the files that you have access to. (Sometimes, logging on is called *signing on*.)

Windows XP lets many different users create their own *accounts*, with optional passwords. Each account contains all the settings that the account's user likes, such as screen colors, Start menu options, and other preferences. When someone first starts the computer, a Welcome screen appears with each user's account name and an associated icon. You can easily add new users, change an account's icon, and modify your password.

Three *permissions* are available for XP accounts. An account's permission determines how much access to the operating system that account is allowed to have. The permissions are

- Administrator: An administrator account allows changes to other users' account settings and has access to all areas of Windows XP. An administrator account is automatically created when you first install Windows XP, or one will be there when you first start a new computer with Windows XP. That Administrator account does not require a password until you log on as Administrator and assign a password to that account.

- Limited: A limited account allows changing of a user's own account settings and can access the parts of Windows XP that any Administrator account has given access to.

- Guest: A guest account allows the running of some programs with possible limited data file access but cannot access any of the system areas of Windows XP.

The reason for different accounts for different users becomes apparent when you think about how people use the computer. Some people might prefer a desktop wallpaper picture that differs from someone else's favorite. Some people may want to slow down the speed of their mouse movement or work with a desktop that has fewer icons getting in the way.

When you select your account after first starting Windows, Windows loads all your preferred settings. If you later log off and someone else comes along, they will log on with their account and, possibly, see entirely different settings.

Parents can have an account and the kids can have their own accounts. The kids can play games and change the Windows environment without affecting the Windows environment that the parents see when they log into Windows.

The following To Do item shows how to log on.

To Do: Logging into Windows XP

To Do

1. When you see the Welcome screen in Figure 2.1, click on your account name to log on.

2

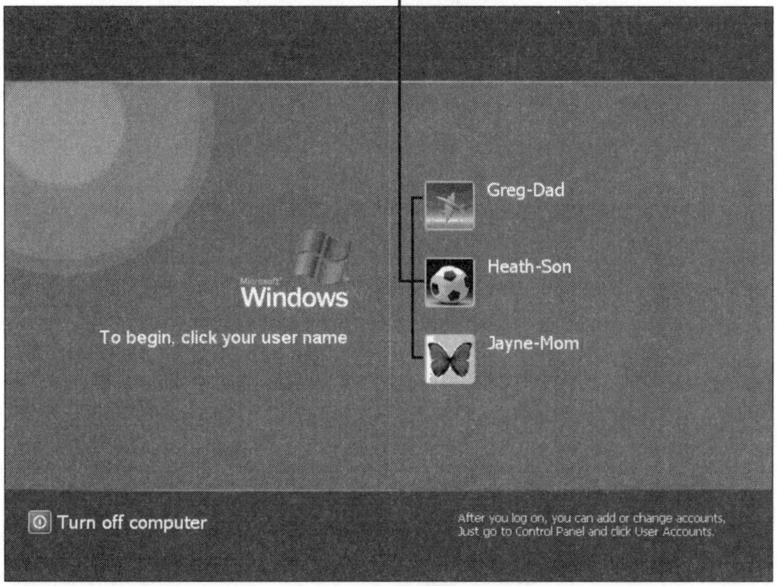

FIGURE 2.1

Each user can have a separate account with special file-access permissions and individual desktop settings.

Click any account to log on

2. Enter your account's password. (Windows XP will not ask for a password if the account has not been set up to require one.) The password will not appear on the screen but an asterisk (*) will appear as you type each character of your password. The asterisks help ensure that you don't reveal your password to someone who may be looking over your shoulder.

3. The Windows XP desktop appears and conforms to your account. If you've recently made changes to your desktop, those changes will be reflected in the desktop that you see. If you make further changes to your desktop, such as change the background wallpaper, Windows XP remembers the change the next time you log on.

▲

Notice that the Welcome screen in Figure 2.1 shows that the account named Greg-Dad has two programs running. If e-mail was waiting for any of the users, Windows XP would also indicate that the mail is waiting for those users.

Windows XP supports *Fast User Switching* of accounts. Unlike most multiuser operating systems, Windows XP allows more than one account to be running at the same time, although only one is visible and available at any one time. Suppose Dad's paying bills with a financial program and little Heath needs to look up a foreign country's location on a Web page's map. Dad can simply log off without having to close programs or stop whatever he was doing. After Heath logs on, looks at the Internet map, then logs off, Dad can return to what he was doing simply by clicking his account at the Welcome screen. All the programs that Dad was running will now be running once again as though he'd never logged off. For example, if Dad was editing a document when he logged off and let Heath log on for a few minutes, the document will reappear when Dad logs back on again.

Your memory may limit the number of concurrent sessions running at any one time. Your computer should have 64 megabytes of memory for each user who will be running programs at the same time under different account settings. A five-member family should, therefore, have only two accounts running programs at the same time if the computer has only 128 megabytes of memory.

Proper Passwords Are Critical

Although passwords might not be as critical in a home setting as in a business environment in which sensitive business and payroll transactions are available, everybody should understand how to invent good passwords.

Make your passwords easy enough to remember but hard enough to make cracking them not worth the effort. Passwords should consist of letters and numbers. Make up a password that is not, by itself, a complete word or common name. Perhaps use your dog's name followed by the year your mother was born. Nonsense passwords are best, such as *qhoil25a*, but remember that you must not forget your password or getting back into your account may be a near impossibility.

One final password tip that will make your computing life safer is to change your password regularly. Even if you don't use passwords for your Windows XP accounts, keep these password suggestions in mind as you surf the Internet and put passwords on your Internet information and sites that require them.

Switching Accounts

If you're using Windows XP and need to log off so that someone else can do something on the computer, the following To Do item shows you how.

To Do: Switching Users

1. Click the Start button to display the Start menu.
2. Click Log off. The Log Off Windows dialog box appears like the one shown in Figure 2.2.

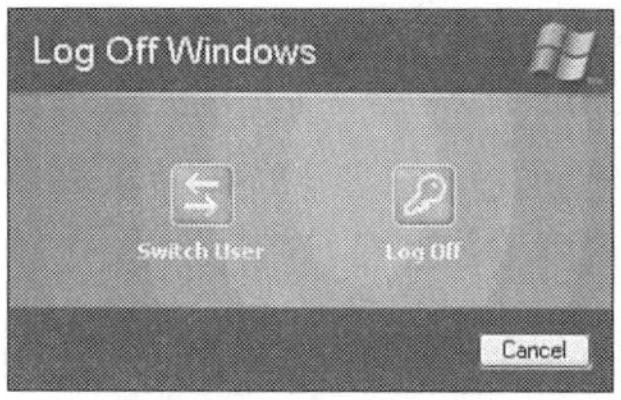

FIGURE 2.2
Tell Windows XP if you want to let someone else use the computer for a while or log off completely.

3. Click Switch User to let another account user log on. Click Log Off if you want to shut down your Windows XP session completely, including shutting down the programs you might be running.
4. If you selected Switch user, the Welcome screen will once again appear and display the list of accounts.

Accounts Aren't Just for Networks

A *network* is a set of two or more PCs connected together in some way. Network connections might consist of a single wire, a wireless connection, or a connection made available by the Internet.

By design, networks enable more than one user access to the same resources such as files and printers. In other words, assuming that you have the proper electronic authorization, you can access files stored on any person's PC that is connected to your PC. The extra benefits that a network provides also require extra security precautions so that unauthorized users do not have access to other people's files.

The nature of different users having their own accounts is critical in a networking environment where multiple users have access to the same files. Some users, such as a business's Payroll Department, might have access to files that other departments should not have rights to. By linking file authorizations to accounts, a Network Administrator can give special file rights to certain users. By adding the security of passwords to accounts, the Network Administrator helps ensure that files remain protected and only available to some people. Others might have read-only access but won't be able to change certain files.

With the Windows XP Home Edition, you don't have to work on a PC networked to another computer to utilize the accounts as you've seen throughout the previous sections of this lesson. Nevertheless, more and more homes are getting on the network band-wagon. Instead of throwing away an old, out-of-date computer, a family can now network that computer to a newer one, keeping the family files on the new computer with the larger disk drive, but allowing access to those files from either computer.

Windows XP simplifies networking computers together and sharing a single Internet connection over the network. Hour 13, "Networking with Windows XP," shows all you need to know to get started with networking.

Assigning and Changing Account Passwords

You can change an account's password as long as you're using an Administrator account or changing your own account. The following To Do item explains how.

To Do: Switching Users

1. Click the Start button to display the Start menu.

2. Select, by clicking, Control Panel. The Windows XP Control Panel, such as the one shown in Figure 2.3, appears. The Control Panel is where the Administrator can make changes to the operating system settings. Often, a user with any permission can make some changes from the Control Panel. Your Control Panel may look different from that of Figure 2.3, depending on your computer's settings. You'll learn all about the Control Panel in Hour 4, "Working with the My Computer Window."

3. Click User Accounts to display the User Accounts window.

4. Click the account you want to change in the bottom portion of the window. A list of options appears.

5. Click Create a password.

6. Type a password. As you type the password, asterisks appear.

7. Press the Tab key to move your *text cursor* (the blinking line that indicates where your next typed character will appear) to the next *field*. A field is a place that accepts data.

8. Retype the password. Windows XP compares the two passwords to ensure they match. This ensures that you actually typed what you wanted to type. (With the asterisks in the password fields, it's not always obvious if you type the wrong character when entering a password.)

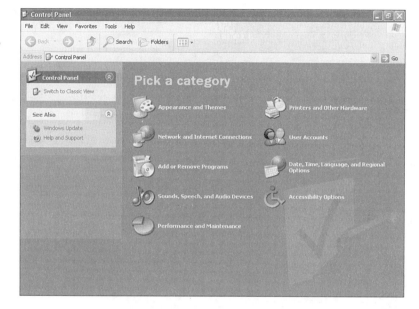

FIGURE **2.3**

Change your Windows XP system and desktop settings from the Control Panel.

9. Press the Tab key to move your text cursor to the next field.

10. Type a password hint. This is a hint that will appear when you log on to remind you what your password is in case you forget it. Make your hint good! You don't want your hint so easy that others figure out your password but you want your hint obvious enough to you to remember your password. Your screen should look something like the one in Figure 2.4.

11. Click the Create Password button. (Since the button's already highlighted and has the focus, you only need to press Enter to trigger the button's action.) Your account will now have the password.

12. Click the X in the window's upper-right corner to close the account window. (You've just clicked the window *Close* button.) The next time you log on with that account, you will be prompted for the password.

FIGURE 2.4
You'll have to type your account password twice and add a hint.

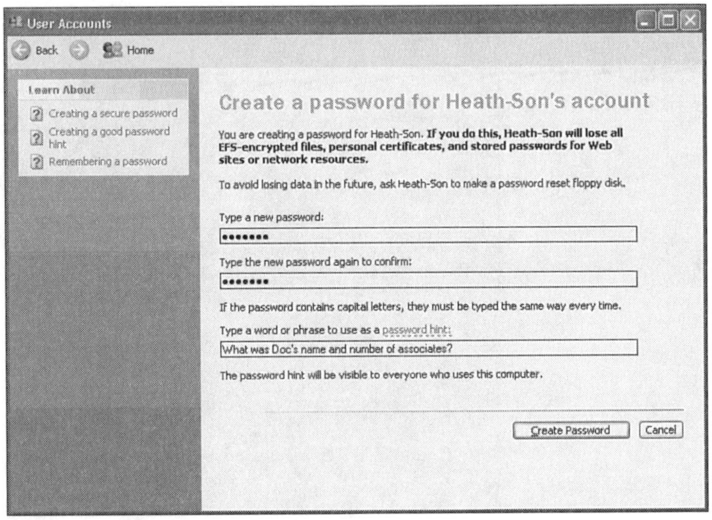

User Accounts

◀ Back ▶ Home

Learn About
? Creating a secure password
? Creating a good password hint
? Remembering a password

Create a password for Heath-Son's account

You are creating a password for Heath-Son. If you do this, Heath-Son will lose all EFS-encrypted files, personal certificates, and stored passwords for Web sites or network resources.

To avoid losing data in the future, ask Heath-Son to make a password reset floppy disk.

Type a new password:
•••••••

Type the new password again to confirm:
•••••••

If the password contains capital letters, they must be typed the same way every time.

Type a word or phrase to use as a password hint:
What was Doc's name and number of associates?

The password hint will be visible to everyone who uses this computer.

Create Password   Cancel

Shut Down Before Leaving

You are probably anxious to get started, but before you learn more about Windows XP, you should learn how to quit Windows XP properly. Because of the integration of Windows XP and your computer's hardware and software, you must take a few quick steps to quit your Windows XP session and turn off your computer.

If you do not properly shut down Windows XP, you can lose work that you just completed. At the worst, you can damage a Windows XP configuration file and cause problems for Windows XP the next time you start your PC.

Your Start menu contains commands necessary to shut down Windows XP and also your computer. Master the Windows XP shutdown process and get used to performing it to ensure that your files remain intact.

The most important command on the Start menu is the Turn off computer command. Before you do too much, even before you really master the ins and outs of the rest of the Start menu, learn how to shut down your computer safely. You don't want to write the first chapter of a best-selling novel only to find that Windows XP sent the chapter into oblivion because you did not shut down the computer properly before turning off the power.

The following To Do item explains how to turn off your computer safely.

To Do: Turning Off Your Computer

1. Close all programs.

2. Press the Start button to display the Start menu.

3. Select the Turn off computer command by clicking on it. Figure 2.5 shows the resulting Shut Down window.

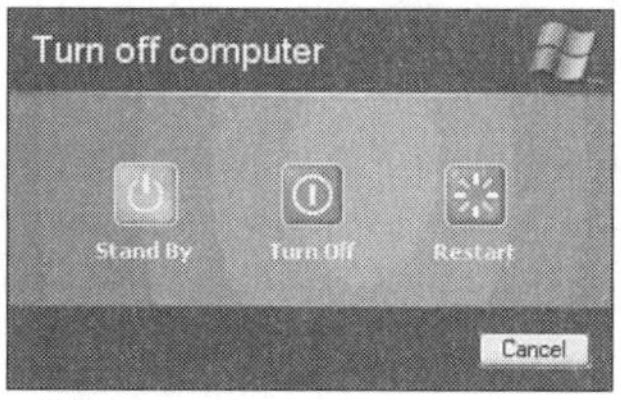

FIGURE 2.5

You must decide how you want to shut down the computer.

4. Select Stand By (by clicking the option) if you want to shut down much of your computer's power but keep your current programs open until you press a key. This option is useful for laptop users who want to temporarily stop working on their computer but who want to save battery life.

5. Select Turn Off to close all programs (if you didn't close them first) and shut down your computer. Depending on your monitor's support for XP's power-off signals, your computer screen might also power down.

6. Select Restart to simulate a power-down and power-up sequence to refresh your computer and restart Windows XP, displaying the log on screen.

If you change your mind about the shut down, you can select Cancel to return to your Windows session.

Develop the habit of shutting down Windows XP properly before turning off your computer. Perhaps you can stick a note to the computer's on/off switch until you get used to running the command. Again, this proper shut down procedure is cheap insurance against data loss, and a good habit to develop.

I Do Windows!

The rest of this lesson focuses on managing the individual windows within Windows XP. You must know how to maneuver throughout the multiple windows on your Windows XP desktop so you can effectively use your computer.

The example window primarily used here is a special window named the *My Computer* window. Hour 4 explains how to use the contents of the My Computer window. The rest of this lesson uses the My Computer window only as an example window to show you how to manage windows.

First, select the My Computer option on your Start menu to open the My Computer window. (A new button appears on your taskbar showing the new open My Computer window.) Most Start menu entries open to windows or start programs running when you select them, as you'll see throughout this book. Some menu options produce additional menus from which you can select.

Figure 2.6 shows the My Computer window with all its control buttons and components labeled. You will find this same window structure in almost every window that you open, as well as in applications that you run, such as a database program. Although you'll often see other kinds of windows, such as the dialog box you studied in the previous hour, the window in Figure 2.6 is more typical of the general windows with which you will work. Your My Computer window, and your other windows, might differ slightly from the look of Figure 2.6's window depending on how your system is configured. As you progress in this 24-hour tutorial, you will learn how to customize windows to look the way you prefer.

FIGURE 2.6
Use a window's controls and menus to manage the window.

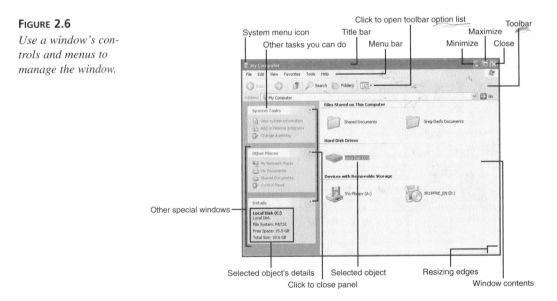

Familiarize yourself with the buttons and window sections pointed out in Figure 2.6 because almost every window contains these window controls or a subset of them. Here are some of the more general things you can do with such a window on the screen:

- *Minimize* the window down to an icon on the taskbar, eliminating the window from the screen, while keeping it open.

- *Maximize* a minimized window to partial- or full-screen size.

- Move a window from one location to another on the screen.

- Bring a window to the top of a stack of windows so that you can work within that window. (Because of the Windows XP multitasking capability, hidden windows can still perform data processing, such as calculating and printing.)

- Display different windows by clicking one of the Tasks or Other Places options. If you display new window contents, you can click the back toolbar button to return to the window's previous contents.

- Drag items, with the mouse, from one window to another if you have two or more windows on the screen at once. You can also drag an item to a different location within the same window.

- Close a window completely, removing its icon from the taskbar and stopping the application that is running inside the window.

You can have one or more windows on your screen, some overlapping other windows, some completely covering others, and you will sometimes see windows side by side or above others. The taskbar indicates the contents of all your open windows. In a typical Windows XP user's day, the user might have two or more applications running at the same time. Each of those applications might display one or more windows of its own.

Don't jump to the conclusion that multiple windows result in confusion. On a typical desk, even the desks of the most organized people (the author not being one of them!), you'll find all sorts of paper stacks, and those stacks don't imply disorganization. The desk's user simply has to know how to organize the stacks and bring the most important stacks to the forefront when he wants to work on them. It is the same with Windows XP.

Some applications open single windows. Other applications might open multiple windows. For example, there are word processors that can display two documents side by side in two different windows. Almost all windows in Windows XP look and act just as all the others.

Minimizing Windows

Minimizing a window clears the window from your desktop, but the program is still loaded, active, and out of sight until you are ready to return to the program. The taskbar continues to list the window or application until you completely close the application as the following To Do item explains.

To Do: How to Minimize Windows

1. Locate your My Computer window's Minimize button.
2. Click the button. Look closely at the screen as you minimize the window. Notice that Windows XP graphically and quickly shrinks the outer edges of the window into the taskbar button labeled My Computer.

When you minimize a window, whichever window or icon is behind it appears. Remember that a window is active when its icon and description still appear on the taskbar.

Enlarging Windows

Windows supplies several ways to enlarge windows. You can enlarge a minimized window from its taskbar status to the window's regular size. You can also maximize a window that's already showing to take up the entire screen space. You can alter the size of a window by doing one of the following:

- Click the window's taskbar button when the window is minimized.
- Click the window's Maximize button to enlarge the window to full screen. (The Maximize button changes to a Restore button as soon as you maximize a window.)
- To manually expand or shrink a window, drag one of the window's outward or inward.

As long as a window contains a Maximize button, you can maximize that window to the screen's full size. (Some windows are designed to be no larger or smaller than a preset size; these windows have Maximize or Minimize buttons that are disabled, indicated by grayed-out buttons.) When you want to dedicate the entire screen to a window, you can usually maximize the window by clicking the window's Maximize button.

> You also can maximize a window by double-clicking the window's title bar. Double-click once again, and the window returns to its previous size.

To Do: Maximizing Windows

1. Click the My Computer window's Maximize button. The window grows to consume the entire screen. The My Computer window does not often contain many items, so maximizing it is not very beneficial other than for this practice. The more a window contains, the larger you will want to make it so that you can see contents that might not fit in a nonmaximized window.

There is no need for Windows to keep a Maximize button on a window that's already maximized; thus, the Restore button takes the Maximize button's place when maximized. The Restore button always restores the window to the size it measured before you maximized it.

2. Click the My Computer window's Restore button. The window resizes (down) to its original size. As soon as you restore the window's size, you will see that the Restore button switches back to a Maximize button once again.

3. This time, double-click the My Computer window's title bar (point the mouse anywhere over the title in the window's title bar before double-clicking). Double-clicking the title bar maximizes a window just as pressing the Maximize button does.

4. Restore the My Computer window's original size again by clicking the Restore button.

You will often want to maximize a window if you are doing a lot of work within that window's program. For example, most word-processor users maximize the word-processing window while typing a document so that more screen real estate goes to that document and, therefore, more of it appears on the screen at one time.

> If you have loaded several programs and one program's window is covering up another program, you can click the taskbar button that matches the hidden program to bring that covered window to the top of the window stack and into view.

Manually Changing Window Sizes

When you point to any window's edge or corner, the mouse pointer changes from its default shape (the pointing arrow) to a bidirectional arrow. The bidirectional arrow indicates that you are at one of the edges of the window and that you can drag the edge or corner inward or outward to change the size of the window.

When you drag one of the four straight edges, the window grows or shrinks left, right, up, or down. When you drag one of the four window corners, the window grows or shrinks in both height and width in the direction of the cursor's bidirectional diagonal shape.

> You cannot always resize every window that appears on your monitor.

Moving Windows

The windows that appear on your Windows XP desktop don't always appear in the location you want. That's okay. By using the mouse, you can easily drag a window to another location on the screen. The title bar acts like a handle for the window—to move the window, you click and drag the window's title bar.

Closing a Window

Windows is obviously full of windows that contain executing programs that work with data values of all kinds. When you run several programs at once, you open many windows that do not relate to each other. This multiwindowed operating system concept provides a flexible and manageable way to run and control several programs at once.

When you're finished with an open window, you must close the window. Closing a window eliminates the window from view, and if that window contained a running program (as most do), it will cease executing. The window's taskbar button will no longer appear on the taskbar.

> Remember that closing a window differs from minimizing the window. Closing a window stops a program; minimizing a window keeps it running in the background and on the taskbar, so you can quickly return to using the program once again.

If a program icon appears on your Windows XP desktop, you can double-click the icon to start the program. Closing the window eliminates the window from your desktop area, but the icon remains on the screen in its original place.

> You can rearrange icons on your screen by dragging them with the mouse just as you rearrange windows. In addition, if you right-click over your desktop and select Arrange Icons By, a pop-up menu appears that enables you to select the order of your desktop icons (such as alphabetically, by type, size, and date).

You also can close its primary window and terminate the entire program by double-clicking the program's icon in the upper-left corner of the window or by selecting File, Exit (for programs) or File, Close (for windows such as My Computer) from the program's menu.

A Window's Menu

Most of Windows XP's windows contain a menu bar. Even non-program windows such as the My Computer window displays a menu bar. You can use the menu bar to close the window, open additional windows, copy, cut, and paste information from one window to another, get help, and even access the Internet for related information. (The Internet's never far away in Windows.)

As you progress over the next 22 lessons, you'll learn ways to use the window menu bar options to traverse windows and to find the information you need. When you select an option from a menu bar, that option's menu opens (drops down) to display a list of actions. For example, Figure 2.7 shows an open View menu. Throughout the remaining lessons, when asked to select View, Details, for example, you will click the View menu bar option and select Details with your mouse or arrow keys.

FIGURE 2.7

Windows contains menus that enable you to control operations on and within the window.

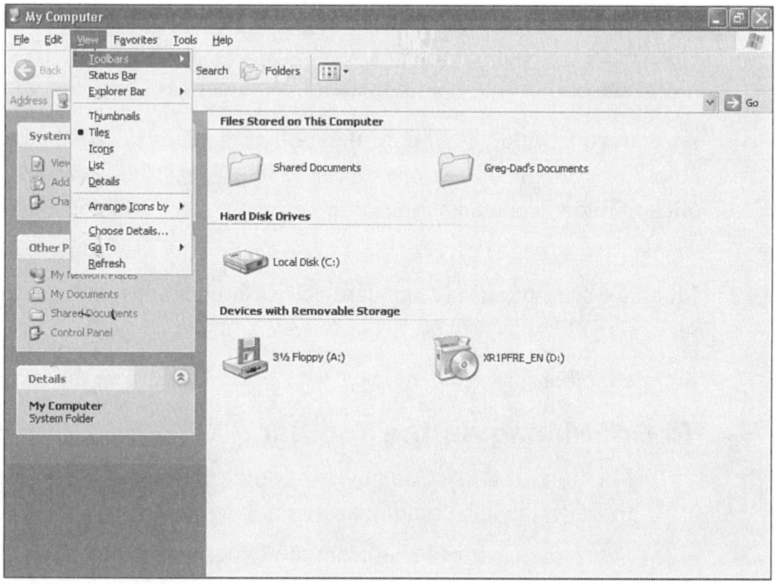

The menu bar enables you to control the way that the window looks and behaves. If the window's icons are too large to hold all of a window's contents, you can select smaller icons or change the window to a list view format as the following To Do item demonstrates.

To Do: Managing the Window Contents

1. From the open My Computer window, select View, Icons. The window's icons become smaller so that they can display in a smaller space. (Before, the icons were tiled and enlarged to show as much detail as possible.)

2. Select View, Details to see the window's contents compacted even further. The list view shows extra information about the window's contents such as the size, date created, free disk space, and other statistics relative to the item in the window.

Use a window's menu bar to change the window's appearance and behavior. More of the menu bar options will come in handy as you learn more about Windows XP.

A Window's Toolbar

A *toolbar* is a ribbon of buttons across the top of a window. Some programs have multiple toolbars. The toolbar you see atop the My Computer window is fairly common and appears throughout most windows that appear in Windows. Toolbar buttons give you push-button access to common actions you perform with the window.

As you work within a window, the toolbar changes to reflect actions that become available. For example, if you open a folder icon located in a window, not only does the clicked folder's contents replace the window's original contents, but the toolbar changes, as well.

Many toolbar buttons are standard across applications and windows, so you will learn to recognize them quickly.

Simple toolbar management is easy, as you will learn in the next To Do item.

To Do: Managing the Toolbar

1. Maximize the My Computer window. Notice that the Back toolbar button (the button with the left-pointing arrow) is grayed out.

2. Select the Control Panel from the Other Places area then click the Printers and Other Hardware option found in the Control Panel's window. A new folder appears containing, among other items, an icon that enables you to set up a new printer that you might add to your system, as well as icons for existing printers you've already designated. Notice that the Back toolbar button is now available, enabling you to return to the previous window contents.

3. Click the Back button and the original My Computer contents return. (Forward takes you to the Printers folder.) No matter how many windows and subfolders you open within a window, you always can retrace your steps backward and forward with the Back and Forward buttons.

▼
4. Modify the way the toolbar looks. Right-click over the right end of the toolbar (an area in which no buttons appear) and click Customize. Click the down arrow next to Text Options and click on No text labels to select that option (assuming that it was not already selected). Click Close. Your toolbar buttons now display in less space without text descriptions. (You also can control the toolbar's appearance from the View, Toolbar menu bar option.) If your toolbar already displayed the text labels, the labels will now be gone. Select Show text labels from this same dialog
▲   box to show labels once again.

One Last Note About Windows

You can completely change the way a window looks by selecting Tools, Folder Options and clicking Use Windows classic folders. When you click OK, the left task pane disappears and the window contains only the icons that represent your computer hardware. Figure 2.8 shows the My Computer window shown in this classic format. This format gives more screen space to your window contents but eliminates some of the tasks you could do from within the window. If you now want to display the Control Panel, for example, you would have to display the Start menu and select Control Panel from there.

FIGURE 2.8

You might like your windows in the classic format.

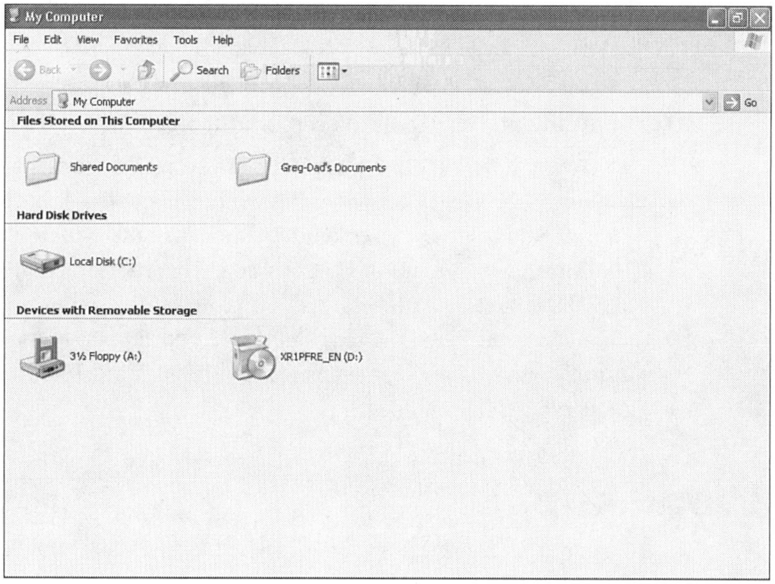

Summary

Perhaps you're beginning to see that Windows XP makes things simple. Changing user accounts has never been easier than it is with Windows XP. Depending on your account's permissions, you can modify the way your account behaves and you can assign a password so that others can't access your account.

Mastering fundamental windows management, as you've done so far this hour, is like learning to drive a car. You must learn the basics before getting into traffic. Now you are ready to begin racing down the road by seeing what Windows XP can really do.

Q&A

Q When will I have to log on to Windows XP?

A If your computer is connected to a network, chances are good that you will have to log on before you can use Windows XP. In a network environment, computers have connections to each other so users have physical access to other people's files. By delegating usernames and passwords, the system administrator assigns protection and privileges to all users on the system.

Q Why do asterisks appear when I enter my account password?

A Asterisks appear in place of the actual characters that you type so that someone looking over your shoulder cannot steal your password.

Q Don't the pop-up ToolTips replace the need for toolbar labels?

A When you hide a toolbar's text labels, you make room for more buttons and you get more screen real estate for the window's contents. If you forget what a button is for, rest your mouse cursor on the button without clicking the button, and the ToolTip shows the button's description. The ToolTips don't appear when you display the buttons' text labels. As you grow more familiar with Windows Me toolbars, you won't need the text labels and you'll want to make more room for the rest of your window elements. You can rely on the ToolTips when you need to know what a button does.

Workshop

The quiz and exercise questions are designed to test your knowledge of the material covered in this hour. The answers are in Appendix C, "Answers to Quizzes."

Quiz

1. What is the difference between an administrator account and a guest account?
2. What can happen if you don't properly shut down Windows XP before you turn off your computer?
3. What is the difference between closing and minimizing a window?
4. *True or false*: When you minimize a window, its taskbar button goes away.
5. How does a toolbar differ from a window menu?

Exercises

1. Open the Control Panel by opening the Windows Start menu and then clicking Control Panel. Minimize, maximize, and resize the Control Panel window. Drag the Control Panel (when it's not maximized) to a different location on the screen. Close the window.
2. Open several windows at once, such as the My Computer, Control Panel, and the Help and Support windows from the Start menu. Notice how Windows XP arranges them. Click on the title bar of any window to bring that window into view and to make it the active window. The other windows remain open, but the active window shows completely.

Hour **3**

Managing the Windows XP Interface

The taskbar and the Start button are closely related. Most people use the Start button to display the Start menu and then execute their programs. When a program begins running, the taskbar displays a button with an icon, along with a description that represents the running program.

The taskbar, the Start button, and the Start menu are the most fundamental components in Windows XP. The taskbar is the cornerstone of Windows XP. This hour explains how to customize the taskbar to best suit your computing style.

In this hour, you will

- Learn more about where the Start menu comes from
- Move, resize, and change the appearance of the taskbar
- Learn why the Start menu's Programs command might not execute all programs
- Arrange windows on your desktop
- Play Solitaire

A Quick Taskbar and Start Button Review

In the previous hour's lesson, you used the Start menu to shut down your computer properly. Clicking the taskbar's Start button produces the Start menu.

The Start menu does all these things and more:

- It makes itself available to you no matter what else you are doing in Windows XP.
- It displays a list of programs and windows on your system using the Start menu's cascading system.
- It provides easy access to recently-used data documents that you can view or edit.
- It provides a search engine that navigates through all your files looking for the one you need.
- It activates the Windows XP help engine, which provides online help for working within Windows XP.

The next few sections explain how you can customize the taskbar and its associated Start menu so that the Start menu acts and looks the way you expect.

Sometimes the Start button temporarily disappears (when you're working in a full-screen command prompt session, for example). When this occurs, you can press Ctrl+Esc to display the Start menu when it disappears. If your keyboard contains a key with the Windows logo, that key also displays the Start menu.

Moving the Taskbar

The taskbar does not have to stay at the bottom of your screen. You can move the taskbar to either side of your monitor or even to the top of your screen. The taskbar placement is easy to change. Some people prefer their taskbar at the top of the screen or attached to the left or right edge of the screen.

Figure 3.1 shows that the taskbar does not have the width necessary to display lengthy descriptions when you place it on the side of the screen. When you place the taskbar at the bottom or top of the screen, the taskbar has more room for longer descriptions.

The newly placed taskbar

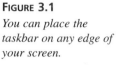

FIGURE 3.1

You can place the
taskbar on any edge of
your screen.

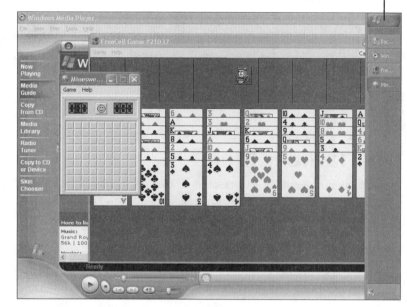

3

If you place the taskbar at the top of the screen, the Start menu falls from the Start button, whereas the Start menu pops up from the Start button when you place the taskbar at the bottom of the screen.

When working on a wide spreadsheet or document, you might want as much screen width as you can get. You then want the taskbar at the bottom or top of your screen. When working with graphics, you usually need more vertical screen space, so you can move the taskbar to either side of the screen.

Moving the taskbar to any of the four edges of your screen is easy. Simply drag the taskbar to the new location as the following To Do item demonstrates.

To Do: Relocating the Taskbar

1. Find a blank spot on your taskbar and point to the spot with the mouse cursor. Be sure that you are pointing within the taskbar and not over a button.

2. Drag the taskbar to another edge of the screen. As you drag the mouse, the taskbar moves with the mouse and appears at the edge of the screen where you release the mouse.

3. Release the mouse button to anchor the taskbar at its new position.

The Taskbar Menu

A right mouse button click often displays a *pop-up menu* (sometimes called a *context-sensitive menu*) of options available to you. Windows XP looks at what you are doing when you right-click. Depending on the context, Windows displays commands appropriate to that task. The taskbar is one such location where the right mouse button brings up a helpful menu. You can use it to change the appearance and performance of the taskbar and the windows controlled by the taskbar. After finding a blank spot on your taskbar, right-clicking brings up the taskbar's pop-up menu shown in Figure 3.2.

FIGURE 3.2

A right-click on a blank space of the taskbar displays a pop-up menu.

The taskbar's pop-up menu

| Toolbars ▶ |
| Adjust Date/Time |
| Customize Notifications... |
| Cascade Windows |
| Tile Windows Horizontally |
| Tile Windows Vertically |
| Show the Desktop |
| Task Manager |
| ✓ Lock the Taskbar |
| Properties |

start   Backup or Rest...   Windows Med...   FreeCell Game...   Minesweeper

The taskbar menu is not necessarily a menu you want to display often. Most users play around with different taskbar and window settings for a while until they find preferences that suit them best. Thereafter, those users might rarely use the taskbar properties menu.

The taskbar actually displays several menus, depending on where you right-click and how you've configured the taskbar. For example, if you right-click over the notification area, the area at the far right (assuming your taskbar's on the bottom of the screen), several more options appear that don't otherwise show.

The Taskbar Properties Menu

When you select Properties from the taskbar menu, the Taskbar and Properties dialog box appears as shown in Figure 3.3.

FIGURE 3.3

Adjust your taskbar and Start menu settings from this properties dialog box.

 If you have too many windows open to locate a blank spot on your taskbar to right-click upon, you can display the Taskbar and Start Menu Properties dialog box by selecting Appearance and Themes from the Control Panel and then selecting Taskbar and Start Menu.

 In Hour 7, "Improving Your Windows Desktop Experience," you'll learn how to use the Taskbar and Start Menu Properties dialog box to change the contents of the Start menu.

The Taskbar and Start Menu Properties dialog box accepts information that controls the way the taskbar appears on the screen. You can allow (or disallow) windows to overlap the taskbar if those windows are large enough to do so, you can eliminate the clock from the taskbar, and you can even minimize the taskbar so that it does not appear until you need it.

The following To Do item lets you practice changing some of the taskbar's properties.

To Do: Working with Taskbar Properties

1. Display the Taskbar and Start Menu properties dialog box by right-clicking over the Start button and selecting Properties.

2. Click the first option, Lock the taskbar. This option enables you to lock the taskbar so you cannot move it to another edge of the screen.

▼   3. Check the option labeled Auto-hide the taskbar. When you click the Apply button,
          the taskbar disappears. The taskbar hasn't gone far—point the mouse cursor to the
          bottom of the screen and the taskbar will reappear. You can now have your taskbar
          and hide it, too! (When you click a dialog box's Apply command button, Windows
          XP implements your selected options immediately without closing the dialog box.
▲   You then can make further changes or click OK to close the dialog box.)

> If you display the Taskbar and Start Menu Properties dialog box but decide
> that you don't want to make any changes after all, click the Cancel com-
> mand button.

Remaining Taskbar Properties

The Taskbar and Start Menu Properties dialog box ensures that the Taskbar always stays
on top of whatever might appear on your window below it. When you uncheck this
option, a window could overlap the taskbar and hide some or all of it.

The fourth option is labeled Group similar taskbar buttons. Microsoft Word users will
appreciate this option which is checked by default. Windows XP watches how you open
windows and, if checked and if the taskbar is already full of buttons, Windows ensures
that only one taskbar button appears for all files you open with the same application. In
other words, you can open three documents in Microsoft Word and all three buttons will
appear next to each other on the taskbar even if you opened another program before you
opened all three documents. In addition, if the taskbar cannot comfortably show all three
buttons, Windows XP combines the buttons into one button, thus saving room on your
taskbar.

The notification area contains the time of day if you've checked the option labeled Show
the clock. The other icons that you find on the notification area represent special notices
such as the new mail icon that alerts you that you have unread mail. To save taskbar
space, only those notification icons that you've clicked recently appear if you check the
last option labeled Hide inactive icons.

Using Dialog Boxes

When Windows displays a tabbed dialog box, it is offering you more than one dialog box
at the same time. (Each box, or page, is called a *property sheet*.) Instead of displaying
two or more dialog boxes on the screen at the same time, the tabs give you a way to
select which dialog box you want to respond to. You can even respond to one dialog box

and then click another tab, and that tab's dialog box then appears so that you can respond to it. Windows often puts an OK command button on a dialog box that you can press when you are finished responding to the dialog box's controls.

Toolbars on Your Taskbar

Right-click over the toolbar and select Toolbars to see an array of choices. Table 3.1 explains each kind of element you can place on the taskbar from this menu.

TABLE 3.1 You Can Add These Toolbar Elements to Your Windows XP Taskbar

Toolbar Element	Description
Address	Displays a drop-down list box on your taskbar where you can enter a Web address to open that Web page from your Windows XP desktop.
Links	Displays popular Web links that you can quickly return to with the click of a button. You can modify the list of links.
Desktop	Displays an icon bar that match those on your Windows XP desktop. You can click one of the icons to start that icon's program or open that icon's window instead of having to return to your desktop to locate the icon.
Quick Launch	Adds Internet access control buttons so that you can quickly get on the Web. In addition, the Show Desktop icon appears in the Quick Launch section so that you can minimize all open windows with a single taskbar click.
New Toolbar	Enables you to select a disk drive, folder, or Web location whose contents appear as a secondary toolbar slider control on the taskbar. Subsequently, the taskbar's right-click menu contains the new toolbar that you can deselect to hide once again.

The Quick Launch toolbar is extremely helpful, especially due to its Show Desktop button. The following To Do item explains how to display and use the Quick Launch toolbar.

To Do: Working with the Quick Launch Toolbar

1. Right-click over a blank area on your taskbar to display the pop-up menu.

2. Select Toolbars to display the list of available toolbars.

3. Select Quick Launch to place the Quick Launch toolbar on your taskbar. Although the Quick Launch toolbar consumes some taskbar space, it contains one-button access to popular programs such as your Internet Web browser and e-mail. If you

▼   don't yet have an e-mail program installed, the e-mail program's icon will appear
in the Quick Launch area when you install the e-mail program. You can also drag
any program icon from your my Computer window to the Quick Launch area.
Figure 3.4 shows the Quick Launch toolbar with icons available for you to click.

FIGURE 3.4   Quick Launch toolbar

The Quick Launch
toolbar puts your
favorite programs
right on your taskbar.   Show Desktop icon

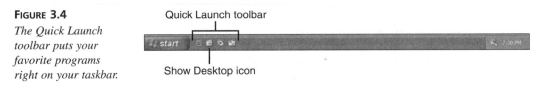

4. Open your My Computer window and the Control Panel.

5. Click the Quick Launch toolbar's Show Desktop button. Immediately, your desktop
appears. Windows XP did not close the windows but only minimized them. The
Show Desktop button is handy when you need to return to your desktop without
▲   closing any programs you have open.

> You can easily remove icons from the Quick Launch toolbar. Right-click on
> an icon and select Delete from the pop-up menu. Windows XP removes the
> icon but does not remove the associated program from your computer. You
> can add more programs to the Quick Launch toolbar by dragging their icons
> from the Start menu to the Quick Launch area. You can even place your
> favorite Web pages on the Quick Launch toolbar by dragging the Web
> page's icon that appears to the left of its address in your Web browser to
> your Quick Launch toolbar. When you subsequently click that Web page's
> icon, Windows XP will display that Web page, starting your Internet Web
> browser if needed first.

When you want to return to all the windows that you had open before clicking Show
Desktop, right-click your taskbar to display the taskbar's pop-up menu and select Undo
Minimize All.

Adjusting Your System Clock and Date

You can change your computer's date and time by double-clicking your notification
area's clock. The Date/Time Properties dialog box shown in Figure 3.5 will appear.

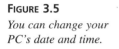

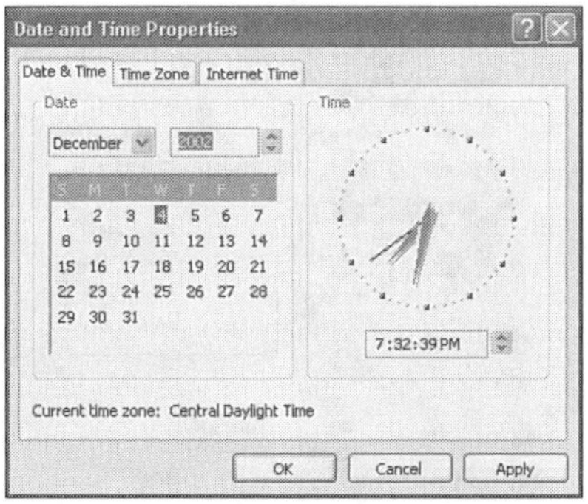

FIGURE 3.5

You can change your PC's date and time.

Managing Multiple Windows with the Taskbar

The taskbar's pop-up menu includes menu options that help you work with more than one open window at the same time. These menu options offer three ways of arranging your open windows so that they are more manageable. If you open two or more windows at once, all those windows can be difficult to manage individually. You could maximize each window and display only one window at a time. There are many reasons, however, to keep more than one window open and displayed at the same time, such as when you want to copy data from one window to another. (Hour 5, "Navigating Files with Windows Explorer," explains how to copy between windows.)

Tiling Windows

When you want to see more than one open window at a time, the taskbar properties menu gives you tools that provide quick management of those windows so that you do not have to size and place each window individually. Figure 3.6 shows how too many windows open at the same time can be confusing.

Three ways exist to organize several windows that are open at once: You can cascade them, horizontally tile them, or vertically tile them. The following To Do item demonstrates the cascade option.

Too many open windows can quickly cause disorganization.

To Do: Working with Cascading Windows

1. From a clean desktop without any open windows, open your My Computer window. If My Computer opens maximized, click the Restore button to shrink the window down in size.

2. Open the Control Panel.

3. Open the Help and Support window. These open windows are open just to put some things on your desktop to work with for this task.

4. Now that you've opened three windows, ask Windows XP to organize those windows for you. Display the taskbar's properties menu by right-clicking after pointing to a blank spot on the taskbar.

5. Select the menu item labeled Cascade Windows. Windows XP instantly organizes your windows into the cascaded series of windows shown in Figure 3.7.

   Notice that the title bars of all open windows appear on the Windows desktop area. When you want to bring any of the hidden windows into focus, click that window's title bar and the window will rise to the top of the window stack. The cascading effect always gives you the ability to switch between windows. As long as any part of a hidden window is peeking out from under another, you can click the title bar to bring that hidden window into focus.

FIGURE 3.7

*The windows are now
more manageable.*

6. Sometimes, you need to see the contents of two or more windows at the same time. Windows enables you to *tile* the open windows so that you can see the actual body of each open window. Windows supports two kinds of tiling methods: horizontal tiling and vertical tiling. Display the taskbar's properties menu and select Tile Windows Horizontally. Windows will properly resize each of the three open windows, as shown in Figure 3.8. (If a window's title bar is hidden but another part of the window is visible, you can bring that window into focus by clicking the part of the window that is visible.)

At first glance, the tiling might seem too limiting to you. After all, to fit those three open windows on the screen at the same time, Windows cannot show you a lot of any one of the windows. Keep in mind that all the window resizing and moving tools that you learned about in Hour 2 work even after you've tiled windows. Therefore, you can move the Help window toward the top of the screen, after tiling the windows, if you want to see more of that window. (Scrollbars automatically appear in tiled windows if the contents of the window consume more space than can be displayed at once. Click the arrows at each end of the scrollbar to move window contents into view.)

▼

FIGURE 3.8

The windows are now tiled horizontally.

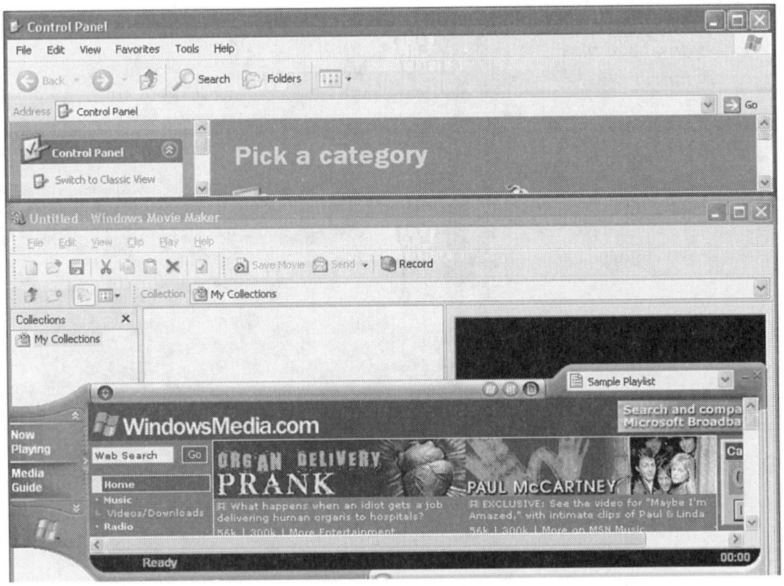

![Screenshot showing Control Panel, Windows Movie Maker, and Windows Media Player windows tiled horizontally. The Control Panel window shows "Pick a category". The Windows Movie Maker window shows "My Collections". The Windows Media Player window shows WindowsMedia.com with "ORGAN DELIVERY PRANK" and "PAUL McCARTNEY".]

7. The vertical tiling method produces side-by-side windows that are fairly thin but offer yet another kind of open window display. Select Tile Windows Vertically and Windows reformats the screen again. Now that you've vertically tiled the open windows, you can restore the original placement of the windows by selecting Undo Tile. (The Undo option appears only after you've selected the Cascade, Tile, or Minimize option.)

8. The Minimize All Windows taskbar properties menu option attempts to minimize all open windows at the same time. The problem with the Minimize All Windows option is that not all windows can be minimized. Therefore, the option minimizes only those windows that have a minimize button (most do). The Show Desktop icon does minimize all open windows.

▲   9. Close all open windows.

> No matter how you tile or cascade the windows, each window's Minimize, Maximize, and Restore buttons work as usual. Therefore, you can maximize any cascaded window at any time by clicking that window's Maximize button.

Sizing the Taskbar

What happens if you open a number of windows by starting several programs? The single-line taskbar fills up very quickly with buttons and icons and descriptions that represent those open windows. The taskbar can become extremely full if you display multiple toolbars on the taskbar. Figure 3.9 shows such a taskbar.

Click here to see
more buttons

FIGURE 3.9
*This taskbar needs
more room.*

Two programs on one button

You can click the up and down arrows that Windows XP places on the toolbar to the right of your program buttons to see additional buttons. Windows cycles through all the taskbar buttons that are active.

Just as you can resize a window, you also can resize the taskbar. Simply point to the top edge of the taskbar (or the inside edge if you've moved the taskbar to an edge or top of the screen) and drag the edge toward the center of the screen. The taskbar enlarges as you drag your mouse. Figure 3.10 shows a wider version of Figure 3.9's taskbar. Notice how all the taskbar buttons are more readable and have room to be noticed.

FIGURE 3.10
*This taskbar now has
breathing room—at the
expense of the screen
space.*

When you enlarge the taskbar, it can more comfortably hold several buttons for open windows, and the descriptions on those buttons can be longer. Use the pop-up ToolTips if you need a reminder of the purpose of the taskbar buttons, such as the Show Desktop button. Of course, the larger taskbar means that you don't have as much screen space as you might need for your programs.

Starting Programs with the Start Menu

The Start menu offers an extremely simple way for you to start the programs on your computer. Two or three clicks start virtually any program on your disk drive. When you install new programs on your computer, those programs add themselves to your Start menu. (Hour 8, "Installing Programs with Windows XP," explains how to install programs on your computer.)

As you open programs and use your computer, Windows XP keeps track of your most recent programs and places them in a handy position on the Start menu as Figure 3.11 shows.

FIGURE 3.11

The Start menu keeps track of the programs you've used recently.

Recently run programs —

The More Programs command on the Start menu enables you to launch any program on your disk. To start a program, you display the menu that contains that program and then click the program's name or icon.

Microsoft gives you the Solitaire card game. You can practice starting programs from the Start menu's More Programs command by starting Solitaire.

To Do: Playing Solitaire

1. Click the Start button to display the Start menu.
2. Select the More Programs command. A cascaded menu will appear next to the Start menu.

   Each of these items in the menu represents either a program or a folder of programs. When you buy a program such as a word processor, the word processor might come with several related programs that help you manage the word processor environment. The word processor folder opens to yet another window (you can tell by the presence of an arrow at the right of the word processor's folder) that then lists all the related programs in the folder.

▼   3. Select the Games option to display the programs in the Games folder. If you don't see Games, first select Accessories and look there.

4. Select the Solitaire option. You'll see the opening Solitaire card game screen.

5. There's no time to play right now! This hour's closing quickly. Therefore, terminate the Solitaire program by clicking the window's Close button (the button with the X, as you learned in Hour 2). Solitaire goes away and you are back to the regular Windows XP desktop.

Using the Run Command

In addition to the Start menu's Programs command, you can use another method to start programs that aren't set up on the Programs' cascade of menus. The Run command on the Start menu provides a way for you to execute specific programs.

Reaching Your Files

A *pathname* is the exact computer system location of a file. The document and folder concept in Windows makes working with paths much easier than before Windows. Most often, you specify pathnames visually by clicking folder icons instead of typing long pathnames, as you had to do before Windows.

The folders in Windows used to be called *directories*. A directory is just a collection of files and other directories. In file listings, Windows often displays a folder icon with a name to represent a directory that holds other files. Folders can hold subfolders, so the location of a file, the file's path, might be deep within several nested folders on a disk or CD-ROM drive.

A full pathname begins with a disk drive name followed by a colon (:) followed by a backslash (\). If the file resides in the disk drive's top folder (called the *root directory*), you then type the filename. If, however, the file resides in another folder, you must list the folder after the backslash. If the file resides in several nested folders, you must list each folder in order, from the outermost to the innermost, and separate each folder name with a backslash. Both of the following are full pathnames to specific files:

c:\autoexec.bat

d:\Sherry\WordProc\Home\Insure\Fire and Casualty

The first filename is autoexec.bat located in the root directory. The second filename is Fire and Casualty located within a series of nested directories.

The Start menu's Run command offers a tedious way to execute any program on your computer. If you want to run a program that would not properly set up in Windows (perhaps the program is an old MS-DOS–based program), you have to execute the program using Run.

To run a program from the Run menu option, display the Start menu and select the Run command. Windows displays the Run dialog box.

There might or might not be text next to the Open prompt. Windows XP needs to know the exact name and path of the program you want to open (and run).

Almost all users install Windows XP on drive C:. If your Windows XP system is installed on another drive, substitute your drive name for the C: and type the following exactly as you see it (using either uppercase or lowercase letters): **C:\WINDOWS\SOL** and press Enter.

The Solitaire game is normally installed on the Windows directory on drive C:. The name of the program is SOL.EXE. To execute any program with an .EXE filename extension, you need to type only the first part of the filename, such as SOL. If Solitaire does not start, you might have typed the line incorrectly. Try again and be sure that you use backslashes and not forward slashes.

You might be one of the lucky few who never needs the Run command. Nevertheless, there are many programs on the market that Windows cannot execute in its environment. Using Run, you can execute any program on your computer as long as you know the program's pathname and filename.

> Windows supports a strong data document concept. It is data-driven more than program-driven. If you type a data file (such as a Microsoft Word document) instead of a program name with the Run command, Windows automatically starts the program needed to work with that data file and loads the data file for you. Therefore, you worry less about your programs, and you can concentrate more on your data. In addition, you can type an Internet address (often called a uniform resource locator, or, URL) at Run and Windows XP automatically starts your Internet browser and takes you to the Web site you entered.

Summary

This hour concentrated mostly on the taskbar. The taskbar gives you a play-by-play status of the open windows on your system. As you open and close windows, the taskbar updates with new buttons to show what's happening at all times. If you start more than one program, you can switch between those programs as easily as you switch between cable TV shows: Click a button on the taskbar.

The taskbar works along with the Start menu to start and control the programs running on your system. Use the Programs command on the Start menu to start programs with a total of two or three mouse clicks. Although you can use the Run command to start programs, the Programs menu is easier to use as long as the program is set up properly in Windows XP.

Q&A

Q Why would I use the taskbar properties menu to organize my open windows when I can do the same thing manually by dragging them where I want them?

A The taskbar properties menu gives you the ability to adjust the appearance of your screen's open windows with one mouse click. If you select a cascading window scheme, Windows XP ensures that all open window title bars appear on the screen, with the most recently opened window as the front window of focus. You can bring one of the hidden windows into focus by clicking the window's title bar. If, instead, you select the horizontal or vertical tiling options, Windows XP displays a little of all open windows on top of each other or side-by-side.

If you normally work in only one window at a time, you won't use the taskbar properties. However, you can use the taskbar properties menu to change the appearance of the taskbar itself.

Q How can I use the taskbar properties menu to change the appearance or performance of the taskbar?

A The taskbar is set by default to appear, no matter what else is on your screen. Microsoft thought it best to keep the taskbar on the screen so that you can switch between programs and adjust the Windows XP performance easily. However, to maximize the screen space and clear away as much as possible, you can change the taskbar's performance so that onscreen windows cover the taskbar, giving you an additional line for the open window. In addition, you can select that Windows XP always hide the taskbar completely, showing you the taskbar only when you point to the bottom of the screen with the mouse cursor. If you increase the size of the taskbar, you can still hide it through the properties' Auto hide feature. The increased size will appear when you show the taskbar, but the taskbar will not be in the way when hidden.

Q Help! My taskbar has fallen and I can't get my Start menu up! What did I do and how can I fix it?

A You've changed the options in the Taskbar Properties dialog box to hide the taskbar, or you've dragged the top of the taskbar to the bottom of your screen to

3

shrink the taskbar. The taskbar is not gone for long, however. To see the taskbar again, all you need to do is point to the bottom of the screen with the mouse, and the taskbar appears once again.

Workshop

The quiz and exercise questions are designed to test your knowledge of the material covered in this hour. The answers are in Appendix C, "Answers to Quizzes."

Quiz

1. Which option enables you to keep the taskbar off the screen until you're ready to use the taskbar?

2. What happens when you right-click over a blank area of the taskbar?

3. What are the two ways to change your PC's date and time?

4. What does it mean to *tile* windows?

5. How can you make more room for your taskbar when you start a lot of programs at the same time?

Exercises

1. Move your taskbar to each edge of the screen. Determine which is best for you. Remember that you can hide the taskbar with the Auto Hide option if the taskbar consumes too much screen real estate.

2. Locate the Start menu item that contains the Solitaire game. Drag the icon to the left of the game's name to the Quick Launch toolbar. The icon appears on the toolbar so that you can now play the game quickly when you get a chance.

   One problem with doing this is that Solitaire will no longer appear on the Games menu. You can drag the icon right back when you're tired of Solitaire, but doing so is rather tricky because you first drag it to your Start button, wait for the Start menu to appear, then drag the icon to the More Programs command; then wait for the menu to appear, and then keep on until you place the icon back on the Games menu. Whew! To save this effort, if, when you first move an icon to your Quick Launch toolbar, instead of using your left mouse button to drag the icon you use your right mouse button, Windows XP asks you if you want to copy or move the icon to the Quick Launch toolbar when you drop the icon there. If you select Copy, the Solitaire icon will appear both on your Quick Launch toolbar and on the Games menu where it belongs.

PART II

Morning Windows Desktop Exploration

Hour

HOUR 4

Working with the My Computer Window

The My Computer icon opens to a window, as you learned in Hour 3, "Managing the Windows XP Interface," and contains information that relates to your computer's hardware and software. You will often open the My Computer window when you add or remove both hardware and software. The My Computer window provides access to many different areas of your computer.

Many computer beginners and advanced users ignore the My Computer window more than they should. The My Computer window, which always appears on your Windows XP desktop, enables you to access every hardware device on your system in a uniform fashion.

In this hour, you will also begin using the Control Panel window to change the behavior of your mouse and also to modify the screen background that you see. You must look at the desktop often, so changing the graphics behind the desktop can break the monotony that you might otherwise face with a dull Windows XP desktop screen. People often spend the first few sessions with any new operating environment getting to know the environment and modifying the appearance to suit their preferences.

In this hour, you will

- Discover the contents of the My Computer window
- Use the Control Panel to change your computer mouse's behavior
- Change your desktop's wallpaper
- Learn to place program icons on your desktop for easy access

Looking at My Computer

Your computer system is comprised of hardware (the system unit, monitor, keyboard, CD-ROM, networked components, and so on), firmware (the internal memory), and software (for example, Windows XP and its auxiliary programs such as Media Player, word processors, spreadsheets, and games). There are several ways to access your computer's hardware and software through different areas of Windows XP. The My Computer window contains one of the most helpful hardware and software management resources available in Windows XP.

Open your My Computer window now by selecting its entry from the Start menu. Windows XP displays the My Computer window like the one shown in Figure 4.1. The My Computer window contains icons for your computer's primary components such as the disk drives. The computer in Figure 4.1 is fairly comprehensive and your My Computer window might contain fewer or more devices. In addition, your My Computer window's format might be set up to look slightly different from the one in the figure.

The Tasks and Other Places sections enable you to jump to other Windows XP windows to perform other tasks. You can get to these other areas from the Start menu and from other program windows as well. Windows XP almost always gives you multiple avenues to its various areas.

FIGURE 4.1

The My Computer window displays your computer's storage hardware.

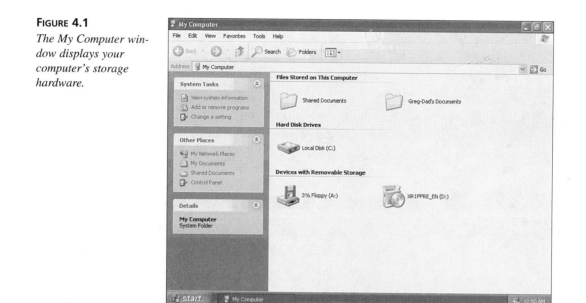

Working in the My Computer Window

People's needs for the My Computer window differ greatly, depending on which hardware they use to run Windows XP. For example, a network user probably displays the My Computer window more often than a single user working primarily on a spreadsheet program. The network user might have more reason to check the properties of a shared folder or disk drive.

Before looking at a sample My Computer window work session, you should understand that there are several ways to view the My Computer window, as well as most other Windows XP windows:

- In the tiled view shown in the previous section in Figure 4.1 with the links to other places on the left and icons for each hardware component on the right
- In the icon view so that more icons can be seen if your computer has many shared folders and drives
- In the detail view that shows disk drive sizes and free space

The tiled view is the default view that is set when you install Windows XP. The next hour's lesson, "Navigating Files with Windows Explorer," explains how to move files from one disk drive to another by dragging a file to the disk icon in which you want to put that file instead of typing a disk drive name, as computer users of older operating systems have to do.

As you progress, you might prefer to switch to a detail view to view more information about the items inside My Computer. Select View, Details from the menu to change to the detailed view. Although small icons still appear next to most of the items in a list view of the My Computer window, the icons are extremely small.

Figure 4.2 shows the detailed view. The detailed view becomes even more important if you display additional information in a window. The detailed list view shows the filename, size in bytes, file type, and the most recent date modified. You will learn in the next section how to display additional information inside My Computer and the detailed view shows more information than the tiled view can show.

FIGURE 4.2

The My Computer window shown in a detailed list view.

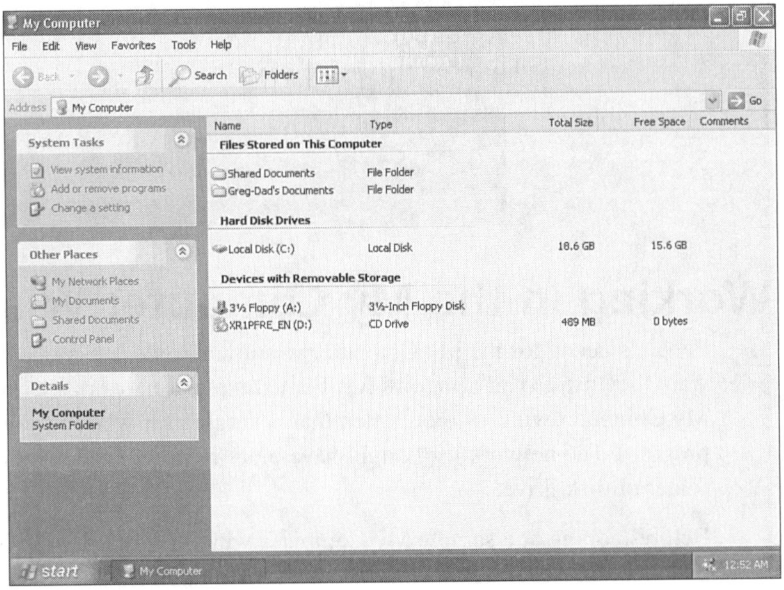

As you add hardware and as you traverse additional windows from within the My Computer window, your current view might no longer be adequate to display the data. For example, for only a few icons, the tiled view works well to show an overview of your machine.

Working with My Computer

The best way to begin learning about the My Computer window is to work within it. Follow the next To Do item to see some of the things that are possible with My Computer and, therefore, with all windows that you need to manage.

To Do: Working in the My Computer Window

1. Open the My Computer window if you don't have it open already.

2. From the menu bar, select View, List. The view instantly changes to the list view.

3. Select View, Details. The list view expands to tell you more about each item, such as free space and total space on the disk and CD-ROM drives.

4. Go back to the tiled view.

5. If not maximized already, maximize your My Computer window by clicking the Maximize button or by double-clicking the title bar.

6. Click the C: disk drive icon once to select it. The Details section shows the disk's size.

7. Now double-click the C: disk drive icon. When you do, you should see a window of folders and other icons. Each folder represents a folder on your disk drive named C:. A folder is a list of files (and subfolders) stored together in one group. The folder name appears under each folder icon. If you also see a hand holding the folder, the folder is known as a *shared folder* available to others on the network you're working on.

   You might see some grayed-out icons in the list. These are hidden system files that you generally do not need access to and you generally shouldn't change or delete. To protect these from view, if you can see them, you can select Tools, Folder Options and click the View tab to designate whether you want to see all hidden files and folders (in which case Windows XP grays out the system and normally hidden files and folders), all files except the hidden ones, or all files except both the hidden and system files. You generally won't work with system or hidden files, and by turning off their display, you clean up your file listings considerably. Click OK to save your changes.

> Folders enable you to group similar files together so that you can work with the entire group at once instead of having to work with individual files. For example, you can keep all your personal correspondence in a single folder so that you can copy it easier to a disk when you want to back up that set of files.

The icons that look like pieces of paper are document icons that represent individual files, including programs and text files, on your system's C: drive. You find other kinds of icons as well. If you see the list view when you display the C: disk drive, select View, Tiles to see the icons.

▼   8. To look at the contents of a file folder, double-click the file folder. When you do,
        yet another window will open up, or possibly the current window will change to
        reflect the new file folder depending on the options set in your Tools, Options
        menu.

        If you have lots of files on drive C:, and most people do, you might have to use the
        scrollbars to see all the window's contents. As you open additional windows by
        opening new folders, you can always return to the previous folder window by
        clicking the toolbar's Back button.

       9. Click the Back button to return to a previous view.

      10. Every time you change the window contents from the My Computer window by
        double-clicking an icon such as the C: drive icon, a new set of window contents
        appears. You can traverse right back through all the windows you visited and return
        to the My Computer window contents by pressing the Back button on the toolbar,
▲   just as you do to traverse back through Web pages you might have traveled.

Click the arrow next to the My Computer toolbar's Views button. A view list
drops down from which you can quickly select *Thumbnails,* Tiles, Icons, List,
and Details. Thumbnails are small pictures that represent the contents of
your file, unlike icons that only represent the file type.

Other Start Menu Windows

You will master other Start menu windows besides the My Computer window as you
learn more about Windows XP. The previous three lessons began describing many of
these windows, such as the My Pictures, My Music, and the Control Panel window.

Here are two Start menu windows that you're not yet familiar with:

- My Documents—Contains a list of data files for many of your application programs.
- My Network Places—Contains a list of computers that are networked to yours
  (although you might not see this option if you do not use a network).

All the windows view commands you've learned so far work throughout the
Windows XP environment. Therefore, you can now change views for all
windows you work with using the same View menu commands you learned
earlier about the My Computer window.

Accessing the Control Panel

The Control Panel enables you to adjust and manage the way hardware devices are attached to and respond to your computer. Open the Control Panel from the Start menu and you'll see a window like the one in Figure 4.3.

FIGURE 4.3

Modify the system settings from within the Control Panel.

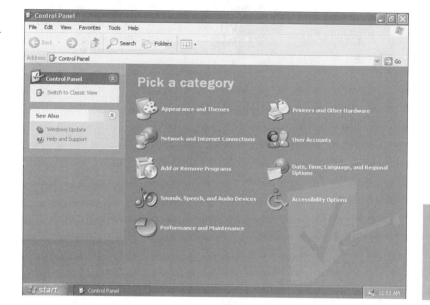

Notice the option on the left pane of the Control Panel labeled, Switch to Classic View. When you click this option, Windows XP changes your Control Panel's view to the *classic view* used in previous Windows versions. The classic view, as opposed to the *category view* that you saw previously, groups all available icons located in your Control Panel window by function. Figure 4.4 shows the Control Panel classic view.

The Control Panel's toolbar and menus work in a similar manner to those of the My Computer window. When you master windows basics for one kind of window, you can apply that talent to all other windows. From the Control Panel, you can change or modify system and hardware settings.

Be very sure that you know what to change before modifying values within the Control Panel. You could change a required setting that might be difficult to reverse later.

FIGURE **4.4**

*You can see all the
Control Panel's icons
from the classic view.*

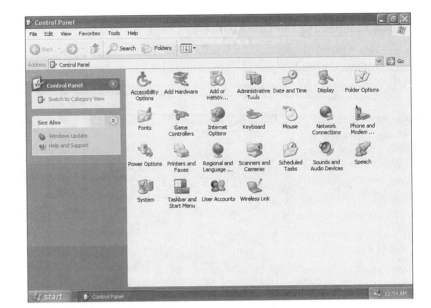

Modifying the Mouse Properties

Some operations inside the Control Panel are complex and could violate your system's
setup. Many tasks are safe inside the Control Panel, however. Follow the next To Do item
to learn how to modify the way your mouse behaves.

To Do: Modifying the Way the Mouse Behaves

1. Open the Control Panel window if you have not yet done so.

2. Select the Mouse icon. The icon indicates that the mouse settings are found here.
   You see the Mouse Properties dialog box appear, as shown in Figure 4.5.

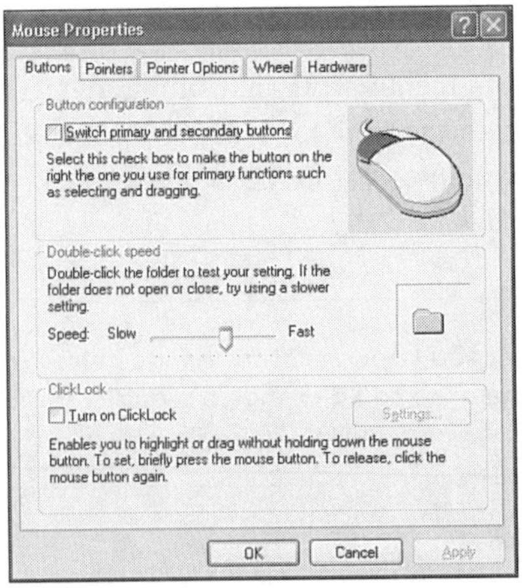

FIGURE **4.5**

*You can change the
behavior of the mouse.*

3. If you are left-handed but your mouse is set for a right-handed user, you can select the option labeled Switch primary and secondary buttons to change the mouse button orientation. The buttons will change their functionality as described in the text beneath the option. (The change will not take effect until you close the Mouse Properties dialog box or click the Apply button.) You can change the button back to its original state by clicking the option once again.

4. Click the tab marked Pointers at the top of the Mouse Properties dialog box. From the Pointer portion of the dialog box, you can change the default appearance of the mouse. A scrolling list of mouse shapes indicates all the kinds of cursor shapes that appear when certain Windows XP events take place.

5. To change the default mouse pointer (called the Normal Select shape), double-click the row with the Normal Select text. Windows XP displays another screen, shown in Figure 4.6, with different mouse pointers you can use. The mouse pointers are stored in files on your system. Some pointers (those whose filenames end with the .ani filename extension) are animated cursors that move when you select them and use the mouse.

FIGURE 4.6

Select a mouse cursor shape file.

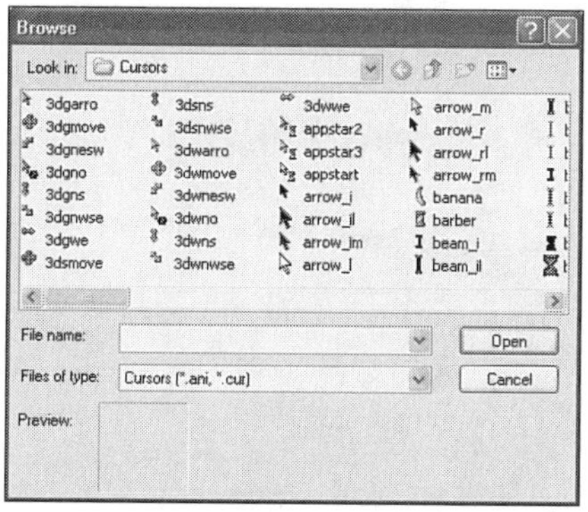

4

6. Windows XP can change the *theme*, or overall look of all your mouse pointers, to make them uniform. Just for grins, click the down arrow next to (None) inside the Scheme area and point to 3D-Bronze in the list. Windows changes all your mouse pointers to three-dimensional bronze shapes.

7. Before leaving the Mouse Properties window, click the Use Default button to return the standard mouse cursor to its default pointer shape unless you want to keep another selection.

8. Click OK to close the Control Panel.

Different Wallpaper

In Hour 1, "Taking a Bird's-Eye Look at Windows XP," you learned that wallpaper is the name for the background you see on the screen when you start Windows XP and work within its windows. You can change that wallpaper to a different picture or eliminate the wallpaper altogether.

To Do: Modifying Your Wallpaper

1. Open your Control Panel window.

2. Select the Appearance and Themes category. Here, you can change several desktop elements such as the wallpaper background and your *desktop themes*. Desktop themes are predesigned icons and colors and desktop settings, combined in a single collection, so that you can easily change the overall look of your desktop and other windows elements. Instead of modifying the entire look of Windows XP, you should probably keep most of the default settings as they are until you learn how to navigate the default Windows XP theme. For this To Do item, you will change only your desktop wallpaper's background.

3. Select the option labeled Change the desktop background to display the Display Properties dialog box shown in Figure 4.7.

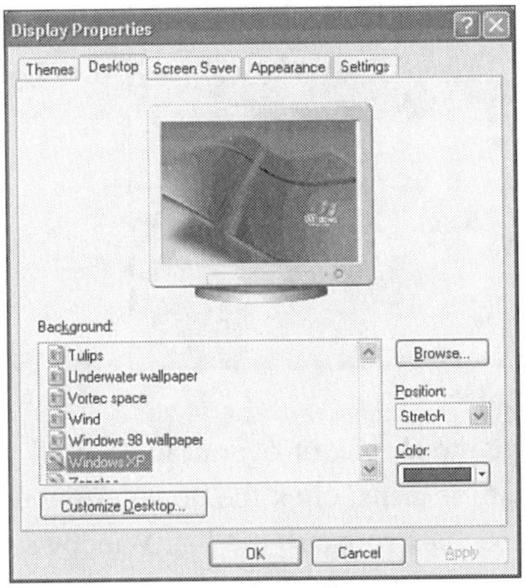

FIGURE 4.7

You can change your desktop's appearance.

4. The Background list of choices determines the wallpaper pattern you might want to use for your desktop's background. Scroll through the list of choices looking for an interesting name, such as Azul and click on that selection. Windows models the new wallpaper style in the small screen to give you a preview of it. You can go with that selection or choose another.

5. When you are happy with your selection, click the OK button, and presto, you've hung new wallpaper without messy cutting or gluing!

You can change your wallpaper without first displaying the Control Panel. Simply right-click over a blank spot on your desktop, select Properties, and click the Desktop tab.

> When surfing the Internet, you can quickly set any image you find on a Web page as wallpaper. Just right-click over a Web page's picture, select Set as Wallpaper, and Windows XP transfers the picture to your desktop immediately, replacing whatever wallpaper you had there before.

Adding Handy Desktop Icons

You already know that the taskbar's Show Desktop icon quickly minimizes all open windows and returns you to the desktop. Some Windows users prefer to place program icons on their desktop so that they can keep common windows and routine programs handy. When you place an icon on your desktop that represents a window such as the My Computer window, you only need to double-click that icon, while at your desktop, to see the window or start the program.

The following To Do item explains how to place programs on your desktop.

To Do: Putting Program Icons on Your Desktop

1. Click the Show Desktop Quick Launch toolbar button to minimize any windows you may have open.

2. Locate the program in your Start menu that you want to represent with a desktop icon. You may have to open a few cascading Start menu folders to locate the program.

3. Click and hold your right mouse button and drag the program's icon from its Start menu location to your desktop and release the mouse button.

4. Select Copy Here from the pop-up menu that appears and Windows XP places the icon on your desktop. You now only need to double-click this icon from the desktop to start the program.

> You can also place icons that take you to specific Web pages on your desktop. When viewing a Web page in your Internet browser, drag the icon to the left of the Web page's address to your desktop. The next time you double-click that desktop icon, the Web page appears, dialing your Internet connection first if needed.

Summary

This hour taught you how to use the My Computer window. Don't be dismayed that this hour just skimmed the surface of what's available in the My Computer window because the My Computer icon provides a launching point for many powerful hardware and software interactions that sometimes take a while to master. The typical Windows XP user does not have to know all the details of the My Computer window to use Windows XP effectively.

Q&A

Q Will I use the My Computer window a lot?

A This question's answer varies. Some people use their computers primarily for one or two application programs. These people don't modify their computers very often and do not perform a lot of file interaction or system management, so they would rarely, if ever, need to open the My Computer window.

On the other hand, if you modify the hardware on your computer often, you might have to access the My Computer window often. Windows XP is designed for use with *plug-and-play hardware*, which means that you don't only need to install a new device and Windows XP, in theory, should recognize the device. You, therefore, won't have to configure Windows XP every time you change hardware on your computer. Not all hardware devices are truly Plug-and-Play, however, and you might have to modify some Windows XP system settings using the My Computer window when you install new computer hardware, such as a second printer.

Q I like the animated cursors, but will they slow down my computer?

A If you use a slow computer, you don't want to do anything that will drain more speed from the processor. Nevertheless, the animated cursors do not seem to cause much of a drain on the processor's resources. The animated cursor icons are small and efficient. Therefore, you should feel free to use whatever cursors you want to use.

Workshop

The quiz and exercise questions are designed to test your knowledge of the material covered in this hour. The answers are in Appendix C, "Answers to Quizzes."

Quiz

1. What are some of the items you can manage from the My Computer window?

2. Why does Windows XP offer multiple views of the same window?

3. How can you tell if a folder is shared?

4. If you need to modify the way your mouse behaves, where would you go?

5. *True or false:* You can start a program both from your Start menu as well as from your desktop?

Exercises

1. Change your mouse button's orientation to swap the left and right mouse buttons. Close the Mouse dialog box and use the mouse for a while. You'll see that the buttons are reversed. Change the buttons back. You'll learn many ways to adjust your computer's behavior as you explore the rest of this 24-hour tutorial.

2. Change the desktop theme from your computer's current theme to another. Open some windows and look at the Start menu and taskbar to see how the new theme affects the way your Windows XP looks. Additional themes are available on the Internet if you have access as you'll see from the Display Properties dialog box. Even if you find a theme you like, you probably should restore the default theme for the rest of this book's lessons so that your screens match the figures in this text. By the way, each account can specify a different theme. If you find one or two themes you like, you may even create additional accounts for those themes and log on under one of the accounts when you want to work inside one of the theme's environments.

4

HOUR 5

Navigating Files with Windows Explorer

Windows XP includes a comprehensive program that you might use every time you turn on your computer, the *Windows Explorer* program, which graphically displays your entire computer system, including all its files, in a hierarchical tree structure. With Explorer, you have access to everything inside your computer (and outside if you are part of a network or on the Internet).

This hour demonstrates the Windows Explorer, a program that enables you to manipulate all of your computer's program and data files. After you've learned about Explorer, the hour wraps up by showing you some time- and disk-saving features of Windows XP.

In this hour, you will

- Change the various displays of the Windows Explorer
- Learn why Explorer makes managing your computer almost painless
- Learn what shortcuts are all about
- Use the Recycle Bin

Introducing the Windows Explorer

Often, Windows users call the Windows Explorer program just *Explorer*. You'll find Explorer listed on the Start menu system. Click the Start button to display the Start menu. Select More Programs, Accessories, and then select Windows Explorer. (Do not select Internet Explorer as that's your Internet browser.) The Windows Explorer window opens to look like the one shown in Figure 5.1. By default, Explorer opens to your My Documents folder located on your Windows disk drive. Your Explorer window might look somewhat different from the one in the figure. As Figure 5.1 shows, you can make Explorer point to any drive and folder, including a My Documents folder on a non-Windows drive if one exists. Simply type the location you wish to view in the Address bar.

FIGURE 5.1

Explorer's opening window shows folders and files.

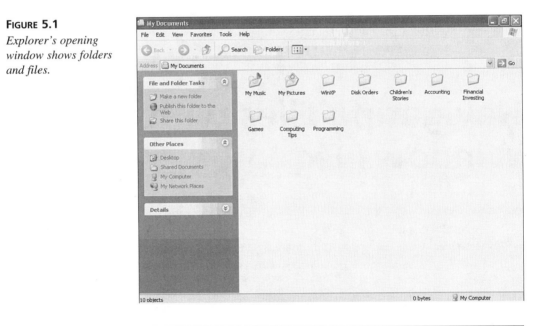

 You'll see how to customize your Explorer screen throughout this section.

Although the figure shows the Explorer screen fully maximized, you can run Explorer in a smaller window if you want something else to appear on your screen as well. In addition, your Explorer screen might differ slightly from the figures depending on your computer's files, disks, and theme.

You can quickly start Explorer by right-clicking over the Start menu and selecting Explore from the pop-up menu that appears. Even faster, locate your Windows key, the one with the flying Windows logo on it, and press Windows+E to start Explorer.

You can replace the task area of your Explorer screen with a hierarchical overview of your computer system by selecting View, Explorer Bar, Folders. You will recognize many of the icon entries from your My Computer window. If a vertical scrollbar appears on the left window, scroll to see the rest of the hierarchical system tree. You can replace the task area once again by selecting View, Explorer Bar, Folders so that common tasks are available to you.

If a folder icon appears in the Explorer bar with a plus sign to the left of it, that folder contains additional folders and files. Folder icons without the plus sign contain only data files (called *documents* throughout Windows XP) but not additional folders. When you open a folder and display its contents, the plus sign changes to a minus sign, as you'll see in the To Do item a little later.

The right side of the Explorer window contains a pictorial overview of the contents of whichever device or folder you select in the left window. The overview might contain large or small icons or a list view, depending on the view you select.

As with the My Computer window, you can display a thumbnail view that shows a small version of any Web page or graphic file that appears in the Windows Explorer window. As you select different items (by clicking to open folders or by selecting from a displayed Explorer bar), the right window changes to reflect your changes. The task area contains tasks you'll often perform inside the Explorer window as well as quick links to other places you may need to see such as the My Computer window or your desktop.

The following To Do item guides you through an initial exploration of Explorer.

To Do: Working with Explorer

1. Start Windows Explorer.
2. Select View, Explorer Bar, Folders to display your computer disk drive hierarchy.
3. Scroll through the Explorer bar's hierarchy until you see the icon for the C: drive in the window.

4. If you see a plus sign next to your C: icon in the left window (you might have to scroll the window's scrollbar to see the C: icon), click the plus sign to display the contents of the C: drive. The plus becomes a minus sign, and the left window opens the C: icon showing the list of folders and documents on the C: drive. Click the drive's minus sign again to close the window. Click once more to turn the plus to a minus and watch the right window. As you change between these two views of the C: drive (detailed and overview), watch the right window.

> Notice that the right window does not change as you click the C: icon in the left window. The reason is that the right window always displays the contents of whatever you highlight in the left window. Whether the C: icon is open (with a minus sign) or closed (with a plus sign), the C: icon is highlighted. If you were to click one of those documents on the C: drive, the right window would then update to show the contents of that folder (don't click a folder just yet).

5. Click the highest level in the left window, labeled Desktop, and Windows XP displays the contents of your desktop in the right window.

6. Click the C: icon to display the contents of the C: drive. Depending on the contents and size of your C: drive, the right window can contain a few or many document files.

7. Press Alt+V to open the View menu on the menu bar. Select Toolbar to display a list of tools you can display on your toolbar. Whatever you know about other windows applies to the Explorer window. For example, you can add text labels to the toolbar icons if you right-click the toolbar and select Customize.

8. Type a Web address inside the Address Bar's textbox to replace the contents of your Explorer window with a Web page. Press Back to return to the Explorer window. As you can see, Windows XP attempts to blur the distinction between your computer and the online world. Whether data is on your hard disk or on the disk of a computer across the globe, Explorer gives you quick access.

9. Select View, Details. Windows XP Explorer displays the items in a detailed format that describes the name, type, and modified date of each item. Actually, given the detail that you normally have by using Explorer, you will almost always want to display the right window in this detailed list view. When you work with files, you will often need to know their size, type, or last modified date.

   Click Name, the title of the first detailed column in the right window. Watch the window's contents change as you then click Modified. Explorer sorts the display to appear in date order (earliest first). Click Modified again and Explorer displays the items in reverse date order from the oldest to the most recent. If you click any column twice in a row, Windows sorts the column in reverse order. You can always sort columns in order or reverse order by clicking the column's name when working in a columnar Windows window.

10. If you want to see more of one of Explorer's windows, you can drag the edge of the left window pane (the pane marked Folders) left or right. For example, if you want the left window to be smaller to make room for more large icons, drag the right edge of the Folders pane to the left and release the mouse when the left window is as small as you want it. (Remember that the mouse cursor changes shape when you place it at the proper position on the dividing column.) Figure 5.2 shows the Explorer screen with the Explorer bar and no task window. Perhaps you'll prefer this configuration over the Task pane appearing. You'll learn which window configuration works best for you as you gain more experience with Explorer.

FIGURE 5.2

Make more room by closing the Folders window pane and changing the view.

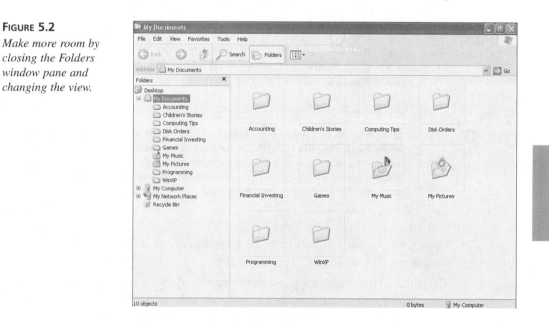

11. Click the toolbar's Folders button to see the Folders pane once again. As you can see, the Folders button quickly changes between the Explorer bar and your Task pane.

Explorer does not update the display every time you resize a window or change the size of the Folders pane. Therefore, if you enlarge the right window while in an icon view, Explorer does not automatically rearrange the right window's icons to fill up the newly enlarged space. You will almost always want to select View,

▼ Refresh after modifying Explorer's window sizes because Refresh analyzes any changes you've made to your disk while inside Explorer and updates the Explorer window. Perform Refresh when you open Explorer in a window and then add or delete files from another window.

> If you make the left or right window too small, Windows XP adds a horizontal scrollbar to the small window so that you can scroll its contents back and forth to see what's highlighted or to select another item.

12. The Explorer environment is always updating itself to reflect your current actions. Therefore, the right-click menu commands change, depending on whether you select a text document, folder, sound document, graphics document, disk drive, or network drive. Click a folder and right-click to see the menu that appears. Now, right-click over a document file to see a slightly different menu. The actions you might want to perform on a document are often different from the actions you might want to perform on a folder, and the menu reflects those differences. The right-click's pop-up menus are context-sensitive, so they contain only the options you can use at the time.

> Open a folder by double-clicking it, and then return to the previous (parent) folder by clicking the Up icon on the Explorer's toolbar. Use the Up toolbar button to return to your previous Explorer window's contents. You can return to the previous folder you opened (which is not necessarily the parent folder) by clicking the toolbar's Back button instead of Up.

13. Many Explorer users copy files to and from disk drives and other kinds of drives, such as networked drives.

You can use Explorer to copy and move individual files or multiple files at once. Often, you want to put one or more files from work on a diskette to use on your home computer for weekend overtime. (Sure, you want to do that a lot!)

To select a Windows file (called a document, remember), click that document. To select more than one document at a time, hold down the Ctrl key while clicking each document that you want to select. You can select folders, as well as documents. When you select a folder and other document files to copy to a disk, for example, Windows XP copies all the document files within the folder, as well as

▼ the other document files you've selected, to the disk. Figure 5.3 shows an Explorer screen with several document files and a folder selected. The File, Send To command (from the right-click pop-up menu) is about to send those files to the disk in the A: drive. The Send To command is useful for sending copies of selected files and folders to a disk, a fax recipient, or one of several other destinations you've set up.

FIGURE 5.3

Select multiple documents and folders if you need to copy several at a time.

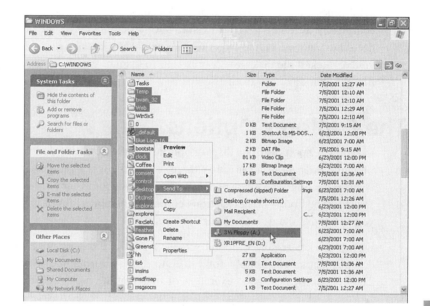

If you want to select all but one or two documents and folders inside a window, first Ctrl+click the one or two that you don't want to select (which selects those) and choose Edit, Invert Selection to reverse the selection. All the items that were not selected are now selected, and the one or two that were selected are no longer selected.

14. When you want to move or copy a file to another location (the Send To command works only for diskettes and other nonhard disk devices), select the file (or select a group of files) in the right window and drag while holding down the *right* mouse button to the folder or disk where you want to move or copy the file. Windows opens a pop-up menu when you release the files from which you can select a move or copy operation.

▼   15. Rename files and folders if you need to by selecting the file or folder and pressing
               the F2 shortcut key. (F2 is the shortcut for the File, Rename menu command.)
               Windows XP highlights the name, so you can edit or enter a new name. When you
▲   press Enter, Windows XP saves the new name.

The strength of Explorer is that your entire computer system appears in the left window
at all times. When you want to drag a document or folder to a different directory on a
completely different drive (or even to another computer on the network if you are connected to a network), the target disk drive always appears in the left window. As long as
you've clicked the disk drive's plus sign to display that disk's directories, you can drop a
file into that directory from elsewhere in the system.

The Explorer Options

Explorer supports various display options for the items inside its windows. Files have
filename *extensions*, a file suffix three or more letters long that appears after a filename.
A filename might be MyPayments.TXT or All Accounts.act (filenames can contain
spaces). The Tools, Folder Options command displays tabbed dialog boxes that enable
you to control the way Explorer displays items.

Different users require different screens from the Explorer program. There are types of
documents that you simply don't need to display during normal work inside Explorer.
The system files are good examples of files that the typical user does not need to see.

In addition, the actual location of the file—its pathname—does not always match the
system of embedded folders. In other words, a document might be located inside two
embedded folders shown with the Explorer display, but the actual file might be embedded three levels deep on your hard disk. The system of folders—usually but not
always—matches the system of directories on your disk. If you need to know exactly
where folders and documents are located on your disk drive, you can request that
Explorer display the full pathname of those folders and documents using these steps:

1. Select the Tools, Folder Options command to display the Folder Options tabbed
   dialog box shown in Figure 5.4.

2. Click the View tab to see the folder display options.

3. If you click the option labeled Display the full path in title bar, Explorer displays a
   full pathname of selected documents in the title bar every time you select one of
   the items in the left window.

FIGURE 5.4

The Folder Options dialog box determines the appearance of Explorer.

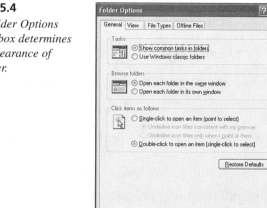

4. Another option, Hide file extensions for known file types, determines how Windows responds to known file types. Windows comes installed with several types of files already *registered*, and you might not ever need to register additional types. Registered files are files that Windows recognizes by their filename extensions. When you install a program whose data file is not registered, the installation program registers the file type with Windows.

   The file type's registration tells Windows the required program needed to process files with that extension. Once registered, when you double-click that file's icon, Windows starts the program you've associated with that file. For example, when you double-click a file with a .cda extension, Windows starts the CD Player application because CD Player is the application associated to all files that end with the .cda extension.

5. Look through the remaining items to see the other folder options that Windows provides. Click OK to finish your selection.

> If you are familiar with MS-DOS and filenames, you might feel more comfortable if you display the file extensions on the Explorer screen documents. Hiding the extensions reduces clutter in the right window, but with the extension, you can determine the exact name of the file when you need the exact name. Fortunately, with or without the extensions, the icons next to the filenames help remind you of the file's type.

5

> If you hide filename extensions in Explorer, Windows hides those extensions in almost every other file listing. For example, if you hide Explorer's extension display, you will no longer see extensions in WordPad's Open dialog boxes. You won't even see them in applications that you purchase in addition to Windows applications, such as Microsoft Excel.

Managing Documents with a Right Mouse Click

After you display the Explorer (or any other file list in Windows XP), you can point to any folder or document and click the right mouse button to perform several actions on the document. Here's what you can do with documents:

- Select documents by clicking them to highlight them
- Play sound or video files and view graphics
- Print selected documents
- Copy selected files to a disk
- Cut or copy selected text to the *Windows Clipboard* (an area of memory that holds data that you copy there until you replace the Clipboard's contents with something else or log off Windows)
- Create a shortcut access to the file so that you can later open the file without using the Open dialog box
- Delete documents
- Rename documents
- Change documents' system attributes

Right-clicking a folder's name produces a menu that enables you to perform these actions.

The following To Do item walks you through many of these right-click actions.

To Do: Practicing with the Right-Click

1. Inside an Explorer window, point to a text file on your C: drive. Text files use a spiral notepad icon. Open your Windows folder if you see no text files in your C:'s root folder. Point to the file and right-click. A pop-up menu opens to the right of the document, as shown in Figure 5.5.

FIGURE 5.5

A right-click displays a pop-up menu.

The Open command always attempts to examine the document's native format and open the document with an appropriate program such as the Windows's Notepad program. Although the first command is Open for text files, the command is Play if you right-clicked a sound file. For now, don't select Open.

2. Find a blank formatted diskette. Insert the diskette in the A: drive. Right-click over the text document and select the Send To command. The disk drive appears in the list that appears when you select Send To. When you select the disk drive, Windows XP begins sending an exact copy of the text file to the disk. Windows graphically displays the sending of the document to the A: drive with a flying document going from one folder to another.

3. Point to the text file once again and right-click. Select Delete. Windows displays the message box shown in Figure 5.6. Don't choose Yes because you need to keep the text file where it is.

The *Recycle Bin* is a special location inside Windows that holds the documents you delete. The Recycle Bin's icon appears on your Windows desktop. Windows gives you one last chance to recover deleted documents. When you delete a document file of any type, Windows sends that file to the Recycle Bin. The documents are then out of your way but not deleted permanently until you empty the Recycle Bin. Remember that you can delete documents directly from any Open dialog box.

5

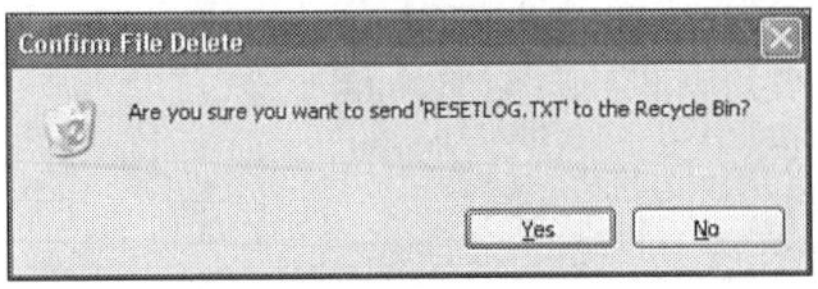

FIGURE 5.6

The Recycle Bin holds deleted documents for a while.

Confirm File Delete

Are you sure you want to send 'RESETLOG.TXT' to the Recycle Bin?

[Yes]   [No]

4. Click No because you should not delete the text file now.

5. It's extremely easy to rename a document. Right-click to display the document's pop-up menu and select Rename. Windows highlights the name, and you can edit or completely change the name to something else. Change the filename now to XYZ. Press Enter to keep the new name. (If you want to cancel a rename operation you've started, press Esc.)

Do not supply an extension when you rename the file unless you've turned on the filename extension display. For example, if you renamed a Readme document (that is really named Readme.txt) to NewName.txt, the document would actually be named NewName.txt.txt! Fortunately, Windows XP warns you if you change a file's extension, so you can accept or reject the change before it becomes permanent.

6. Try this: Move the mouse pointer to an area of the Explorer's right pane where no icon appears and right-click. A new menu appears.

The Undo Rename command reverses the previous renaming of the document. Select Undo Rename, and the XYZ text file you just renamed reverts to its original name.

Undo Rename remembers a long list of past names. For example, if you change a document's name three times in a row, and then select Undo Rename three times, Windows reverts the name to its original name.

You now understand the most important commands in the Explorer's primary right-click pop-up menus. These menus differ slightly depending on the kind of document you click (folder, video, sound, graphic, program, text, word processor document, and so on), but the fundamental menu of commands stays the same and works the way this section describes. If you want to make copies of files on the hard disk or move the file to a different location, you should master the techniques described in the next section.

Right-Click to Copy and Move Documents

A file icon's right-click menu offers advanced copying and moving of files. You'll use the Windows Clipboard as the go-between for all Windows copy, cut, paste, and move operations. When you want to copy a file from one place to another, you can place a copy of the file on the Windows Clipboard. When you do, the file is on the Clipboard and out of your way, until you go to where you want the file copied. You'll then paste the file to the new location, in effect copying from the Clipboard to the new location. When you copy a file to another location, the file remains in its original location and a copy is made elsewhere.

> The Clipboard holds one item at a time. If you copy a document to the Clipboard, a subsequent copy overwrites the first copy.

> If you want to copy a file to diskette, use the Send To command explained in the previous section because Send To is easier to use than copying to a floppy disk.

When you move a file from one location to another, Windows XP first performs a cut operation. This means that Windows XP deletes the file from its current location and sends the file to the Clipboard (overwriting whatever was on the Clipboard). When you find the location to which you want to move the file, Windows XP copies the Clipboard's contents to the new location (such as a different folder or disk drive).

5

> **About the Clipboard**
>
> In a way, the Clipboard is like a short-term Recycle Bin, which holds all deleted files until you are ready to remove them permanently. The Clipboard holds deleted (or copied) documents and pieces of documents, but only until you send something else to the Clipboard or exit Windows XP and log off Windows XP.

▼ To Do: Practicing with Move and Copy

1. Right-click a text file's icon.
2. Select the Copy command. Windows sends a complete copy of the document to the Clipboard. The Clipboard keeps the document until you replace the Clipboard's

▼ contents with something else or until you exit Windows. Therefore, you can send the Clipboard document to several subsequent locations.

3. Right-click a folder in Explorer's right window. The menu appears with the Paste command. Windows knows that something is on the Clipboard (a copy of the text file), and you can send the file's copy to the folder by clicking Paste. Don't paste the file now, however, unless you then open the folder and remove the file. There is no need to have two copies of the text file on your disk.

4. Right-click once again over the text file. This time, select Cut instead of Copy. Windows erases the document file from the Windows folder and places the file on the Clipboard.

> Windows keeps the name of the document in place until you paste the document elsewhere. The name is misleading because it makes you think the document is still in the Windows folder. A ghost outline of an icon appears where the document's icon originally appeared. As long as the name still appears in the Windows folder, you can open the file and do things with it, but as soon as you paste the Clipboard contents elsewhere, the file permanently disappears from the Windows folder.

5. Right-click a folder. If you select Paste, the text document leaves its original location and goes to the folder. Don't paste now but press Esc twice (the first Esc keypress removes the right-click menu, and the second restores the cut file).

6. Windows lets you change your mind. If you change your mind after a copy or cut operation, you can always reverse the operation! Right-click the icon area and the pop-up menu contains an Undo command that reverses the most recent copy or cut.

> Here's a much faster way to move a document to another folder listed in the Explorer windows: Drag the document to the folder! Try it by dragging a test file over to another hard disk or to another folder on the same disk. An outline of the document travels with the mouse cursor during the drag. When you release the mouse button, the file anchors into its new position. Want to restore the item? Right-click the mouse and select Undo Move or Undo Copy. Windows always enables you to undo copies and moves, no matter how you perform the move, through menus or with the mouse.

If you want to use the drag-and-drop shortcut method for copying documents, hold down the Ctrl key while dragging the document to the other folder. (The key combination is easy if you remember that both copy and Ctrl begin with the same

▼

▼ letter.) As you drag an item, Windows displays a plus sign at the bottom of the icon to indicate that you are copying and not moving. To cancel a copy you've started, drag the item back to its original location before releasing your mouse button or press Esc before releasing your mouse button. In addition, if you drag the item while holding the right mouse button, Windows XP displays a pop-up menu, enabling you to specify that you want to move or copy the document.

7. Sometimes, you might need a document for a program outside of the program in which you're currently working. You can place a document on the Windows desktop. Select a text file and copy the document to the Clipboard by right-clicking and selecting Copy. (You also can use drag-and-drop if you want. Hold down Ctrl and drag the document out of the Explorer window, if you've resized Explorer so that you can see part of the desktop, and continue with step 8.)

8. Move the cursor on the Windows desktop to an area of the wallpaper that has no icon on it. Right-click to display a menu and select Paste. The document's file will now have an icon on your desktop along with the other icons already there.

▲ To copy or move the wallpaper document, use the right-click menu or drag the document with the mouse, as explained earlier in this hour.

Placing Documents on the Desktop

The items you place on the desktop, whether by copying or by moving, stay on the desktop until you remove them from the desktop. Even after shutting down Windows XP and turning off your computer, a desktop item will be there when you return.

Although you shouldn't clutter your desktop with too many documents, you might want to work with a document in several different programs over a period of a few days. By putting the document on the desktop, it is always easily available to any application that's running. Of course, if you run an application in a maximized window, you must shrink the window to some degree to retrieve the document because you have to see the desktop to copy and move the items on it. Also, you can even drag Web pages to your desktop.

5

Using the Explorer's Task Pane

A mastery of the previous section is critical to using your computer to its fullest. The file-related copy, cut, and move operations, using the right-click pop-up menus and your mouse for dragging are skills that all Windows users should understand. So many programs support these file operations that their mastery is critical.

Having said that, throughout the previous section, you may have noticed that the Task pane of the Explorer window changed as you selected files. As Figure 5.7 shows, when you select a text file, the Task pane offers to rename, move, copy, publish to the Web (assuming you have the rights to post to an Internet site), send the file as an e-mail, print the file on your printer, or send the file to the recycle bin. For these common file operations, clicking the task is often easier than right-clicking and selecting from the pop-up menu. (Remember, if your Task pane is not showing, click the toolbar's Folders button to display it.)

FIGURE 5.7
The Explorer Task pane simplifies common file operations.

Tasks you can perform

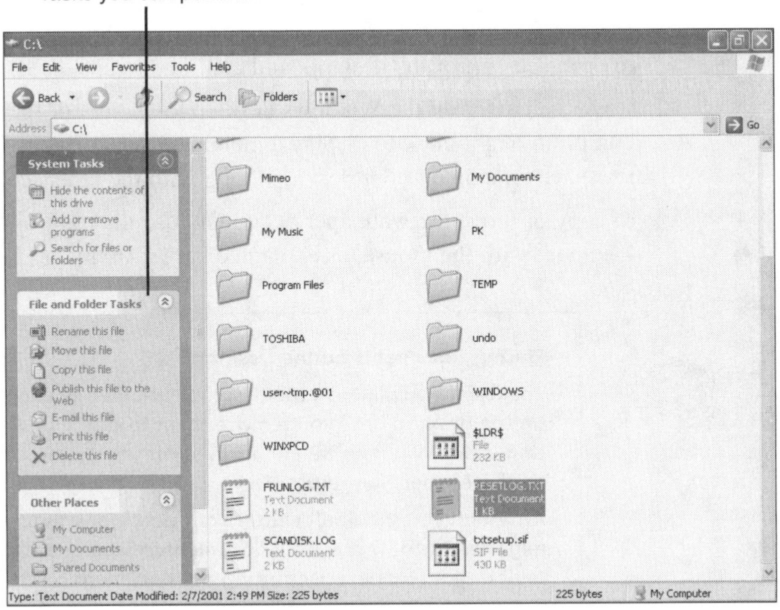

Where Do the Deleted Files Go?

When you delete files by using dialog boxes or Explorer, you now know that those files go to the Recycle Bin. While in the Recycle Bin, those files are out of your way and deleted in every respect except one: They are not really deleted. Those files are not in their original locations, but they stay in the Recycle Bin until you empty it.

Periodically, you will want to check the Recycle Bin for files that you can erase completely from your hard disk. The following To Do item explain the Recycle Bin in more detail.

The Recycle Bin icon changes from an overflowing bin to an empty one when you empty the Recycle Bin, enabling you to tell at a glance whether your Recycle Bin is empty.

To Do: Working with the Recycle Bin

1. Display your desktop by minimizing any open windows you might have on the screen.

2. Double-click the Recycle Bin icon. The Recycle Bin window opens.

3. If you've deleted at least one file, you should have one or two files already in the Recycle Bin. There might be many more, depending on what has taken place on your system. You will recognize the format of the Recycle Bin's column headings; you can adjust the width of the columns by dragging the column separators with your mouse.

The Recycle Bin dialog box contains all deleted files on your system—not just the deleted files on one of your disk drives. You can change the disks that the Recycle Bin uses for its storage of deleted files, but unless you change your Windows XP default values, all files that you delete through Windows XP go to the Recycle Bin.

4. Most of the Recycle Bin dialog box's menu bar commands and toolbar are identical to the ones in Explorer and other windows. When you select an item (or more than one item by using Ctrl+click), your commands apply to that selected item.

5. Right-click any Recycle Bin item to display a Properties dialog box for that item. The box tells you additional information about the deleted item, such as the date you created and deleted the item. Click OK to close the dialog box.

6. Perhaps the most important menu command is Empty the Recycle Bin in the left pane. This command empties the entire Recycle Bin. Select this command now, if there is nothing in your Recycle Bin that you think you will need later.

7. Select File, Close to close the Recycle Bin dialog box.

Although the Recycle Bin adds a level of safety to your work so that you have a second chance to recover files that you delete, if you hold the Shift key when you highlight a file and press Delete (from Explorer or any other window), Windows XP bypasses the Recycle Bin and deletes the files from your system immediately.

Making Windows XP Easier to Use

There are numerous ways to make Windows easier for your day-to-day work. Three time-saving techniques are as follows:

- Changing the Start menu
- Adding single-key access to programs
- Shortcuts

After you create single-key access to a program or a shortcut or you change the Start menu, those time-savers stay in effect, making work inside Windows XP much more efficient.

These time-savers might not help everyone, but they often help users of Windows XP. You have to experiment with the techniques until you find the ones that help you the most. Practice using the time-savers by following this To Do item.

To Do: Saving Time with Windows

1. You can add programs to the top of the Start menu by dragging a program from Explorer or My Computer to the Start button. Open Windows Explorer.

2. Click the Windows folder. The folder's contents appear in the right window.

 Before adding programs to the Start menu, you must know the location of the program you are adding. If you do not know the path to the program, you can use the Find commands described in Hour 9, "Finding Files, Folders, and Friends."

3. Scroll down the window to locate a game called FreeCell (the extension is .exe). FreeCell is a solitaire card game.

4. Drag the FreeCell icon to your Start button. The icon stays in place, but an outline of the icon moves with your dragged mouse cursor.

5. Release the icon over the Start button. You've just added the FreeCell game to the top of your Start menu.

▼ 6. Close Explorer and click your Start button. Your Start menu now includes the FreeCell game, located directly beneath your user account name, as shown in Figure 5.8. You can now start FreeCell without traversing several Start menu layers for those times when the boss is away for a short while. (Other recently-used programs will be there with FreeCell and they are all as close as your Start menu.)

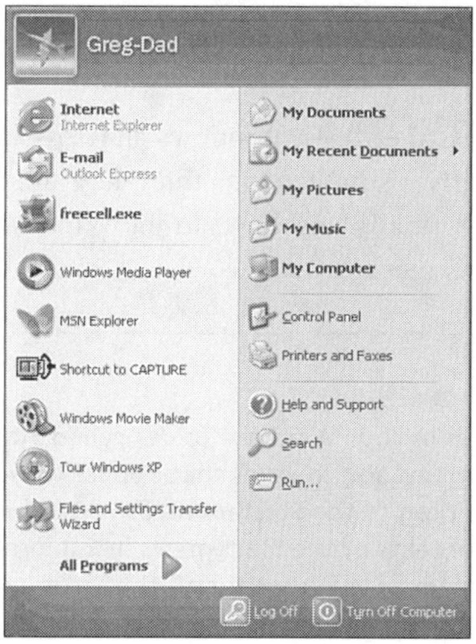

FIGURE 5.8

Your Start menu now includes the FreeCell game.

Windows XP offers a great way to rearrange and modify your Start menu without going through the windows and buttons of the Settings, Taskbar and Start Menu option. Any time you want to move one of the Start menu's entries from one location to another, display that item on the Start menu and drag that item to another location on the menu. (Don't click the item and release the mouse; be sure that you click and hold your mouse button.) If you right-click over any Start menu item, a pop-up menu appears, enabling you to rename or delete that item.

5

7. Remove FreeCell from the Start menu (you can add it later if you really want it there) by right-clicking on the menu entry and selecting Unpin from Start menu.

8. Select More programs and then open the Accessories menu folder to view the contents of the Accessories group. The Calculator program's icon appears in this folder group.

9. Right-click the Calculator icon to display a pop-up menu.

▼ 10. Select Properties to display the Calculator program's Properties tabbed dialog box.

▼ 11. Press Alt+K to move the cursor to the Shortcut key text prompt. Type **C** at the prompt. Windows XP changes the **C** to `Ctrl + Alt + C` on the screen. Ctrl+Alt+C is now the shortcut for the Calculator program. If you run a program that uses a shortcut key you've added to Windows XP, the program's shortcut key takes precedence over the Windows XP shortcut key.

12. Click OK to close the dialog box.

13. Select File, Close to exit Explorer and then close the Taskbar and Start Menu Properties dialog box.

Whenever you now press Ctrl+Alt+C, Windows starts its Calculator program. This single-key shortcut (actually a simultaneous three-key shortcut) enables you to start programs instantly, from virtually anywhere in the Windows system, without hav-
▲ ing to locate the program's menu or icon.

Shortcuts

A subfolder resides in your Windows folder called Start Menu. The Start Menu's folder contains all the items that appear on your Start menu, including the items you drag to the Start menu as you did in the previous task. If you display the contents of the Start menu in Explorer, you'll see small arrows at the bottom of the icons there. The arrows indicate shortcuts to the file.

The name shortcut has a double meaning in Windows XP—one of the reasons that this section's timesavers can become confusing.

A shortcut is actually better termed an *alias file*. When you create a shortcut, such as on the Start menu, Windows does not make a copy of the program in every location where you place the icon. Windows actually creates a link to that program, called a shortcut, that points to the program on your disk wherever its location might be.

If you right-click a document or folder in Explorer's right window, you see the Create Shortcut command that creates a shortcut to the document or folder to which you are pointing. Windows creates a new icon and title (the title begins with Shortcut too) but does not actually create a copy of the item. Instead, Windows creates a link to that item. The link reduces disk space taken up by multiple copies of the same files. The shortcut pointer takes much less space than a copy of the actual file would.

Summary

This hour showed you how to use the Explorer to manage your documents and folders. Copying and moving among folders and documents are painless functions when you use Explorer. You can display the item to be moved in the right window and drag that item to any device listed in the left window. Inside Explorer, you can associate file types to programs, so you can click a document and run the appropriate program that works with a document.

Three shortcuts exist that help you access your programs. You can add a shortcut to the desktop, to the Start menu system, and even to the keyboard to start programs quickly.

Q&A

Q Why does it seem as though many Explorer functions are available elsewhere, such as in the My Computer window and in Open dialog boxes?

A You can find many of Explorer's capabilities elsewhere. Windows is known for giving you the tools you need where you need them. You don't have to hunt for the tools you need.

Q I'm confused; are there three kinds of shortcuts?

A There are three versions of shortcuts in Windows XP. You can add a single-key shortcut to any program. When you press Ctrl+Alt and that key at the same time, Windows starts the program. You can be working in Explorer, at the desktop, or in virtually any other program, but when you press the shortcut keystroke, Windows starts the program you've assigned to that shortcut key.

When you right-click a document or folder and select the Create Shortcut command, Windows creates a shortcut to the item, which is really an alias name that knows the location of the original document or folder, but which acts like a copy of the item.

When you add items to the Start menu (or any menu cascading out from the Start menu), you must create a shortcut to that item because you don't want a copy of the same program all over your disk drive. Therefore, the menu command will be a shortcut to the program that, after you select that menu item, finds the program on the disk drive and starts the program.

Workshop

The quiz and exercise questions are designed to test your knowledge of the material covered in this hour. The answers are in Appendix C, "Answers to Quizzes."

Quiz

1. How does the Windows XP thumbnail view display lists of files?

2. *True or false*: You should start Internet Explorer to manage your computer's drives, folders, and files.

3. Why would you want to display filename extensions in Windows Explorer?

4. How can you rearrange Start menu entries with your mouse only?

5. How can you tell at a glance that an icon represents a shortcut and not a file?

Exercises

1. Place your favorite word processing program at the top of your Start menu for quick access to the program. Then, add a keyboard shortcut to the word processor so that you don't even have to display the Start menu to start the program.

2. Open your Control Panel, select Appearance and Themes, and select Taskbar and Start Menu to display the Taskbar and Start Menu Properties dialog box. Click the Start Menu tab and then click Customize. Study the various ways you can modify the look and behavior of the Start menu, such as changing the size of the icons you see there.

HOUR 6

Calling for Help

This hour shows you how to help yourself! That is—how to help yourself find help when using Windows XP. Although this book is *really* all you'll ever need to use Windows effectively (self-promotion was never one of my weak points), when you get confused, Windows offers a good set of online tools that you can access to find out how to accomplish a specific task.

If you've used previous versions of Windows, you will notice that Microsoft has added a lot to the Windows XP entire help system.

In this hour, you will

- Access the help system
- Ask a remote user for assistance
- Check your hardware and software for compatibility to Windows XP
- Access the help inside individual Windows XP applications

Introducing the Help and Support Center (HSC)

Even Windows XP experts need help now and then with Windows. Windows is simply too vast, despite its simple appearance and clean desktop, for users to know everything about the system. Windows includes a powerful built-in Help system. The Help system connects to the Internet when needed so that help is on your disk and up-to-the-minute help is available from Microsoft's Web site. Help is available whenever you need it. For example, if you are working with the My Computer window and have a question, just search the online help system for the words *My Computer*, and Windows gives advice about using the My Computer window.

Microsoft calls the Windows XP help screens the *Help and Support Center* (the *HSC*). The help system goes far beyond the standard online help you may be used to in other applications and previous versions of Windows.

There are a number of ways you can request help while working in Windows XP. There are also numerous places from which you can get help. This hour focuses on the most common ways that you can use online help and also offers tips along the way.

To use every help feature available to you in Windows, you need Internet access. Microsoft keeps up-to-date advice on the Web, such as bug reports and add-on programs to Windows that you can download to improve your use of Windows XP.

The taskbar is always available to you no matter what else you are doing in Windows XP. Even if you've hidden the taskbar behind a running program, the taskbar is available as soon as you press your Windows key to display the taskbar and Start menu. The HSC's command is located on the taskbar's Start menu. Selecting the Help and Support Center option displays the online help's opening screen by using a Web browser format. To get started, the next To Do item shows you how to access the online HSC.

To Do: Accessing the Help and Support Center from the Start Menu

1. Click the Start button to display the Start menu.

2. Select Help and Support to view the online help window. After a brief pause, you see Windows XP's HSC window shown in Figure 6.1.

FIGURE **6.1**

The Help and Support Center window offers all kinds of help.

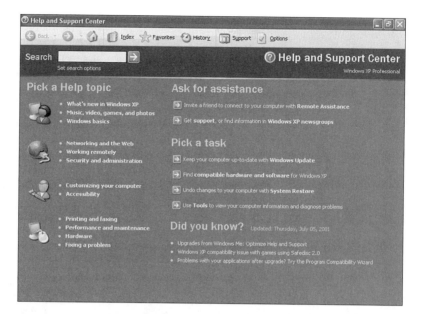

The HSC window offers two kinds of help: local help that searches your PC's Windows XP help files for answers to your questions and Web help resources that connect to your Internet provider and accesses Microsoft's huge online help resource.

> The Help and Support window contains a toolbar that works like a Web-browsing toolbar.

Therefore, when you need help, you aren't limited to your own system help files. Although you can get many answers from your PC's local help files, Microsoft's online Help window makes it easy for you to contact the large online help databases Microsoft stores on the Web.

6

> The HSC window resides on your disk as an HTML file, which is the format behind all Web pages. Web pages can be local or on the Internet—your PC reacts to both in the same manner. Therefore, the HSC window acts like a

Web page. When you rest your mouse cursor over a *hot spot* (a link to another location, also called a *hyperlink*), the mouse cursor changes to a pointing hand to let you know that if you click that hot spot, another page will appear. As with all help pages, you can traverse backward through your help screen travels by clicking the toolbar's Back button.

Any time you click the HSC's History button at the top of the HSC screen, the HSC displays a window that includes every link you've visited recently within the HSC. You can quickly return to any HSC item you've viewed recently by clicking its link in the History window pane.

Getting Topical Help

If you have a question about Windows XP or about a certain utility program that comes with Windows, just ask for help and Windows will supply it. Although the Windows XP help extends to the Web for more complete help topics, you'll find most answers to common Windows questions on your own system and searching your local disk is generally quicker than waiting on a Web search, as the following To Do item demonstrates:

To Do: Requesting Help from Windows XP

1. Open the Help and Support Center window if it is no longer open from the previous section.

2. After a brief pause, the HSC screen that you saw in Figure 6.1 appears.

   The initial Help and Support Center window offers a summary of the help items available to you in an Explorer-like format. Click an item to read more about that topic. When you click a topic, more details emerge from which you can select.

3. Click the entry labeled Music, video, games and photos. Several topics appear in the left window pane for which you can get more detailed help by clicking on one of the topics.

4. Click the Music and sounds topic to open that topic and see the related help topics. An overview of the topic appears in the right pane.

5. Click the Playing and copying music topic to see the help tasks shown in Figure 6.2.

6. Click the toolbar's Back button to see the HSC screen before you displayed the detail. As with any Web page, you can click the Back button to return to the previous help screen. If you view several topics in succession, you sometimes want to return to a previous topic. Return to the detail page once again. You can also return to pages you've backed up from by clicking the Forward button.

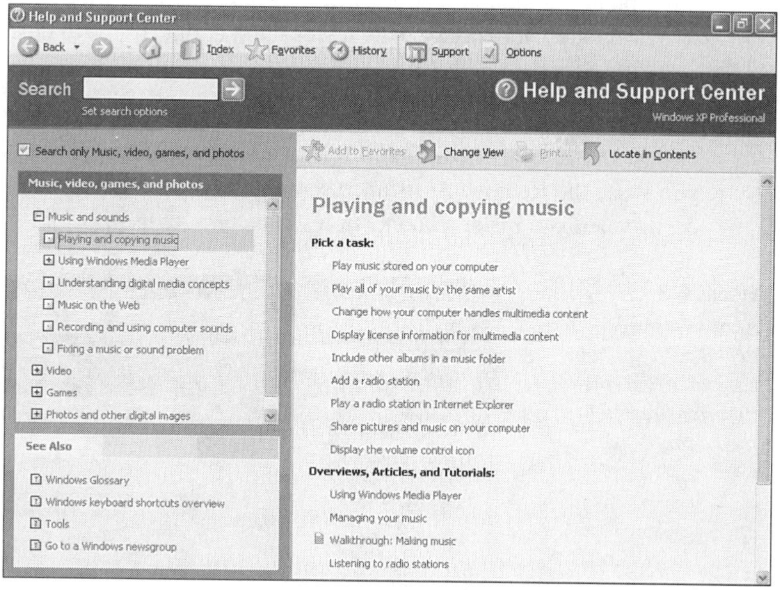

FIGURE 6.2

The Help and Support Center helps you get started with playing and recording music.

You can click the Home link at the top of the Help and Support Center to return to the initial HSC page.

Obtaining Support

The Support area of the HSC contains several topics that provide you with third-party assistance and Internet-based information that can help you get past problems.

Contacting Remote Assistance

When you have a problem with your computer, wouldn't it be nice to ask an expert to come look over your shoulder and explain what's going on? In a way, Windows XP does just that.

The HSC's Support link provides the following kinds of assistance:

- Provides links to Microsoft-based Web sites and other online areas (such as chats and by e-mail) that contain advanced troubleshooting information for Windows XP.

- Provides links to your own computer's system tools, such as the Advanced System Information utility that lists all hardware and software settings currently set for your computer.

6

- Provides *remote assistance*, a system that allows others connected to your computer via the Internet or local network to temporarily take over your computer remotely, looking at your screens and applications, to determine where problems are occurring.

The remote assistance is the most innovative feature inside Windows XP because previous operating systems did not offer such support. When you choose Remove Assistance, you'll see the Remove Assistance screen shown in Figure 6.3 that explains what will occur when you make a connection with a remote user.

FIGURE 6.3

Another user can connect directly to your computer and run your programs remotely to locate problems.

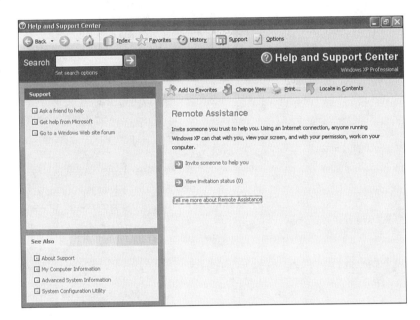

During the remote session, the remote user will be able to look at the same screen you are. Your computer will receive the remote user's keystrokes in a manner that makes the computer believe it is you doing the typing. The remote user will then be able to reproduce the problems you are having and, after seeing your system the same way that you see it, will hopefully be able to suggest solutions.

During the remote session, you and the remote user will be able to chat back and forth in a pop-up chat window. You'll use the chat window to explain what is happening and to answer questions the remote user may have.

Your remote user must be using Windows XP (any version) and must have Internet access or access to your computer through a local area network. Some networks have *firewalls* attached that add security from unauthorized break-in attempts. Such firewalls sometimes wreak havoc with the Remote Assistance and your network's System Administrator will have to help ensure that the firewall allows for remote access before you can be connected to such a user.

So many variations of equipment and connections exist that it would be virtually impossible to walk you through a step-by-step To Do task that would work in all readers' cases. Nevertheless, the general steps that you must take to connect to a remote user are fairly common. Here are the general steps you'll go through when using the Remote Assistance:

1. Display the Help and Support Center window.

2. Click the Remote Assistance link beneath the first topic in the Support area.

3. Click the link labeled Invite someone to help you. Before connecting to a remote user, you need to send that user an invitation to connect to your system. As Figure 6.4 shows, you can send the invitation by e-mail, by the *MSN Messenger* service (provided by Microsoft), or save the invitation in a file that your remote user can retrieve.

FIGURE 6.4

The HSC offers three ways to send an invitation to your remote user.

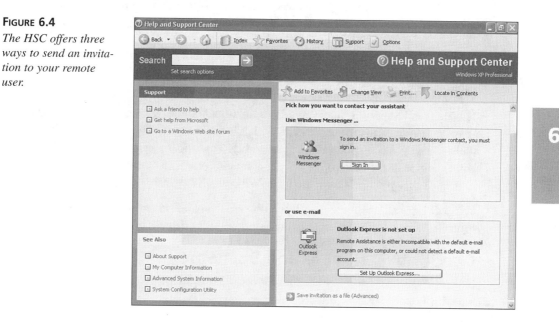

You'll learn in Hour 12, "Tying Windows into the Web," how to sign up for Microsoft's free MSN Messenger, an online service that provides free e-mail, chat sessions, phone calls, and other features.

If you send an e-mail or save your request as a file, the e-mail or file-based invitation will expire at the time you designate. After all, if you need help in the next two hours but your remote user happens to be on vacation, you don't want your remote user getting back in a week and trying to respond to the invitation long after you no longer need the response. If you use the MSN Messenger service, your remote user must be logged on to respond immediately but you can also send an e-mail to the user through the MSN Messenger system so the user learns of your invitation the moment that user logs into the Internet.

4. After your remote user responds to your invitation and agrees by clicking the appropriate link on the remote computer, Windows XP will connect your machine to your remote user and give control over to the user. You will still be able to control your computer as well and you can communicate with the remote user during the session using the pop-up chat window.

Don't send an invitation to a remote user you don't trust. Obviously, the ability to access your computer's resources is not a gift you'd offer to someone you don't know. Some software and hardware firms will surely be offering to provide remote assistance through XP's Remote Assistance service. Generally, if you initiate the support request to a company you trust, and you'll be at your computer watching the session, your files should be fine. You can terminate the Remote Assistance session any time you want to.

Updating Windows

The Help and Support Center provides a link to an online Microsoft site that checks your Windows XP files to ensure they are the latest and that you have all the needed system files to keep your computer running smoothly. This update feature is not actually an online help feature but if you're having computer problems, the problems may be related to the fact that you don't have the latest Windows XP patch.

You will learn all about this link labeled Keep your computer up-to-date with Windows Update in Hour 18, "Giving Windows XP a Tune-Up."

Checking Hardware and Software

If you suspect that a graphics adapter or other hardware device is having problems working with Windows XP, or if a program does not behave the way you expect, you can click the link labeled Find compatible hardware and software for Windows XP to see if the item in question is approved to work within Windows XP. You must have an Internet connection available to use this HSC feature.

When you click the Find compatible hardware and software for Windows XP link, the HSC provides a Product Search dialog box that you can type the name and model of your hardware device or the name and version of the software you're having trouble with. When you click Search, the HSC goes to Microsoft's Web site and checks to see if the hardware or software program is compatible with Windows XP. If not, you may have to upgrade your hardware or program. If so, then you know the problem you might be having is not a compatibility issue.

Staying Current with *Did You Know?*

The section labeled *Did you know?* is a section of the HSC that changes periodically. As you use the Internet, the HSC will often download new topics for the *Did you know?* section. These topics are generally guides about using Windows XP features and information about upgrading to newer versions as they become available.

When you go to the HSC for help, you might want to glance at the *Did you know?* section to see if something interests you there. Click any of the links to learn more about that link's topic.

Searching the Index

As good and complete as the HSC is, you may have difficulty locating exact help on a specific topic that you need help with. The times that you are not sure where to look, check the HSC's Index link. The Index link helps you zero in to a specific item for which you need help.

Follow this To Do item to use the Index link.

To Do: Using the Index in Your Search

1. Click the Index link at the top of the Help and Support Center window. An alphabetical list of all items within the help system appears in a scrollable window pane, as Figure 6.5 shows.

2. To find something in the index, scroll the indexed list to the item you want to find. You can quickly move to an item by clicking the text box and typing your requested entry. As you type, the index item that matches your typed letters begins to appear.

3. Scroll through the entries, looking at the various index items.

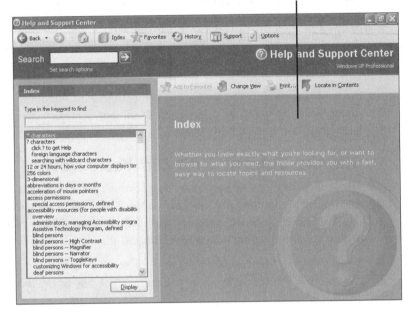

FIGURE 6.5

The Index enables you to find details quickly.

Your selected item's detail will appear here

4. Locate the indexed entry, direct cable connections, and double-click the overview entry below the main topic. A detailed overview window opens in the right window pane. A hot spot appears in the right window labeled Related Topics. The help pages are often cross-referenced to other related help pages and Windows accessory programs, so you can read all the information related to the topic in which you are interested and start that topic's program when needed. You can move to other topics by clicking on the index pane's items or by selecting hot spots in the right pane. As you move to various hot spots, the Back button always returns you to the previous help page, so you can always get back from where you came in the Help system.

5. Every once in a while, an indexed topic requires additional information. Sometimes the Help system narrows a search to a more specific item. For example, if you click the indexed item labeled overview, located beneath the entry named accessibility resources (for people with disabilities), a Topics Found dialog box appears like the one in Figure 6.6. When you select one of the dialog box's topics and click the Display button, that topic's Detail page appears.

FIGURE 6.6
Help needs you to be more specific.

6. Click Home to return to the main Help and Support Center window.

If you know with which specific Windows XP element you need help, you can often locate the help quicker by selecting from the Index page instead of the more general Contents pages that first appears when you request help.

The Search box at the top of the Help and Support Center screen allows you to type an entry and search your computer's help files for any topic. Surprisingly, the Search box doesn't always produce an extremely helpful list of topics (this is true of the early versions of Windows XP at least), but you'll sometimes find exactly what you need. If a quick search doesn't produce good results, you can use one of the other methods discussed in this hour's lesson to locate exactly the help you need.

Other Forms of Help

The help you obtain in Windows XP does not always come from the help system itself but from auxiliary help systems that add support to the tasks and programs you work with.

Using Application Help

When you use a Windows XP program, you often need help with the program rather than Windows. Almost every Windows application's menu bar includes a Help option you can click for help with that program.

For example, if you select Help, Help Topics from the Windows XP Calculator program, a Help dialog box appears with tabs at the top of the window that list helpful help divisions such as Contents, Index, and Search. The Contents pages offer a general overview of the program. You're already familiar with the Index page because it mimics the Index page in the Help and Support Center window described in the previous section. Figure 6.7 shows the Calculator's Index page.

6

FIGURE 6.7
*Most applications
provide indexed help
topics.*

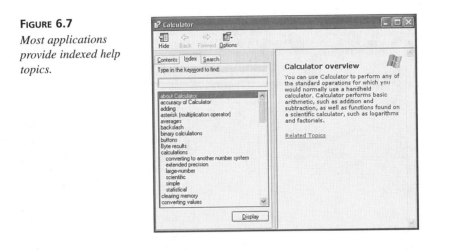

The Search tab on many applications' help screen makes looking for a particular topic
not indexed on the Index tab easier. To search for a topic, click the Search tab, enter a
topic, and then click the command button labeled List Topics. If the help engine locates
your search candidate, a list of all help pages that include your search topic appears, and
you can open that help page to view its details in the right pane by clicking the Display
button.

Using Pop-Up Help

Sometimes, you'll be in the middle of a dialog box working inside Windows when you
spot a command button or other control that you do not understand. Look in the upper-
right corner of the window for a question mark on one of the command buttons. If you
find such a question mark, you've found the Windows *Pop-Up Help* command button and
cursor (sometimes called *Roving Help*).

The Pop-Up Help enables you to narrow the focus and request help on a specific screen
item. Not all dialog boxes or screens inside Windows contain the Pop-Up Help feature,
so look for the question mark command button, which is to the left of the window minimizing and resizing buttons.

As long as the dialog box contains the Pop-Up Help button, you can request Pop-Up
Help for any item on the dialog box as the following To Do item demonstrates.

▼ To Do

To Do: Requesting the Pop-Up Help

1. Right-click on the Start button to display the Taskbar and Start Menu Properties
   dialog box (you can also access this dialog box from the Control Panel). The dialog box displays the Pop-Up help button with the question mark in the upper-right
   corner.

2. Click the question mark once and your mouse cursor changes to a question mark that follows the mouse pointer as you move the mouse.

3. Point the question mark mouse cursor over the link labeled Show the clock and click the option. Windows displays the Pop-Up Help message box shown in Figure 6.8.

FIGURE 6.8

The Pop-Up Help helps you when you point to a place on the screen.

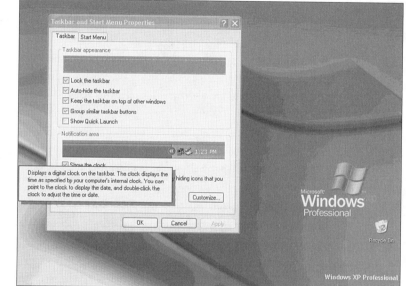

4. Press Esc to get rid of the pop-up description box and return to the regular mouse cursor shape.

Another way exists that produces the Pop-Up help. Point your mouse cursor over an item. Right-click and select What's This? from the single-option menu that appears to display the pop-up description.

Summary

This hour showed you how to access the powerful Help features in Windows XP. When you have a question about Windows XP, you can ask Windows XP for help. There are several ways to access the helpful dialog boxes about a variety of topics. The most common method of getting detailed help is to select the Help and Support command from

6

the Start menu. You can access your local PC's help files, search the Internet for the answers you need, or ask a remote user to take a look. Most Windows XP programs contain a Help command that displays a tabbed dialog box containing different kinds of help search screens.

Q&A

Q **There are so many kinds of help available; which one should I use?**

A The method of help that you access depends on the task you're trying to accomplish. Generally, there are several ways to get help on the same topic. If you want help on a procedure such as moving files, you can probably find related topics grouped together in the Index listing. There, you can find topics, grouped by subject, which you can browse.

For help on a dialog box element that you don't understand, click the question mark button (if one is available in the dialog box's upper-right corner) and click over the item you want help with. A description pops up that describes that item in more detail.

If you are having problems making something work and you've checked your hardware and software from the Compatible Hardware and Software link, it may be time to ask a remote user for assistance.

Workshop

The quiz and exercise questions are designed to test your knowledge of the material covered in this hour. The answers are in Appendix C, "Answers to Quizzes."

Quiz

1. How can an Internet connection help improve the help you get from Windows XP's Help and Support Center?

2. In what ways does the Windows XP Help and Support Center mimic an Internet Web browser?

3. What are the three ways to send an invitation for the Remote Assistance feature?

4. If you know exactly which Windows XP topic you need help with, which is the fastest way to go directly to that topic's help information?

5. *True or false*: Many dialog boxes provide a pop-up help for their items that do not require that you use the HSC.

Exercises

1. Read all about Windows Explorer from the Windows Start menu's HSC window. Many topics reside under the Windows Explorer entry. You'll learn a lot about Explorer by seeing what the HSC has to say about Explorer.

2. If you have a friend who also uses Windows XP and has an Internet connection, start a Remote Assistance session. Send your friend an invitation and let your friend control your computer for a while. Chat in the chat window as you do so. Perhaps let your friend play a game on your machine. Once you're finished, reverse the roles. You should understand what it's like to be on the other end so that you can help others. Ask your friend to send you an invitation, accept the electronic invitation, and do something on your friend's computer. But don't check your friend's bank statements; some friends don't like it when other friends do that.

6

Hour **7**

Improving Your Windows Desktop Experience

This hour differs somewhat from the others. Instead of studying a single central aspect of Windows XP, such as Explorer, this hour contains a potpourri of desktop-management tips and procedures that improve the way you use the Windows XP environment. Previous hours studied topics in depth, but this hour offers advice that you can use while working within Windows XP.

You can activate your desktop with the Windows Active Desktop feature. Place Web pages and other files directly on your desktop to customize your Windows wallpaper. Windows XP comes with several screensaver designs, and you can purchase and download additional screensavers. Screensavers not only provide something for your computer to do while it is idle, but they also offer security features.

This hour also offers a collection of tips that help you customize Windows XP to suit your preferences. Walk through this hour, trying the shortcuts and advice, to decide which topics best suit your needs. Now that you've mastered the major Windows XP tools, such as Windows Explorer and the My Computer window, you are ready to streamline the way you use Windows XP.

In this hour, you will

- Place Web pages on your desktop as wallpaper
- Use screensavers to personalize your PC
- Protect your computer with a password
- Locate the computer's time and date settings

Activate Your Desktop

Windows XP includes an *active desktop* feature that allows you to place Web page content directly on your desktop. The Web page acts like part of your wallpaper. The Active Desktop is Windows XP's way of more seamlessly integrating your Windows desktop into the online Internet world.

Web pages are the result of their underlying language, *HTML*, which defines the colors, pictures, embedded *applets* (small programs that activate Web pages by using yet another language called Java), and information that appears on those pages. HTML stands for *HyperText Markup Language*.

HTML documents end with the .html filename extension and use a Web page icon in Windows Explorer views. Some document names still follow the pre-Windows 95 filename limitations that require a maximum 3-letter extension; therefore, some HTML documents end with a filename extension of .htm.

Previous versions of Windows required that you specify that you want to use an active desktop before you stored live Internet content on your desktop. With Windows XP, you simply have to select a Web page to place on your desktop and Windows XP puts it there; the active desktop is always available.

You can learn about the active desktop by following along with this To Do item.

To Do: Working with the Windows Desktop

1. Right-click over your Windows wallpaper to display the pop-up menu.
2. Select Properties and click the Desktop tab. The Display Properties dialog box appears, as shown in Figure 7.1. (As with most of Windows, you can access the Display Properties dialog box from other locations, such as from the Control

Panel's Appearance and Themes category.) The Desktop page enables you to set up a wallpaper file. You can select one of the supplied wallpaper files by scrolling and selecting from the list box.

FIGURE 7.1

You can control your desktop's settings from the Display Properties dialog box.

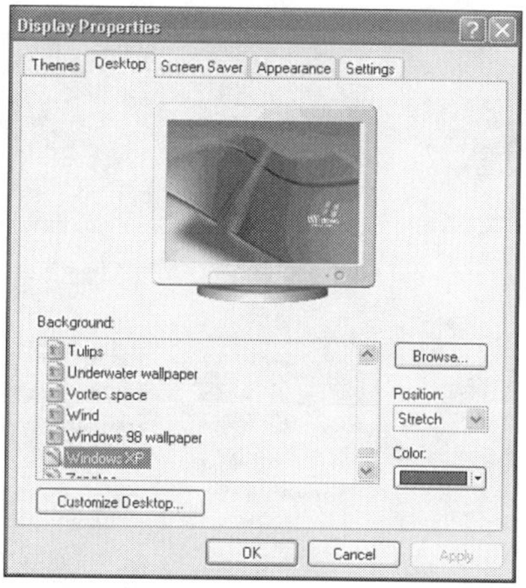

3. If you've stored a Web page on your disk, you can click the Browse button to search for any HTML file to use as your wallpaper. When you locate the HTML file you want as your wallpaper, click the Open button to select the file. The file and its pathname now appear in the Wallpaper list for subsequent selections.

4. Instead of a stored Web page, you can place an online Web page on your desktop. Click the Customize Desktop button to display the Desktop Items dialog box.

5. Click the Web tab and select from the list of Web pages in the list (initially, your default home page will be listed) or click New to type a new Web page address. When you click OK to close each of the open dialog boxes, the Web page will be part of your desktop, such as the one in Figure 7.2.

You can resize and move the desktop Web page (assuming you did not choose the option labeled Lock Desktop Items when you placed the Web page on your desktop). As Figure 7.2 shows, the Web page will not show with a title bar that includes the Minimize, Maximize, Restore, or Close buttons. However, if you point to the top of the Web page, Windows XP will add the title bar and the buttons so that you can move, resize, and close the Web page when you want to do so.

7

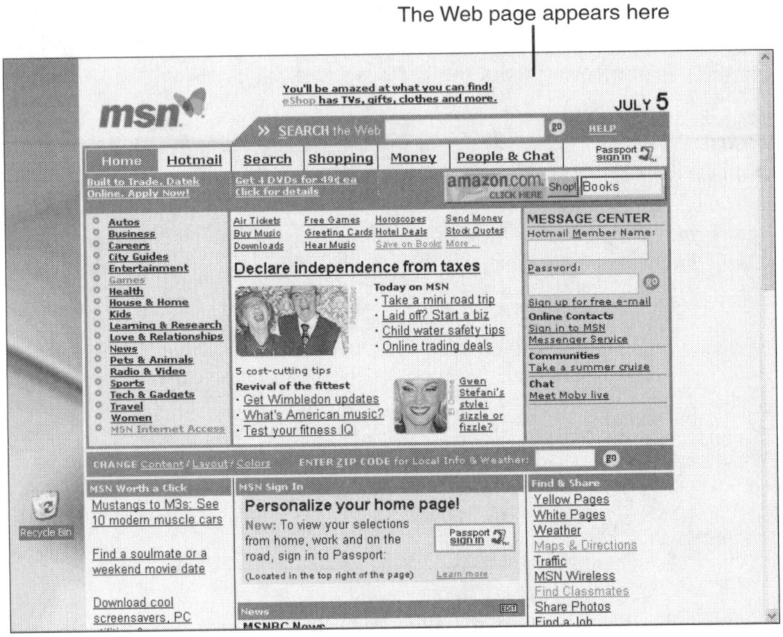

FIGURE 7.2

You can set wallpaper to any HTML or graphics file.

The Web page appears here

Synchronizing Your Web Page Desktop

The advantage of placing a Web page on your desktop is that, unlike regular wallpaper, the Web page content can frequently change. The Web page will not change on its own after you place the page on your desktop. Windows XP stores the page in an *offline format*, meaning that the Web page contains whatever it contained when you first placed it on your desktop. You can close your Internet connection after placing the Web page on your desktop because the Web page content will already be on your computer's hard drive, as a snapshot of what it contained when you placed the page.

If you want the Web page to be updated regularly, you must tell Windows XP to *synchronize* the page, or go to the Internet and update the page at specified time intervals.

The following To Do item explains how to synchronize your Web page.

To Do: Synchronizing Your Web Page-Based Desktop

1. At any point, you can right-click over a blank area of the Web page to display a pop-up menu and select Refresh to synchronize the desktop Web page to its current Internet. Windows XP starts your Internet connection automatically if needed to refresh the page. Instead of manually synchronizing the page, you can request that Windows XP do so as the remaining steps show.

▼   2. To specify a time interval that you want Windows XP to use to synchronize the
         Web page, display the Display Properties dialog box and click the Customize
         Desktop button to open the Desktop Items dialog box.

     3. Click the Web tab.

     4. To synchronize immediately, click the Synchronize button. Doing so performs the
         same action as manually selecting the Refresh pop-up menu option as described in
         Step 1. To set up a synchronization schedule for automatic synchronization, click
         the Properties button and then click the Schedule tab to display the Schedule page.

     5. Click the option labeled Using the Following Schedule(s) and click the Add
         button to display the New Schedule dialog box shown in Figure 7.3.

FIGURE 7.3

Tell Windows XP how
often to synchronize
the Web content.

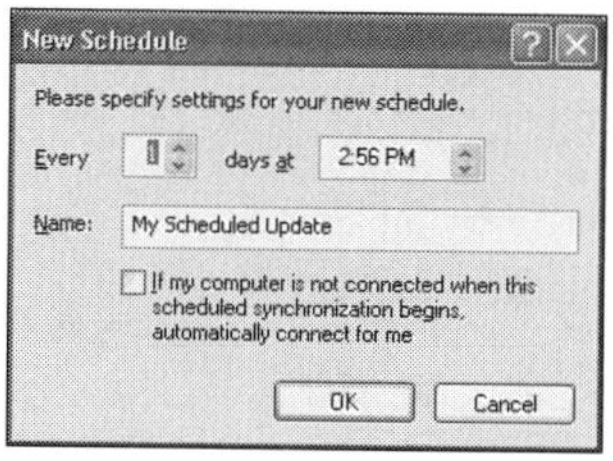

New Schedule	? X
Please specify settings for your new schedule.	

Every [1] days at [2:56 PM]

Name: My Scheduled Update

☐ If my computer is not connected when this
   scheduled synchronization begins,
   automatically connect for me

[OK]   [Cancel]

     6. Select a time when you want Windows XP to synchronize your desktop Web
         page's content and choose how often to synchronize. Click the check box at the
         bottom if you don't have an always-on Internet connection (such as a T-1, DSL, or
         cable modem line).

     7. Click OK and close all the open dialog boxes. At the time you scheduled, Windows
         XP will handle the synchronization automatically so that you can keep a fresh Web
▲   page on your desktop.

Active Content

Instead of putting a Web page on your desktop and having Windows synchronize it every
once in a while, you can have extremely active content, such as a moving stock ticker or
weather and news ticker flying across your desktop. The following To Do item explains
how.

To Do: Placing Active Content on Your Desktop

     1. Display the Display Properties dialog box and click the Customize Desktop button
         to open the Desktop Items dialog box.

     2. Click the Web tab.

     3. Click the New button.

7

4. Click the Visit Gallery button. A Web page appears that shows the Microsoft Desktop Gallery Web page, such as the one shown in Figure 7.4. The Desktop Gallery contains a stock ticker, news service, weather service, and several other items that you can place on your desktop. As long as your Internet connection is active, the items update. Therefore, during market hours, you will be able to see the price of a stock, news, or other information updated regularly.

FIGURE 7.4

Locate the content you want to place on your desktop.

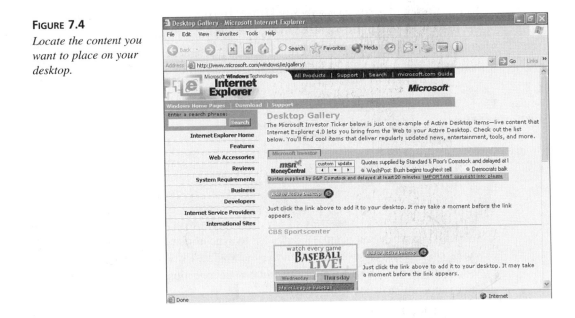

5. Click the Add to Active Desktop button next to the feature that you want on your desktop. Depending on the kind of gallery item you select, Windows XP will ask you to customize the content, perhaps by providing the stock symbols you want to track or the area of the country in which you live so you can get the local weather. When you return to your desktop, the content will be active.

SOS—Save Our Screens!

Almost everyone has heard of screensavers. Computer software stores contain shelf after shelf of screensaver programs that display pictures of your favorite television characters, cartoons, and geometric and 3D designs. Microsoft designed Windows XP to include several screensavers, so you don't have to buy one.

Want to know an insider's computer industry secret? Here it is: Screensavers really don't save many screens these days. In the past, computer monitors, especially the monochrome green-letters-on-black kind, would *burn in* characters when left on too long without being used. In other words, if you left the monitor on for a long time and did not type anything, the characters on the monitor would begin to leave character trails that stayed on the monitor even after you turned it off.

To combat character burn-in, programmers began to write *screensavers* that blanked the screen or displayed moving characters and pictures. The blank screens had no burn-in problems, and the moving text never stayed in one place long enough to burn into the monitor. The screensavers kicked into effect after a predetermined length of non-use. When you wanted to start work again, you could press any key to restore the computer screen to the state in which you left it.

Today's monitors don't have the kind of burn-in problem that previous monitors had. Screensavers aren't typically needed. Although a color monitor that is turned on all day and displays the same information will still get the burn-in effect, the effect is less pronounced than a few years ago. Why, during an age when they are not needed, are screensavers more popular than ever before? The answer is simple: Screensavers are fun! Screensavers greet you with designs and animated cartoons when you would otherwise look at a boring screen. It's *cool* to use a screensaver. After you master Hour 14, you will be able to use even live Web pages as your screensaver!

Screensavers aren't just for fun and games. Windows screensavers offer an additional benefit over entertainment: The Windows screensavers provide password protection. If you need to walk away from your screen for a while but you want to leave your computer running, you can select a password for the screensaver. Although you can add a password to your Windows XP account and log off before you leave your computer, you might not always remember to do this. After the screensaver begins, a user has to enter the correct password to use your computer. This ensures that payroll and other departments can safely leave their computers without fear of disclosing confidential information. Often, computer stores display their PCs with password-protected screensavers to keep customers from tampering with the systems.

Setting Up a Screensaver

Windows contains several screensavers from which you can choose. Through the Screensaver dialog box, you can set up a blank screensaver or one that moves text and graphics on the screen. You control the length of time the monitor is idle before the screensaver begins. The following To Do item explains how to implement a screensaver.

To Do: Requesting a Screensaver

1. Open the Display Properties dialog box and click the Screen Saver tab. (You can also open the Control Panel window, select Appearance and Themes, and then select the option labeled Choose a Screen Saver to display the same Screen Saver page.) Windows XP displays the page shown in Figure 7.5.

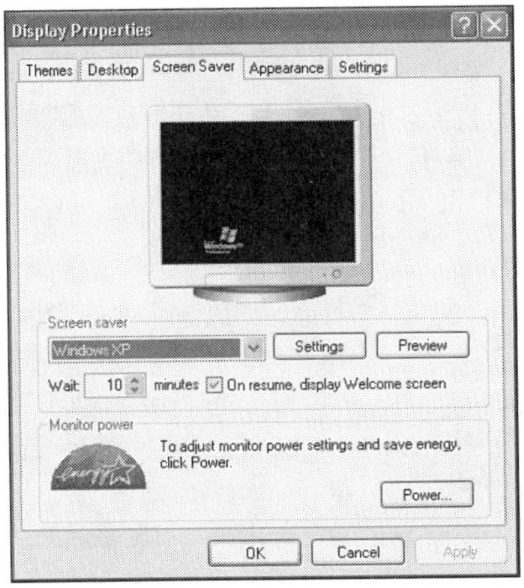

FIGURE 7.5

The Screen Saver tab controls the screen-saver's timing and selection.

If your monitor is designed to be *Energy Star-compliant*, meaning that your monitor supports energy-efficiency options, the lower dialog box settings will be available to you. You can adjust these options to save electricity costs. The Energy Star controls work independently and override any screensaver settings you might use.

2. The drop-down list box—directly below the Screen Saver prompt—that you display when you click the down arrow contains a list of Windows screensavers. Click the box now to see the list. When (None) is selected, no screensaver will be active on your system.

3. If you select Blank Screen, Windows uses a blank screen for the screensaver. When the screensaver activates, the screen goes blank, and a keypress (or password if you set up a password) returns the screen to its previous state.

The remaining screensavers are generally more fun than a blank screensaver. If you want to see the other screensavers, click any one of the remaining screensavers in the list (such as 3D Flying Objects or 3D Maze), and Windows will display a preview of it on the little monitor inside the dialog box, as shown in Figure 7.6.

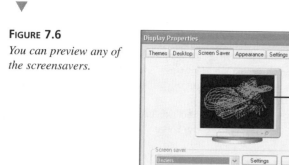

FIGURE 7.6

You can preview any of the screensavers.

Preview

4. The animated screensavers can move fairly fast. To adjust their speed, click the Settings button. In some cases, you can also adjust the number of animated items that appear on the screensaver screen. Click OK when done.

5. The Preview button enables you to view the screensaver full-screen if you want a better preview than the small screen inside the dialog box provides. Click Preview to see the actual screensaver in action. Press any key or move the mouse to terminate the screensaver preview and return to the dialog box.

6. The Wait prompt determines how many minutes your computer must remain idle for the screensaver to activate itself. By pressing Alt+W (the shortcut key combination for the Wait prompt), you can enter a new minute value or click the up and down arrow keys to change to a new minute value.

7. When you click the OK command button at the bottom of the dialog box, Windows activates the screensaver program. The screensaver remains active in all future Windows XP sessions until you change it again by using the Screen Saver dialog box.

8. The screensaver operates in the background but never shows itself, even on the taskbar of program buttons, until your computer sits idle for the specified time value. If you keep your hands off the keyboard and mouse for the waiting time period, you'll see the screensaver go into action. Press any key (or move the mouse) to return to the desktop.

7

Windows XP now lets you create your own screensaver! Store pictures in the following folder: c:\Documents and Settings*yourLogonName*\My Documents\My Pictures. You can capture these pictures from a digital camera or scan the pictures with an attached scanner. Select the My Pictures Slideshow and Windows randomly displays your pictures on the screen when the screensaver begins its work. You can adjust settings such as the length of time each picture appears by clicking the Settings button after you select the My Pictures Screensaver option from the Screen Saver tabbed page.

If you click the option labeled Return to the Welcome Screen, Windows XP returns to the account logon screen. There, you or another user will have to log on once again (and possibly enter a password if your account is password-protected) to use the computer after pressing a key to stop the screensaver.

Paint Windows XP

Windows offers several color schemes for you to select. Microsoft designed multiple color schemes that work well together. Depending on your taste, you can choose from conservative to very wild colors.

The color schemes that you can select have nothing to do with the colors of icons, wallpaper, or screensavers on your system. The color schemes determine the color for various systemwide items such as screen title bars, window backgrounds, and dialog box controls.

By selecting from various color schemes, you can determine the colors that Windows XP uses for common system-level items such as window controls. You'll use the Display Properties dialog box to change the color of your Windows XP environment as the following steps show:

1. Right-click over a blank area of your desktop and select Properties. The now-familiar Display Properties tabbed dialog box appears.

2. Click the Appearance tab to display the Appearance page, shown in Figure 7.7.

3. If you want to take the time, you can change the color of every item on the Windows screen including dialog boxes, window borders, and title bars. However, it's much easier to pick a color scheme from the list of the many choices that Microsoft supplies.

   On the top half of the Appearance page, you see the currently selected color scheme. If you select a different color scheme, you will see that scheme's color appear at the top of the dialog box.

FIGURE 7.7

Change system colors in the Appearance page of the Display Properties dialog box.

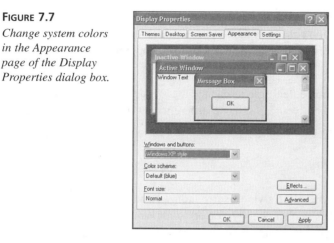

4. The color scheme of your Windows installation does not instantly change. You're still in the process of selecting colors at this point. If you don't like your selected color scheme, try another. As a matter of fact, try *all* of them to find one you really like.

High contrast color schemes work well for times when you take your Windows laptop outdoors.

5. Click the Effects button to display the Effects dialog box shown in Figure 7.8. Use the Effects settings to determine how menus and ToolTips appear and disappear, whether large icons appear for Windows XP items such as menus, whether a shadow appears under menus, and other special effects that transpire as you use Windows XP.

FIGURE 7.8

Select from several screen effects.

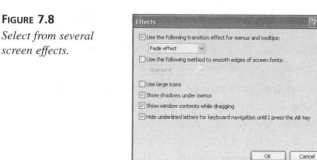

7

6. When you find a color scheme that you really like, click the OK button to close the dialog box and change the color scheme to your selected colors. You can now begin working with the new color scheme. As soon as you open a window, you'll see the difference.

As you change your color scheme, feel free to change the Windows display font as well. From the Appearance dialog box, you can select a different font for almost every kind of text Windows XP displays.

Summary

This hour took a brief detour from the style of surrounding hours and gave you some tips and desktop-management tools that can help you work with Windows more effectively. After completing the first part of this book, you should have a good understanding of the tools that are available to you as a Windows user. Now that you've become more comfortable with these aspects of Windows, you'll appreciate some of this hour's time-saving tips.

In this hour, you learned how to improve your computer's desktop wallpaper by adding your own graphics or HTML-based wallpaper. Your PC's idle time can be occupied by setting up a screensaver. By sending the screensaver to your logon screen, you can add security to your system so that you can safely leave for a few minutes without exiting the program in which you're working.

Windows has many customization features. These customization tools help both the novice and the advanced user enjoy Windows XP more fully.

Q&A

Q How does the wallpaper pattern differ from the screensaver pattern? Are they the same?

A The wallpaper is your desktop's background. You always see the wallpaper when you first start Windows and when you minimize or close programs you are using within Windows. You will never see the screensaver unless you quit working on your computer for a few minutes and the screensaver begins running.

The screensaver must be a moving pattern (or be completely blank) to accomplish the goal of a screensaver. The screensaver's original purpose was to keep a program running that changed constantly to eliminate the burn-in of the screen's characters that could occur on the monitor. Since the burn-in problem is not common today, a secondary goal of a screensaver is to display an animated and often fun screen during your computer's idle times. As mentioned earlier in this hour, you can turn your Web-based wallpaper into a screensaver so that a designated Web page (or HTML document on your disk) appears when the screensaver wakes up.

Q Why would I need to synchronize a Web page that I place on my desktop?

A When you place a Web page on your desktop, Windows XP takes a snapshot of the current Web page and puts that content on your desktop. If the Web page changes, your desktop will not reflect that change until you synchronize the Web page.

Workshop

The quiz and exercise questions are designed to test your knowledge of the material covered in this hour. The answers are in Appendix C, "Answers to Quizzes."

Quiz

1. Where are HTML files often found?

2. *True or false*: Without a screensaver, characters can burn themselves into your monitor.

3. What does *Energy Star compliant* mean?

4. How can a password-protected screensaver help secure your system?

5. Where do you change the color of Windows items such as title bars and menus?

Exercises

1. Create your own screensaver. If you don't have a scanner or digital camera, you might not be able to complete this exercise until you find a way to put digitized pictures on your disk.

2. Change the color scheme of your desktop. Try setting your own colors for individual Windows elements, such as title bar text. You can always return to one of the supplied Windows color schemes after your experiment if your colors don't work well together. If you create a good color pattern, save the scheme under a filename that you'll remember. You then will be able to switch back and forth between your scheme and others without having to re-enter the color settings.

7

PART III

Early Afternoon Windows Exploration

Hour

HOUR 8

Installing Programs with Windows XP

By itself, Windows XP doesn't help you directly with your work. Your application programs do the work. You use application programs to write documents, create graphics, explore the Internet, manage database files, and play games. Somehow you have to get application programs onto your PC. Programs come on CD-ROMs or are downloadable from the Internet. You must run new programs through an *installation routine* so that Windows XP properly recognizes them.

Some application programs require their own unique, one-of-a-kind installation routines, although, fortunately, you'll install most of today's programs using a uniform method. This hour looks at Windows XP's support for adding programs, discusses unique installation problems you might encounter, explains how to make older programs run, and reviews how to remove programs that you've installed and no longer need.

In this hour, you will

- Learn why proper installation is critical
- Use the Add/Remove Programs dialog box effectively
- Discover where to go when you need to add or remove a Windows component
- Uninstall programs properly
- Learn what to do when no adequate uninstall procedure exists

Using the Add or Remove Programs Window

Before Windows, you could add a program to your computer simply by copying a file from the disk you purchased to your hard disk. To remove the program, you only had to delete the file. Things got messier with Windows, however, because Windows expected a lot from application programs. Programs are no longer simple to add or remove unless you familiarize yourself with the proper techniques.

If you don't follow the proper program-installation techniques, your application probably won't run correctly. Even worse, with the Windows integrated set of files, a program you add to your PC incorrectly might make other programs fail.

The Windows Control Panel contains an entry that you'll frequently visit to manage the programs on your PC. This icon is labeled Add or Remove Programs. When you open this icon, the tabbed dialog box shown in Figure 8.1 appears. Depending on the number of your PC's installed applications, you'll probably see different applications listed in the lower half of your PC's Add or Remove Programs window.

To the left of the dialog box contains an Add New Programs button that you can click to install new software. Surprisingly, you'll rarely, if ever, use this button when installing Windows XP programs because most programs install automatically, as explained later in this hour. The dialog box's lower half contains a list of many application programs on your PC. Not every program on your PC will appear in the list. The list contains programs that you can *uninstall* from your system. If you uninstall using the Add or Remove Programs dialog box, you can be assured that the application will completely disappear.

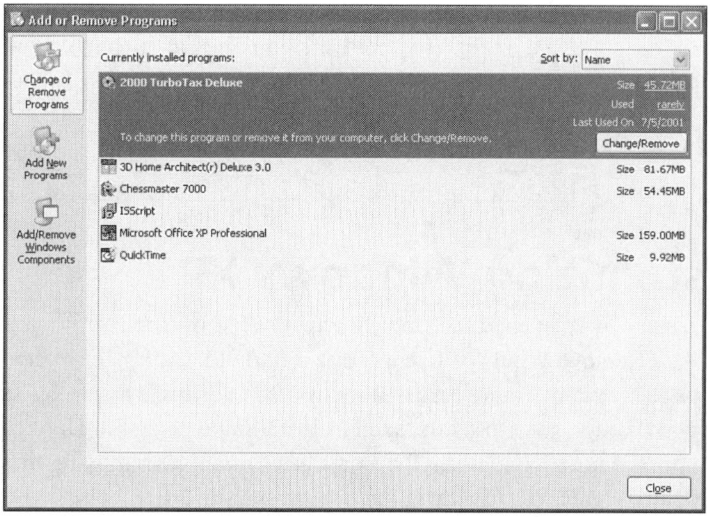

FIGURE 8.1

You manage your installed programs from the Add or Remove Programs dialog box.

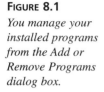

8

Although you can uninstall most Windows applications, occasionally an application will share a support or system file with another application. Even more common, sometimes the uninstallation routine detects *incorrectly* that the file is shared by another program. Therefore, during some uninstallation routines, you might see a dialog box message asking if you want the routine to remove one of the shared files. Generally, it's difficult to know what to do. The safest advice is to keep the file by responding as such to the dialog box if it appears. Although in many cases retaining the file simply wastes disk space, you'll avoid possible trouble with other applications that might use the file.

If you make a system backup before uninstalling an application, you can safely remove the file and then keep the backup handy until you're convinced that the system is stable. Again, it's often simpler just to keep the file in question when the uninstallation program prompts you about it. These orphaned files often make for heated discussions among the PC community—and rightly so. Windows and uninstallation routines should be written so that they work together more accurately without requiring the user to make such ambiguous file-deletion decisions.

Sometimes you'll rerun an application program's installation routine to change installation settings. The Add or Remove Programs window contains a button labeled Change or Remove Programs that many applications utilize to let you change program options or remove the program altogether.

> If a program stops working properly, you might have to reinstall it com-
> pletely. Although you can rerun the installation again in some cases, you're
> probably better off uninstalling the program first to remove all traces of it
> and then running the installation from scratch again. (Be sure to back up
> your data files before you do that.)

Customizing Windows XP

After you've opened the Control Panel's Add or Remove Programs dialog box, click the
Add/Remove Windows Components button to display the Windows Components Wizard
page shown in Figure 8.2. A Windows XP *Wizard* is a step-by-step procedure that guides
you through some process, such as installing a program. Unlike your applications, you'll
never remove Windows XP because you would be removing the operating system that
controls your PC. (You wouldn't sit on the same tree branch you're sawing off, would
you?) When you update to a future version of Windows, the new version will remove
Windows XP, but you can worry about that later. For now, the Windows Components
Wizard lets you add and remove various Windows XP options.

FIGURE 8.2

*Change Windows XP
options from the
Windows Components
Wizard dialog box.*

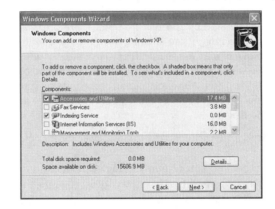

When you make a change to a Windows XP setting, that setting might not show until
you restart Windows XP.

The following To Do item shows you how to change Windows XP installation settings.
Although the various Properties menu options you find throughout Windows XP let you
change settings that affect Windows' performance, appearance, and operation, the
Windows Components Wizard lets you add or remove pieces of Windows XP's
functionality.

Some manufacturers store the Windows XP system on your computer's hard disk instead of supplying a separate CD-ROM. You'll want to keep your system backed up completely in case you need to reconfigure your computer. Other users get Windows XP from a purchased CD-ROM. If you obtained Windows XP on CD-ROM, you might need your Windows XP CD-ROM to change Windows XP options, so locate it. If prompted for the CD-ROM, the Windows XP banner will automatically appear when you insert the CD-ROM. Just close the window if this occurs. Some systems come with the Windows XP operating system stored on the hard disk, so don't worry about locating the Windows XP CD-ROM unless prompted for it.

To Do: Modifying Your Windows XP Installation Settings

1. Select Add/Remove Windows Components to run the Windows Components Wizard. The Components scrolling list box shows which groups of Windows XP options you've installed. An empty check box means that none of those options is installed to run. A grayed-out check mark means that some of the options in that group are installed. A regular check mark means that the entire group is installed. If you didn't install Windows XP, or if you installed Windows XP using all the default options, you might not be completely familiar with all the groups that appear. As you work through this 24-hour tutorial, you'll learn more about the various options available for Windows XP.

2. Click the title for Accessories and Utilities. (If you click the check mark and not the title, you'll change the setting.) Then click the Details button, and a new list appears that shows entries for Accessories and Games.

3. Click Accessories to select the item.

4. Click the Details button to see the details of the Accessories group of programs. You'll see a scrollable list of Accessories programs like those shown in Figure 8.3. Accessories are most of the programs that appear when you select the Start menu's More Programs, Accessories option.

5. Uncheck the Clipboard Viewer. Rarely will you need this leftover from Windows 3.1 days. Unchecking it requests that Windows XP remove it from your system. (You can repeat this task afterward to put it back.)

6. Click OK twice to return to the Windows Components Wizard.

7. Click Next and Windows XP begins the process of removing the Clipboard Viewer from your system. This update can take a while if you have just added or removed several Windows XP components.

8. Click Finish to close the Windows Components Wizard and return to Windows XP.

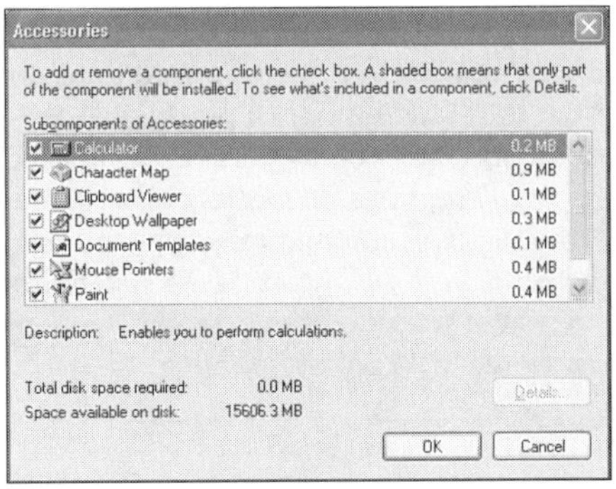

FIGURE **8.3**

See which Accessories options are installed.

Installed Applications

Almost every time you purchase a new application program to install on your PC, you'll insert its CD into the drive, close the drive door, and see an installation screen such such as the one shown in Figure 8.4.

FIGURE **8.4**

An application program is about to install.

In most cases, such an application checks your PC to see if the program is already installed. If it isn't, the program gives you an installation screen such as the one shown in Figure 8.4. The software authors know that you probably wouldn't be inserting the CD into the drive if you didn't want to install the program.

If the program is already installed, the program often, but not always, begins executing (without the installation prompt) after you close the CD-ROM drive door. This is mostly true of some games that require that you insert the actual CD-ROM into your CD-ROM drive any time you want to play the game.

If the application doesn't start, or if you have *AutoPlay* disabled (AutoPlay is a feature of Windows XP that starts reading your CD as soon as you place a CD-ROM in the drive) and you want to leave it that way, you can choose Run from the Start menu and type *d:***Setup**. Replace the d with the letter of your CD-ROM drive.

Not many programs still come on floppy disk; however, if you're installing from a floppy disk, you'll have to insert the first installation disk into the disk drive, choose Run from the Start menu, and type **a:****Setup**.

If you get an error message, choose the Start menu's Run command to make sure that you've entered the drive, backslash, and Setup command properly. If you get an error message again, your program might require a different command. Replace Setup with Install to see what happens. If the Run command still fails, check the program's owner's manual to locate the correct command.

Each application's setup is different. Nevertheless, the following list provides guidelines that almost every installation follows:

- You can often read installation notes (usually called a *Readme* file) by clicking an appropriate selection in the installation window.

- Sometimes multiple installation options are available. Check the manual for the installation that suits you if you can't determine from the opening window which one to use.

- When you start the installation, an installation wizard usually guides you step-by-step through the process.

- You can often accept all installation defaults if you're unsure whether to install an option during the wizard's performance. The wizard asks questions such as which disk drive and folder you want to install to.

- If you don't have adequate disk space, the installation program will tell you. You'll have to remove other files, get more disk space, reduce the installation options, or do without the program if you don't have space for it.

- At the end of the installation, you will probably have to restart Windows for all the installation options to go into effect. If you're asked whether you want to restart Windows, you can answer No, but don't run the installed program until you restart Windows.

Uninstallation Procedures

Most application programs written for Windows XP include a standard uninstallation routine that removes the application from Windows and from your PC. Remember that an application program is often made up of several files. The program's installation routine stores those files in several different locations. Therefore, without an uninstallation routine, removing the application is a tedious task.

Before displaying the Control Panel's Add or Remove Programs window to uninstall a program you've installed, check the Start menu group where the program resides. Sometimes, in a program's menu group, the installation routine sets up the uninstallation routine that you can run from that group. For example, if you installed a game called Side-to-Side, you might start the game by selecting from a series of Start menu options that look like this: More Programs, Side Game, Play Side-to-Side. Look on the same menu and see if you can select an uninstall option, such as More Programs, Side Game, Uninstall Side-to-Side. When you begin the uninstallation process, a wizard steps you through the program's removal.

If no menu option exists for the uninstallation, go to the Control Panel's Add or Remove Programs window. Scroll through the list of items in the lower part of the window to see if the program you want to remove appears in the list. If it does, select that entry and click the Change or Remove Programs button to begin the uninstall wizard.

If no entry appears, you are running out of options! Insert the program's CD once again and see if the opening window contains an uninstall option. If it doesn't, look through the Readme file to see if you can get help. Also, look in the program's owner's manual. Lacking an uninstall routine, try one more place if you have access: the Web. See if you can find the company's Web page somewhere in the Readme file or owner's manual. If you can't find it, try going to the Web address `http://www.companyname.com/` and see if something comes up. Replace *companyname* with the name of the company that manufactured the application you want to uninstall.

A Last Resort

If your search for an uninstall procedure comes up empty, you are forced to do one of two things:

- Leave the program on your system if you have ample disk space
- Manually remove as much of the program as you can

That last option can get messy because it requires searching for the program files. In the next hour, you'll learn how to search for files, so you might want to browse Hour 9 before attempting to manually remove the application. After you've removed the program's files and the folder where the application resides, you need to remove the Start menu entry.

Deleting Start menu entries is simple, but keep in mind that you're only removing items from a menu and not deleting files from your disk. Simply open your Start menu and locate the item you want to delete. Right-click the item and select Delete from the pop-up menu. Confirm the prompt and Windows XP removes the entry. You can remove a program group from the menu, instead of just individual items, the same way.

Summary

This hour described how to install and uninstall application programs on your PC. Before Windows XP came along, program installation and removal was simple because programs rarely resided in more than one file on your disk. Today's Windows XP programs, however, install with multiple files in multiple locations, and their removal can become tedious.

The next hour describes how to use Windows XP's file-searching capabilities to locate files on your computer. You might need to search for a file if you manually need to remove a program from Windows, as described in the last section.

Q&A

Q Why don't I ever use the Add or Remove Programs window's Add New Programs button to install programs?

A Nobody seems to have a good answer for that! It seems as if software companies don't want to access this already-supplied installation resource. If they did, all program installations would basically require the same steps, and, you would think, users would be happier. Nevertheless, companies seem to prefer that the installation routine begin automatically when the user inserts the CD-ROM.

The drawback of this approach is that many times such an installation won't work as expected. Either the AutoPlay feature is turned off, or the user bought the program on floppy disks. (Floppy disk drives don't support the AutoPlay feature.)

Workshop

The quiz and exercise questions are designed to test your knowledge of the material covered in this hour. The answers are in Appendix C, "Answers to Quizzes."

Quiz

1. What Windows Control Panel option helps you install and uninstall application programs?
2. What happens if you insert an application program's CD-ROM in your PC's CD-ROM drive and the application is not already installed?
3. Where can you modify your Windows XP installation options?
4. Name some ways to uninstall application programs?
5. Why would you never want to uninstall Windows XP?

Exercises

1. Open the Add or Remove Programs window. Scroll through the list of installed programs to make sure that programs you no longer use are not installed. If one or more of these programs appear, select them and click the Remove button to remove the application. By regularly checking the installed application list, you will keep your hard disk free of programs you no longer use that consume disk space.

2. Open the Windows Components Wizard. Make sure that all the Windows XP's Accessories options are installed. By doing this, you help ensure that your system is ready for all the remaining lessons in this tutorial.

HOUR 9

Finding Files, Folders, and Friends

Hard disks are getting bigger, more information appears on the Internet by the minute, and you've got to find things fast! Fortunately, Windows XP comes to your rescue with powerful searching tools. Windows can quickly find files and folders that you need. You can search by filename, date, and location. In addition, Windows includes several Internet searching tools that enable you to find people and Web sites that match the exact specifications you want to match.

In this hour, you will

- Master the Start menu's Search command
- Specify wildcard searches
- Learn which search options help you find information the fastest
- Use Internet searching tools that help you wade through huge mounds of data
- Locate people in other parts of the world

Introducing Search

Click the Start menu to select the Search option. When you select Search, Windows XP uses the *Search Companion*, an animated screen character that can help you form your searches, to walk you through searching. You can turn off Search Companion by selecting the option labeled, Turn off animated character. If you elect to use the Search Companion, Windows XP displays the Search Companion pane shown in Figure 9.1.

FIGURE **9.1**

The Search Companion helps you form your searches.

 Click the option labeled Change Preferences if you want to choose a different Search Companion character or search without the character altogether.

Whether you elect to use a Search Companion, the Search window lets you search for many different things as Table 9.1 describes.

TABLE 9.1 Using Search to Locate Information

Target	Description
Pictures, music, or video	Looks for files and folders that are registered as media files.
Documents (word processing, spreadsheet, etc.)	Looks for non-application documents, such as data files and word processor documents.
All files and folders	Looks for any type of file.

TABLE 9.1 continued

Target	Description
Computers or people	Looks for computers networked to yours and people who might be logged onto your network. Each computer on a network has a unique name.
Information in Help and Support Center	Takes you to the HSC to locate what you need.

9

You should master the Start menu's Search command because you'll search for information quite often. Today's computers have extremely large disk drives, and locating a file that you worked on previously is not always a trivial task without some help. Using Search, you won't have to wade through disks, folders, and subfolders looking for an older document. Let Windows XP do the work for you.

> You can quickly display the Search Files and Folders window by right-clicking the Start menu and selecting the Search option or by pressing the Windows key on your keyboard and then pressing F for Find before releasing both keys.

Searching for Pictures, Music, or Video

When you select the Pictures, music, or video option, Windows XP asks you for the type of file for which you want to search such as a picture, a music file, or a file containing video, as well as for a filename. These kinds of multimedia files can take on many different filename extensions; therefore, knowing the exact filename extension is not always easy. Fortunately, by telling Windows XP the file type (picture, music, or video), you don't have to know or care what kind of extension is on your file because Windows XP recognizes most file extensions related to the type of file for which you want to search.

After you select one or more file types, type the name of the file to search. You can type just a few letters of the name including letters from the middle or end of the file and Windows XP will search for all files that contain those letters in their names. The list of files, if any matches are found that meets your search type and name, are listed in the right windowpane.

Searching for Data Documents

Searching for data is similar to searching for multimedia files. Windows XP looks for files with filename extensions that are commonly used for data documents in Windows applications.

Instead of selecting a file type, you must tell the Search window when you last modified the document. Fortunately, you don't have to know for sure. The Search window gives you these choices:

- You don't remember when you last modified the file.
- You last modified the file sometime last week.
- You last modified the file sometime last month.
- You modified the file within the past year.

In addition to the modification date, you also must enter the filename or the part of the filename before clicking the Search button to let Windows XP locate the file or multiple files that match your search criteria.

Searching for Any File

When you search for a file of any type, including program and system files, the Search window provides more search options than the previous kinds of searches provide. The Search window gives you the ability to search based on these criteria:

- Part or all of the filename
- Letters, a word, or a phrase in the file; this works best for data document files
- The drive or drives that Windows XP is to search
- The date you last modified the file
- The approximate size of the file
- Advanced search options you'll learn about later in this hour in the section, "Improving Your Searches."

The Windows Explorer's toolbar's Search button opens a Search pane with the same searching capabilities as the Start menu's Search command. Therefore, after you master the Search command, you'll also know how to look for information from inside Windows Explorer and other windows.

Searching Files and Folders

You'll probably use the Start menu's Search command to search for files and folders on your PC. Search gives you access to many different search criteria. You can search for files in a specific folder, on a disk, or on your entire computer system, including networked drives if you have any.

If you know a partial filename, you can find all files that contain that partial filename. If you want to search for a file you changed two days ago, you can find all files with modification dates that fall on that day. You can even save searches that you perform often so that you don't have to create the search criteria each time you need to search, as discussed in the next section.

Searching Computers and People

You can search for a computer connected to your network by selecting the option labeled `Computers or people` and then selecting `A computer on the network`. After you enter the name or a few characters from the computer's name, the Search window begins looking over your network of computers. If found, a computer icon appears in the results windowpane. You can double-click that icon to search the computer for files, assuming you have the proper network permission to search that computer.

If you select the option labeled `People in your address book`, the Search window searches for people located in your Windows *address book*, a list of names and addresses that you'll automatically have if you use Outlook Express or Microsoft Outlook for your e-mail and address list. (Other contact applications may act as your address book if you use them.) When you click the option labeled `People in your address book`, the Search window displays the Find People dialog box shown in Figure 9.2.

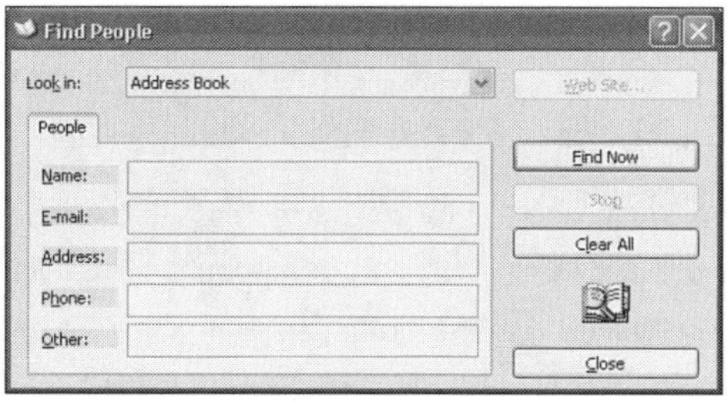

FIGURE 9.2

You can locate people stored in your address book and elsewhere.

You can search for people not only stored in your address book files, but also anybody listed on one of several people-finding Internet search engines. Simply click the down arrow on the drop-down list box labeled `Look in` and select the type of online service you want to use for your search.

If you click the option labeled `Search the Internet`, either from the initial Search Companion pane or from the `Computers or people` windowpane, the Search window displays the Internet search pane shown in Figure 9.3. Type a word or phrase for which you want to search, click the Search button, and the right Search windowpane fills up with a Web page full of Internet search results that match your request. A list of further options you can use to narrow your search will appear if you don't see what you are looking for in the right pane.

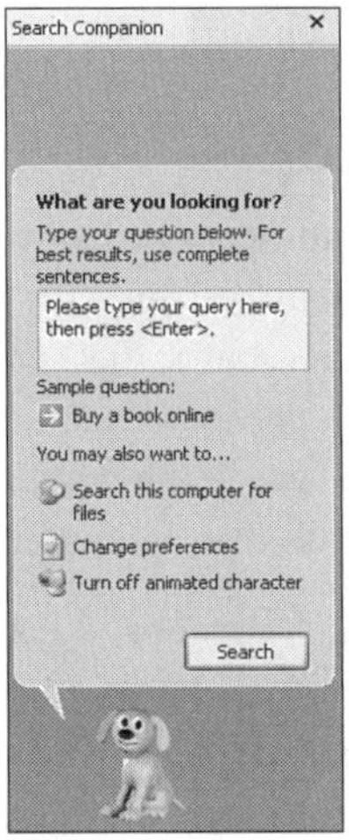

FIGURE 9.3

Enter your search query and Windows XP will search the Internet to fulfill your request.

Improving Your Searches

You can use *wildcard characters* to narrow your search results. A wildcard character stands for one or more groups of characters, just as a joker often functions as a wildcard in card games. Search supports two wildcard characters: * and ?.

* acts as a wildcard for zero, one, or more characters. For example, if you want to see all files that end with the .txt extension, you can specify *.txt as your search criteria. The asterisk wildcard tells Search to locate every file that ends in .txt, no matter what appears before the file extension. The criteria ABC*.* represents all files that begin with the letters ABC, no matter what follows the letters and no matter what extension the file has. (ABC*.* even locates files that begin with ABC and have no extension.)

The question mark wildcard replaces single characters within a criteria. Therefore, ACCT??.DAT finds all files that begin with ACCT, have two more characters, and end in the .DAT extension. The following files would successfully match that criteria: ACCT02.DAT, ACCT03.DAT, and ACCT04.DAT. However, neither ACCT.DAT nor ACCTjun03.DAT would match because the two question marks specify that only two characters must replace the wildcards in those positions.

The following To Do item walks you through a search session that uses wildcard characters.

To Do: Using Search

1. Display the Search window.

2. Click the option labeled All files and folders. The Search Companion's windowpane appears, as shown in Figure 9.4. Your screen might differ slightly if your Search window's toolbar is displayed.

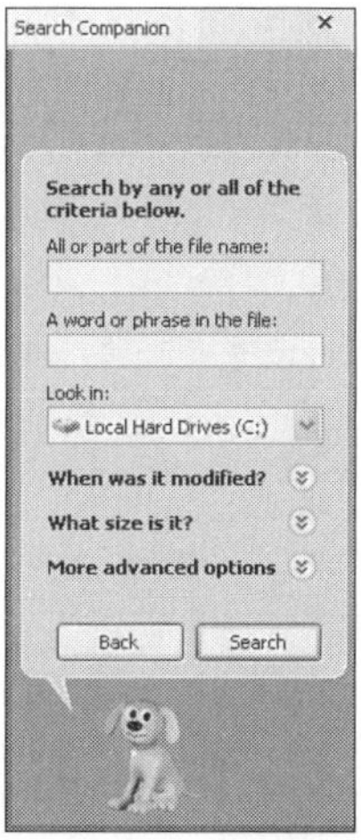

FIGURE 9.4

Search searches across drives for specific documents and folders.

> Search Companion ✕
>
> **Search by any or all of the criteria below.**
>
> All or part of the file name:
>
> A word or phrase in the file:
>
> Look in:
> 💾 Local Hard Drives (C:) ▾
>
> **When was it modified?** ⌄
> **What size is it?** ⌄
> **More advanced options** ⌄
>
> Back   Search

3. Type **winmine.*** at the prompt labeled Part or all of the file name. This wildcard specification looks for all files and folders that begin with the letters winmine. It turns out that you can just type **winmine** to achieve the same result, except that without the wildcard, the Search window will locate all files with the letters *winmine* anywhere in the name, not just at the beginning.

4. Leave the defaults in the other fields and click Search. Windows automatically searches your disks and subdirectory folders, although you can click the option labeled More advanced options to limit the search to top-level, root-folder directories only.

▼ After a brief pause, your dialog box should resemble the one shown in Figure 9.5, although you may show more or fewer results. The list contains not only the document's filename, but also the folder in which the document resides, the size of the document, the type of file, and the date and time that the file was last modified. (You might need to use the horizontal scrollbar at the bottom of the results windowpane to see the file sizes and dates.)

FIGURE 9.5

Search locates your files.

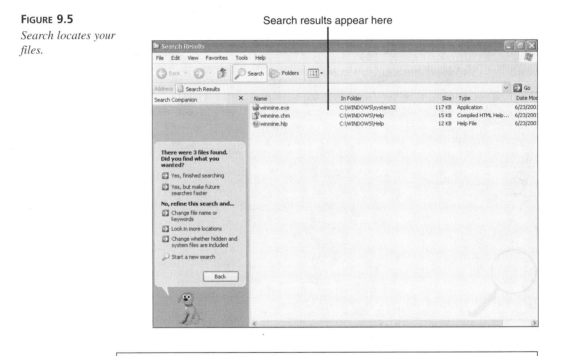

Search results appear here

> If you don't see filename extensions but you want to, select the window's Tools, Folder Options, click the View tab, and uncheck the option labeled Hide File Extensions for Known File Types.

You can drag the edge of any result's column left or right to expand or shrink the width of that column.

If you click any of the result window pane's column title, Search sorts the found information in alphabetical, numerical, or date and time order.

▼ At least four files should appear, and they'll appear in your Windows folder. One of these files has an .exe extension, meaning that you can run that file.

▼   If your filename extensions are turned off, the executable file is the file with the
land mine icon to the left of its Name entry. Now that Windows XP has located the
executable file, you can run the program directly from the Search window.

> When Search finishes, the left Search windowpane offers you several
> choices. You can click the option labeled Yes, finished searching to close
> the left window pane and display the list of results in a wider right window
> pane so you can see all the details. (You can click the toolbar's Search button
> to initiate a new search.) The option labeled Change file name or key-
> words returns you to the initial search windowpane so you can modify the
> search options. The Look in more locations option enables you to change
> the disk drives you are searching to see if the file resides somewhere you
> were not expecting.

5. Double-click the winmine.exe entry, and a Windows game named Minesweeper
   appears. Start clicking away on the squares, but be very careful!

   Windows is smart. If the file you click isn't an executable file, Windows attempts
   to open the file using other resources. For example, if you click a Microsoft Word
   document, Windows automatically looks for the Microsoft Word program on your
   PC and opens the document using Word (assuming that you have Word). If you
   select a help file, Search opens a help window with that file displayed. If you
   select an e-mail message file, Search locates your e-mail reader and displays the
   message there. As long as the file is registered (explained in Hour 5, "Navigating
   Files with Windows Explorer"), Windows can associate the file's parent program
   and display the file.

6. After you've played Minesweeper for a while, close its window and then close the
   Search window.

▲

If your search is taking too long, you may have entered too general a search so that too
many files are being found. Perhaps you entered too many drives to search. If a search
takes too long, click the Stop button. You then can continue the search if you want by
clicking the option labeled Yes, finished searching or refine your search by changing the search drives or locations being searched.

Summary

This hour helped you find information you need on both your own PC and the Internet.
Get in the habit of using Search for your PC, network, and Internet files when you need

to locate information. You can search for the file you want to find and then select the file to open it and begin working with it.

Internet search engines help convert the Internet's information overload to a manageable repository of information. You can search Web sites that fit your exact criteria, as well as look for people's names and addresses.

The next hour's material really gets fun. You'll learn how to use the Windows Accessories programs. Even if you haven't purchased a word processor or a paint program, you can use the ones supplied with Windows to generate virtually any material you want to publish.

Q&A

Q I just bought my PC, and I don't have many files yet. Why will I need to search for anything?

A Sometimes you save a file in an unexpected folder, forget an exact filename, or save multiple copies of the same file on a disk across different folders. Even though you don't yet have many files, you could easily forget what you recently named a file or where you saved it.

Q I don't have Internet access. Can I still access the Internet searching tools?

A Sadly, no. You must sign up with an Internet service provider to gain Internet access before you can use Find's full potential. You will need to subscribe to an Internet service before you can search the Internet for information or people's addresses and phone numbers.

Workshop

The quiz and exercise questions are designed to test your knowledge of the material covered in this hour. The answers are in Appendix C, "Answers to Quizzes."

Quiz

1. Where are some of the areas Windows XP looks for data?
2. What is a wildcard character?
3. What is the difference between the * and the ? wildcard characters?
4. *True or false*: You can execute any found programs from within the search window.
5. What is a search engine?

Exercises

1. Locate all the files you edited, created, or accessed on your most recent birthday.

2. Search for your favorite movie star's e-mail address. If you don't succeed at first, select different options to see what comes up.

9

Hour **10**

Using the Desktop Accessories

Windows XP comes with several application programs you can use right away to do work. These programs—Calculator, WordPad, and Paint—all appear on your Start menu's Accessories menu list. As their names suggest, you can perform calculations, create text documents, and paint pictures by using these three accessory programs.

The Calculator program comes in handy when you want to perform quick calculations without the need of a more powerful program such as an electronic spreadsheet. WordPad does not offer the power of Microsoft Word, but you can create formatted word processed documents quickly and easily with WordPad. Paint is a simple but effective drawing program that you can use to create colorful pictures.

In this hour, you will

- Use the Windows Calculator program
- Discover differences between the scientific and standard calculators

- Create word processed documents with WordPad
- Use Paint to create colorful graphics
- See which advanced Paint editing tools professionally manipulate your images

Calculate Results

The Calculator program performs both simple mathematical and advanced scientific calculations. The Calculator program provides you with all kinds of computing benefits. Throughout a working day, you use your computer constantly, writing letters, printing bills, and building presentations. As you work, you often need to make a quick calculation and, if you're anything like computer book authors, your real calculator is probably covered up beneath papers stacked a foot high. As soon as you start the Windows XP Calculator program, it is never farther away than the taskbar.

> The Calculator program actually contains two calculators, a *standard calculator* and a *scientific calculator*. Most people need the standard calculator that provides all the common mathematical operations required for day-to-day business affairs. The scientific calculator contains additional operations, such as statistical and trigonometric operations.

Working with the Standard Calculator

The Windows standard calculator provides full-featured calculator functions. When you use the Calculator program, you can sell your own desktop calculator at your next yard sale. Windows even enables you to copy and paste the calculator results directly into your own applications. The following To Do item guides you through the use of the standard calculator.

To Do: Using the Standard Calculator

1. Start the Windows Calculator program, shown in Figure 10.1. If you see a calculator window with many more buttons than the figure's, select View, Standard to work with the non-scientific calculator.

2. To steal from an old cliché, it doesn't take a rocket scientist to use the calculator. The calculator performs standard addition, subtraction, multiplication, and division. In addition, the standard calculator includes memory clear, recall, store, and memory add.

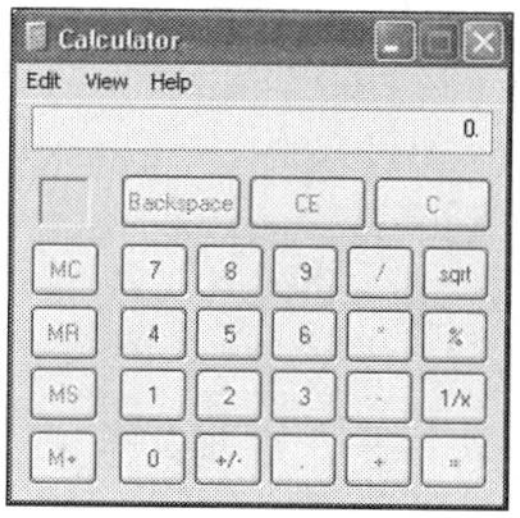

FIGURE 10.1

Windows XP's Calculator emulates a pocket calculator.

All of the calculator operations produce *running totals*, meaning that you can continuously apply operations, such as addition, to the running total in the calculator's display.

10

The calculator has keyboard-equivalent keys. Instead of clicking with your mouse to enter 2 + 2 for example, you can type **2 + 2 =**. The equal sign requests the answer. Not all keys have obvious keyboard equivalents, however. For example, the C key does not clear the total, Esc does. Therefore, you might need to combine your mouse and keyboard to use the calculator effectively.

3. Click the numbers 1, 2, and then 3. You can use your keyboard if you like. As you click, the numbers appear inside the display.

4. Click the multiplication sign (the asterisk).

5. Click the 2.

6. Click the equal sign or press Enter, and the calculator displays the result of 246.

7. Click C or press Esc to clear the display.

The Backspace key erases any character that you type incorrectly.

8. The percent key produces a percentage only as a result of multiplication. Therefore, you can compute a percentage of a number by multiplying it by the percent figure. Suppose that you want to know how much 35% of 4,000 is.

Type **4000** and then press the asterisk. Type **35** followed by the % key (Shift+5 on the keyboard). The value 1400 appears. The result: 1400 is 35% of 4,000. (The word *of* in a math problem is a sure sign that you must multiply by a percentage. Calculating 35% of 4,000 implies that you need to multiply 4,000 by 35%.)

9. When you want to negate the number in the display, click the +/– key. Suppose that you want to subtract the display's current value, 1,400, from 5,000. Although you can clear the display and perform the subtraction, you can also negate the 1,400 by clicking the +/– key, pressing the plus sign, typing **5000**, and pressing the equal sign to produce 3,600.

> The calculator displays a letter M above the four memory keys when you store a value in the memory.

10. To store a value in memory, click MS for *Memory Store*. Whenever you want the memory value to appear in the display, click MR for *Memory Recall*. MC clears the memory and M+ adds the display to the total in memory. If you want to store a running total, click the M+ button every time you want to add the display's value to the memory. The M disappears from the memory indicator box when you clear the memory.

> When you want to switch from your application to the calculator to perform a calculation and then enter the result of that calculation elsewhere such as in your word processor, select Edit, Copy (Ctrl+C) to copy the value to the Clipboard. When you switch back to the other Windows application, you will be able to paste the value into that application.

Using the Scientific Calculator

The second Windows Calculator program, the scientific calculator, supports many more advanced mathematical operations. Despite its added power, the scientific calculator operates almost identically to the standard calculator. The standard keys and memory are identical in both calculators.

To see the scientific calculator, select View, Scientific. Windows displays the scientific calculator shown in Figure 10.2. The scientific calculator offers more keys, operators, and indicators than the standard calculator does.

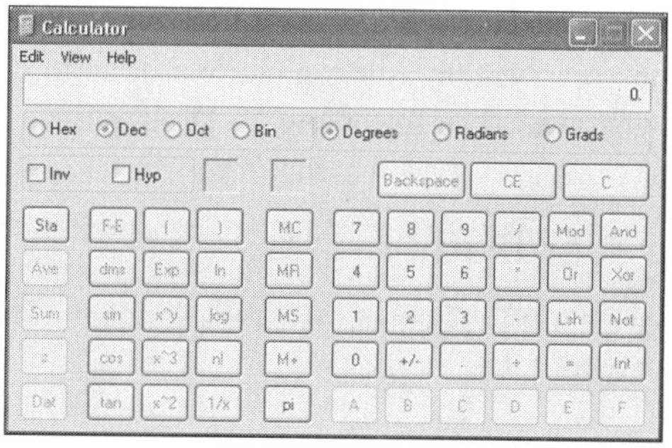

FIGURE 10.2

The Windows scientific calculator provides advanced operations.

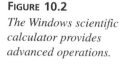

Write with Flair

Windows contains a word processor called *WordPad*, which appears on your Start menu's More Programs, Accessories menu group. Although WordPad does not contain all the features of a major word processor, such as Microsoft Word, WordPad does contain many formatting features and can accept documents created in several word processing programs. This section introduces you to WordPad.

> Notepad also appears in your Accessories menu group, but Notepad is a scaled-down version of WordPad and offers very few of the formatting capabilities that WordPad offers.

WordPad edits, loads, and saves documents in all the following formats: Word for Windows, Windows Write (the word processor available in Windows 3.1 and earlier), text documents, and RTF (*Rich Text Format*) documents. As a result, when you open an RTF or Write or Word for Windows document that contains formatting, such as underlining and boldfaced characters, WordPad retains those special formatting features in the document.

WordPad sports a toolbar that you can display to help you access common commands more easily. WordPad also supports the uses of a Ruler and format bar that help you work with WordPad's advanced editing features. When you type text into WordPad, you won't have to worry about pressing Enter at the end of every line. WordPad wraps your text to the next line when you run out of room on the current line. Press Enter only when you get to the end of a paragraph or a short line such as a title that you don't want combined with the subsequent line. Pressing Enter twice in a row adds a blank line to your text.

10

WordPad contains features for the novice as well as for advanced writers. If you have no other word processor on your system, you can use WordPad to produce virtually any kind of document that you need. The following To Do item leads you through the basic WordPad procedures.

To Do: Using the WordPad Program

1. Start the WordPad program from the Accessories menu. You'll see the WordPad screen shown in Figure 10.3.

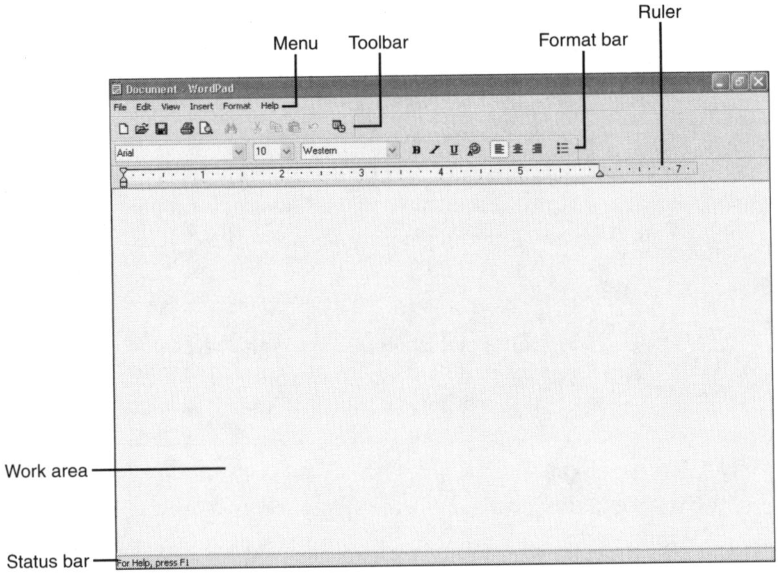

FIGURE **10.3**

WordPad offers many word processing features.

Menu   Toolbar   Format bar   Ruler

Work area

Status bar

If your WordPad screen does not look exactly like the one in Figure 10.3, you can use the View menu to add a check mark to each of the first four menu options—Toolbar, Format Bar, Ruler, and Status Bar—so that you display each of these four optional tools.

2. For this task, you'll practice entering and formatting text. Type the following text: `A large line`.

3. Select all three words by highlighting them with the mouse or keyboard. With the mouse, select by pointing to the first character and dragging the mouse to the last character. With the keyboard, you can select by moving the text cursor to the first letter and pressing Shift+Right Arrow until you select the entire line.

4. Click the format bar button labeled B. The text stays selected but something changes—the text becomes boldfaced. Press any arrow key to get rid of the highlighted text and see the boldfaced text.

5. Select the three words once again. Click the second format bar button with the letter I. WordPad italicizes the text. Now click the third format bar button with the letter U. WordPad instantly underlines the selected text. Keep the text highlighted for the next step.

6. By default, WordPad selects a *font* (a typestyle) usually named Arial or Times New Roman. You can see the font name directly below the format bar. The font's size, in *points*—a point is 1/72 inch, appears to the right of the font name. The default font size is 10 points.

   You can change both the font and the font size by clicking the drop-down lists in which each appears. When you select text, select a font name. WordPad then changes the font of the selected text to the new font name style. After selecting the text, display the font name list by clicking the drop-down list box's arrow and select a font name. If you have the Comic Sans MS (Western), use that font. If you do not have that font name, select another font name that sounds interesting.

   Open the point size drop-down list box and select 36. You can type this number directly into the list box if you want to. As soon as you do, you can see the results of your boldfaced, underlined, italicized, large-sized text displayed using the font name you selected. Press the left or right arrow key to remove the selection. Figure 10.4 shows what your WordPad window should look like.

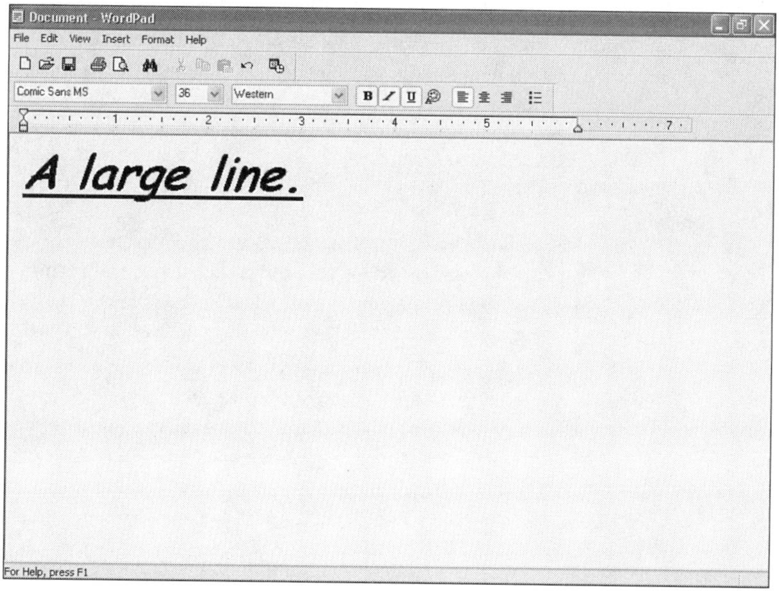

FIGURE 10.4

Select a font and increase the point size to see the large line of text.

▼ WordPad applied all the previous formatting on the three words because you selected those words before you changed the formatting. If you select only a single word or character, WordPad formats only that selected text and leaves all the other text alone.

Don't overdo the formatting of text! If you make text too fancy, it becomes cluttered, and your words will lose their meaning amid all the italic, under-line, and font styles. Use italic, boldfacing, and underlining only for empha-sis when needed for certain words and titles.

7. Press Enter. Click the B, I, and U format bar buttons and return the font name to Times New Roman. Decrease the font size to 10. Type the following: `Windows is fun` and press the spacebar. If you do not like the font size, click the down arrow to the right of the font name list and select a different size.

8. Suppose that you want to italicize your name. If you click the format bar for italic, all subsequent text you type will be italicized. Click the italic format bar button and type your first name. The name will be italicized, but the other text will not be.

9. Click the italic format bar button once again and continue typing on the same line. Type this: `and I like to use WordPad`.

10. As you can see, you don't have to select text to apply special formatting to it. Before you type text that you want to format, select the proper format command and then type the text. WordPad then formats the text, using the format styles you've selected, as you type that text. When you want to revert to the previous unformatted style such as when you no longer want italic, change the style and keep typing.

Font Controls

Ctrl+B, Ctrl+I, and Ctrl+U are the shortcut keys for clicking the B, I, and U format bar buttons. You can also change the formatting of text characters by selecting Format, Font. WordPad displays a Font dialog box, as shown in Figure 10.5, on which you can apply several formatting styles.

As you change the style, the Font dialog box's Sample area shows you a sam-ple of text formatted to the specifications you provide. When you close the Font dialog box, WordPad formats subsequent text according to the Font dialog box settings.

▼

10

FIGURE 10.5

The Font dialog box provides all formatting specifications in a single place.

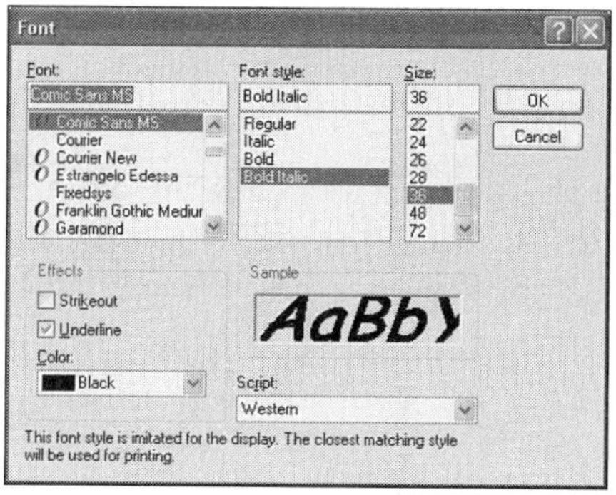

11. Select File, Print Preview to see a *thumbnail sketch* of how your document will look if you were to print it. By looking at a preview before you print your document, you can tell if the overall appearance is acceptable and if the margins and text styles look good. You can quit the preview and return to your editing session by pressing Esc.

12. Close WordPad for now. Don't save your work when prompted to do so.

You've only seen a taste of the text-formatting capabilities available, but there's just enough time left in this hour to discuss one final accessory program called *Paint*. Before moving to Paint, however, browse some of the following word processing features that WordPad supports:

- The Ruler indicates where your text appears on the printed page when you print the document. Each number on the Ruler represents an inch or a centimeter if your computer is set up for a metric setting in the View, Options dialog box. As you type, you can watch the Ruler to see where the text appears as you print the document. If you select the Format, Paragraph command, WordPad displays the Paragraph dialog box in which you can set left and right indentations for individual paragraphs as well as tab stops.

You can place tab stops quickly by double-clicking the Ruler at the exact location of the tab stop you want.

- The toolbar's Align Left, Center, and Align Right toolbar buttons left-justify, center, and right-justify text so that you can align your text in columns as a newspaper does. The center alignment format bar button is useful for centering titles at the top of documents.
- If you have a color printer, consider adding color to your text by clicking the toolbar's color-selection tool.
- The toolbar's Bullet format bar button adds bullets to lists you enter. Before you start the list, click the Bullets button to format the list as a bulleted list.

Paint a Pretty Picture

Paint provides many colorful drawing tools. Before you can use Paint effectively, you must learn how to interact with Paint, and you also must know what each of Paint's tools does. Start Paint by selecting the Start menu's Programs, Accessories, Paint option. The Paint screen contains six major areas, listed in Figure 10.6. Table 10.1 describes each area.

FIGURE 10.6

The six major areas of the Paint screen enable you to create and edit your graphics images.

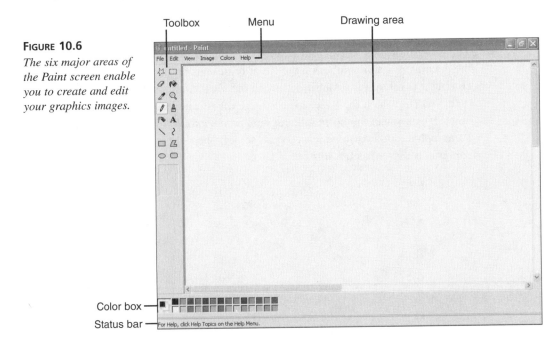

Toolbox   Menu   Drawing area

Color box

Status bar

Paint does not contain a toolbar with buttons as WordPad and other Windows programs do. Paint contains a toolbox that is the most important area of Paint. It is from the toolbox that you select and use drawing tools.

TABLE 10.1   Paint's Six Areas Help You Draw Better

Area	Description
Drawing area	Where your drawing appears. When you want to create or modify a drawing, you work within this area.
Color box	A list of possible colors you can choose to add color to your artwork.
Menu bar	The commands that control Paint's operation.
Status bar	The area that displays important messages and measurements as you use Paint.
Toolbox	The vital drawing, painting, and coloring tools with which you create and modify artwork.
Drawing coordinates	Shows, in pixels, the location of the next item you'll draw.

The two scrollbars on the drawing area enable you to scroll to other parts of your drawing. The drawing area is actually as large as a maximized window. If, however, Paint initially displays the drawing area maximized, you cannot access the menu bar or the tool box or read the status bar. Therefore, Paint adds the scrollbars to its drawing area so that you can create drawings that will, when displayed, fill the entire screen.

The following To Do item helps you learn how to start Paint and navigate around the screen a bit. Practice using Paint and learn Paint's features as you work with the program.

To Do: Getting Artistic with Paint

▲ To Do

1. Start Paint. Paint is located on the Programs, Accessories menu.

2. Maximize the Paint program to full size. Paint is one of the few programs in which you'll almost always want to work in a maximized window. By maximizing the window, you gain the largest drawing area possible.

3. If you do not see the toolbox, the status bar, or the color box, display the View menu and check each of these three important screen areas to ensure that all five areas show as you follow along in this hour.

▼

10

▼   4. Take a look at Figure 10.7. This figure labels each of the toolbox tools. Each tool contains an icon that illustrates the tool's function. The tools on the toolbox comprise your collection of drawing, painting, and coloring tools. When you want to add or modify a picture, choose the appropriate tool. As you work with Paint in subsequent tasks, refer to Figure 10.7 to find the tool named in the task.

FIGURE 10.7

The tools on the toolbox.

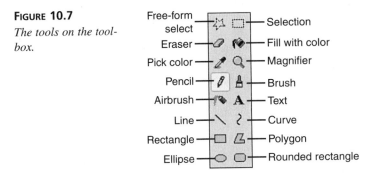

5. Click the Pencil tool.

6. Move the mouse cursor over the drawing area, and the cursor changes to a pencil (the same icon that's on the pencil tool).

7. Hold down the mouse button and move your mouse all around the drawing area. Make all sorts of curves with the mouse. Notice that Paint keeps the pencil within the borders of the drawing area.

8. The default color for the pencil drawing is black. Click a different color on the color bar, such as red or green, and draw some more. The new lines appear in the new color. Select additional colors and draw more lines to beautify the picture even more.

> Every time you change a tool or color or draw a separate line, Paint saves the next group of changes to the drawing area. As with most Windows accessory programs, Paint supports an Edit, Undo feature (Ctrl+Z or Alt+Backspace). You can undo up to three previous edit groups. Therefore, if you've just drawn three separate lines, you can remove each of those lines by selecting the Undo command three times.

9. Erase your drawing by selecting File, New. Don't save your current drawing. Paint clears the drawing area so that you can start a new document image.

10. Click the Line tool. Use the Line tool to draw straight lines.

    A straight line is defined by two coordinates: the starting coordinate position and the end coordinate position. To draw a line, you must anchor the line's starting position and extend the line to its ending position. Paint automatically draws a straight line from the starting position to the end position. You can draw lines, using the Line tool, in any direction.

11. Get used to reading *coordinate pair* numbers in the status bar. The numbers tell you the number of drawing points from the left and top of your window. Move the mouse around the drawing area (do not press a mouse button yet) and watch the pair of numbers at the right of the status bar change.

12. Select a different color and draw another line. Paint draws that line in the new color.

> Now that you've selected the Line tool, look at the area below the toolbox. You'll see five lines, with each line growing thicker than the one before. By clicking a thick line, the next line you draw with the Line tool appears on the drawing area in the new thickness. You can change the thickness, using this line size list, for any of the geometric shapes.

13. Click the thickest line in the list of line sizes. Draw a couple of lines to see the thicker lines. If you change colors before drawing, the thicker lines appear in the new color.

14. The rest of the geometric shapes are as easy to draw as the lines are. Select File, New to clear the drawing area. Don't save the changes.

15. Click the Line tool to change the line thickness size to the middle line thickness (the third thickness size). Always change the Line tool's thickness before selecting one of the geometric drawing tools. The Line tool's line size determines the line thickness for all the geometric tools.

16. Select the Rectangle tool. Rectangles, like lines, are determined by their starting *anchor position* and the rectangle's opposite corner's position. Begin drawing a rectangle at coordinates 190,75. After anchoring the rectangle with the mouse button, drag the mouse until it rests at 385,270. The status line indicator will show 200,200, meaning that the rectangle is 200 by 200 drawing points. When you release the mouse, you will have drawn a perfect square.

10

Drawing a perfect square is not always easy because you have to pay close attention to the coordinates. Paint offers a better way to draw perfect squares. Hold down the Shift key while dragging the mouse, and the rectangle always appears as a square. Shift also draws perfect circles when you use the Ellipse tool.

The three rectangles below the toolbox do not represent the line thickness of the rectangles. They determine how Paint draws rectangles. When you click the top rectangle (the default), all of the drawing area that appears beneath the next rectangle that you draw shows through. Therefore, if you draw a rectangle over other pictures, you see the other pictures coming through the inside of the new rectangle. If you click the second rectangle below the toolbox, the rectangle's center overwrites any existing art. As a result, all rectangles you draw have a blank center, no matter what art the rectangle overwrites. If you select the third rectangle, Paint does not draw a rectangular outline but does draw the interior of the rectangle in the same color you've set for the interior. (The default interior color is white.)

17. Now that you understand the rectangle, you also understand the other geometric tools. Click the Ellipse tool to draw ovals (remember that Shift enables you to draw perfect circles). Click the Rounded Rectangle tool to draw rounded rectangles (or rounded squares if you press Shift while dragging).

    Click the top rectangle selection (to draw see-through shapes) and click the Ellipse to draw circles. Click the Rounded Rectangle tool and draw rounded rectangles. Fill your drawing area with all kinds of shapes to get the feel of the tools.

18. A blank drawing area will help you learn how to use the Polygon and Curve tools, so select File, New (don't save) to clear your drawing area.

19. Select the Polygon tool. The Polygon is a tool that draws an enclosed figure with as many sides as you want. After you anchor the polygon with the mouse, drag the mouse left or right and click the mouse. Drag the mouse once again to continue the polygon. Every time you want to change directions, click the mouse once more. When you finish, double-click the mouse, and Paint completes the polygon for you by connecting your final line with the first point you drew.

20. Clear your drawing area once again. The Curve tool is one of the neatest but strangest tools in the tool box. Click the Curve tool (after adjusting the line thickness and color if you want to do so).

    Draw a straight line by dragging the mouse. After you release the line, click the mouse button somewhere just outside the line and drag the mouse around in

▼   circles. As you drag the mouse, Paint adjusts the curve to follow the mouse. When you see the curve that you want, release the mouse so that Paint can stabilize the curve.

21. The Eraser/Color Eraser tool erases whatever appears on the drawing area. The Eraser/Color Eraser tool comes in four sizes. When you select the Eraser/Color Eraser tool, you can also select an eraser thickness. (The color you choose has no bearing on the eraser's use.) Select the Eraser/Color Eraser tool now and drag it over parts of your drawing to erase lines you've drawn.

▲   22. Clear your drawing area and exit Paint.

The geometric tools generally require you to select a line width, a drawing style (such as rectangles that hide or don't hide their backgrounds), and an exterior and interior color. Then you can draw the shape. You draw most of the shapes by anchoring their initial position and then by dragging the mouse to extend the shape across the screen. If you make a mistake, you can use the Eraser/Color Eraser tool to correct the problem.

Although Paint can only create bitmap files with the `.bmp` filename extension, the Paint program can read both bitmap and PC Paintbrush files. PC Paintbrush filenames end with the `.pcx` filename extension. If you read a pcx file and save the file, Paint saves the file in the bitmap file format when you select File, Save.

Pictures that you draw often need explanatory text in addition to the graphics that you draw, similar to a legend for a map. The Text tool enables you to add text by using any font and font size available within Windows. You can control how the text covers or exposes any art beneath the text. After clicking the Text tool, drag the text's outline box. Text always resides inside this text box that appears. When you release your mouse, select the font and style and type your text. When you click another tool, your text becomes part of the drawing area.

Summary

This hour showed you three desktop accessory programs. The Calculator program offers advantages over its real-world desktop equivalent because the calculator is always available on your Windows desktop as you work with other programs.

WordPad gives you introductory word processing features that enable you to create documents that contain special formatting. WordPad is limited compared to the word processors sold today. For example, WordPad contains no spell checker. Nevertheless, WordPad

10

offers simple, introductory word processing features and supports several file formats so that any WordPad documents you create will be available in other word processors you eventually purchase.

The Paint accessory program enables you to draw. Paint's drawing tools rival many of the drawing tools supplied in art programs that sell for several hundred dollars. Paint includes geometric tools that help you draw perfect shapes. You can color the shape outlines, as well as their interiors, with Paint's coloring tools. The menu bar provides commands that resize, reshape, invert, and stretch your drawn images. If you want precision editing, you can have it by zeroing in on the fine details of your drawing by using the Magnifier tool.

Q&A

Q Why can't I read all the text on the Print Preview?

A The Print Preview feature was not designed to let you read text. The Print Preview feature simply draws a representation of your document when you print the document on the printer. Instead of printing the document and discovering a margin or formatting error, you can often find the errors on the Print Preview screen, allowing you to correct the problem before printing the document.

Q I'm no artist, so why should I learn Paint?

A As just stated, many applications combine text and graphics. In the world of communications, which ranges from business to politics, pictures can convey the same meaning as thousands of words can. Graphics catch people's attention more quickly than text. When you combine the details that text provides with the attention-grabbing effect of graphics, you're sure to have an audience.

There are many other reasons to master Paint, as well. You might want to use Paint to produce these graphics publications:

- Flyers for volunteer or professional organizations
- Holiday greetings
- Letters that include drawings by the kids
- Sale notices for posting on bulletin boards

Perhaps the best reason to learn to use Paint: It's fun!

Workshop

The quiz and exercise questions are designed to test your knowledge of the material covered in this hour. The answers are in Appendix C, "Answers to Quizzes."

Quiz

1. What are the two kinds of calculators available in Windows XP?
2. How does WordPad differ from Notepad and from major word processors such as Microsoft Word?
3. A common type size is the size of *pica,* which is 12 points. What is the actual height, in inches, of pica?
4. How can you center text in WordPad?
5. How can you draw perfect squares in Paint?

Exercises

1. Pick up a daily newspaper and try to mimic the look of the headline article in WordPad. WordPad will not format the text into multiple columns, but you can still learn WordPad by mimicking the headline typeface and size and attempting to make the subheadlines and text look like your newspaper's.
2. You can learn Paint really quickly if you have children or know of some who can show you. Just start Paint and show them the mouse—they'll figure out the rest. Watch and learn!

10

PART IV

Late Afternoon Internet Integration

Hour

HOUR **11**

Surfing the Web with Internet Explorer

In today's world, the Internet is a much larger part of computer users' lives than ever before. Windows XP includes *Internet Explorer*, an Internet *browser* that enables you to access the Internet from within Windows. In designing Windows XP, Microsoft kept the Internet firmly in mind; the browser concept runs throughout Windows and you can access the Internet or your desktop from almost anywhere in Windows. For example, you can access the Internet directly from within the My Computer window without first opening Internet Explorer.

Although the Internet is available throughout Windows XP, you'll probably access the Internet primarily from within Internet Explorer and you'll find the most functionality from within Internet Explorer. This hour introduces the Internet and shows you some of the ways Windows integrates with the Internet. You will learn how to access the Internet with Internet Explorer.

In this hour, you will

- Learn what makes the Internet such an important online tool
- Learn why modern Internet access techniques, such as Web pages, make the Internet more manageable
- Start and use Internet Explorer to surf the Internet
- Navigate the Internet and view the multimedia information you find there
- Enter Web information more quickly with Internet Explorer

Introduction to the Internet

The Internet is a worldwide system of interconnected computers. Whereas your desktop computer is a standalone machine, and cables tie a network of computers together, the Internet is a worldwide online network of computers connected to standalone computers through modems and other kinds of online connections. Hardly anyone understands the entire Internet because it is not one system but a conglomeration of systems.

The Internet began as a government-linked set of computers, progressed to the university levels, and then migrated to business and personal use that now consists of an almost infinite amount of information. The Internet is so vast that nobody could access all of its information today.

No central Internet computer exists. The Internet is a system of connected computers. *Internet* is the term given to the entire system.

The Internet's vastness almost caused its downfall. How does anyone access or find information on the Internet? Fortunately, Internet technicians began standardizing Internet information when it became apparent that the Internet was growing and becoming a major information provider. With the Windows XP interface assisting Internet Explorer's search tools, locating information is simple.

Do not confuse Internet Explorer with Windows Explorer. Internet Explorer is your Internet browser, and Windows Explorer enables you to manage your files. Hour 5, "Navigating Files with Windows Explorer," describes Windows Explorer in more detail.

The WWW: World Wide Web

The *WWW*, *World Wide Web*, or just *Web*, is a collection of Internet pages of information. Web pages can contain text, graphics, sound, and video. Figure 11.1 shows a sample Web page. As you can see, the Web page's graphics and text organize information into a magazine-like, readable, and appealing format.

FIGURE 11.1

Web pages provide Internet information in a nice format.

Web address entry/display   Web page display area

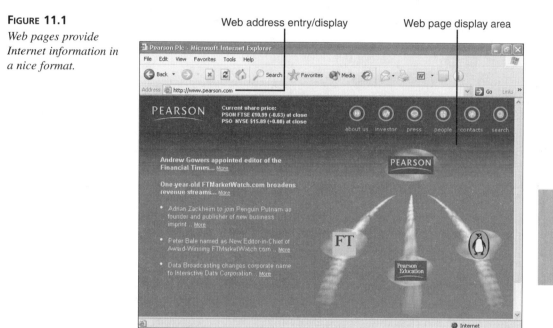

Generally, a Web site contains more information than will fit easily on a single Web page. Therefore, many Web pages contain links to several additional extended pages, as well as other linked Web pages that might be related to the original topic. The first page you view is called the *home page*, and from the home page you can view other pages of information.

Each Web page has a unique location that includes the source computer and the location on that computer, but such locations would be difficult to keep track of. Therefore, the Internet has standardized Web page locations with a series of addresses called *URLs*, or *uniform resource locator* addresses. You can view any Web page if you know its URL. If you do not know the URL, the Internet provides several search engines that find Web pages when you search for topics.

Surely you've run across computer addresses that look like this: www.microsoft.com and www.newsmax.com. These are URLs that access the Web pages. These two happen to be the URLs for Microsoft Corporation and a daily news service, respectively.

Introducing the Internet Explorer Web Browser

Before you can access and view Web information, you need a program that can display Web page information, including text, graphics, audio, and video. The program you need is called a *Web browser*—or just a *browser*. Although several companies offer browsers, Windows integrates one of the best Web-browsing programs, Internet Explorer.

This 24-hour tutorial uses Internet Explorer in the figures and descriptions. Some people prefer to use a competing Web browser, such as Netscape Navigator, to access Web pages. Internet Explorer generally integrates the best with Windows because Microsoft wrote both products.

Before you can access the Internet's Web pages, you need to get Internet access through an *ISP*, or *Internet service provider*. Several national ISPs exist that you've probably heard of such as America Online (AOL) and Microsoft Network (MSN). Many people can access the Internet through a local Internet provider. Whichever provider you use, your provider will tell you how to set up Internet Explorer to access the Internet.

Internet Explorer is easy to start. You literally can access the Internet with one or two clicks by running Internet Explorer. The following To Do item explains how to start Internet Explorer. You must already have Internet access through the Microsoft Network or another provider, and you must have already set up Internet Explorer to access your provider. You can access the Internet through a dial-up modem, satellite, or one of the other connections available today.

To Do: Starting Internet Explorer

1. Select Internet Explorer from your Windows Start menu. If you've displayed the Quick Launch toolbar area, you can click the Internet Explorer icon located on your Windows taskbar.

2. If required, enter your Internet ID and password and click Connect to dial up the Internet. For users with a DSL or cable modem system, the connection will not always require an ID and password.

▼
3. Assuming that you have properly set up an account with a service provider, Internet Explorer dials your provider and displays the page setup to be your initial browser's *home page*. Depending on the amount of information and graphics on the page, the display might take a few moments or might display right away.

▲

Internet Explorer's Home toolbar button displays your browser's opening home page. At any time during your Internet browsing, you can return to Internet Explorer's home page by clicking this Home button. You can change your browser's home page address by entering a new home page address within the Tools, Internet Options dialog box's General page. When you enter a new home page address, Internet Explorer returns to that page whenever you click the Home toolbar button or when you start Internet Explorer in a subsequent session.

Internet Explorer makes it easy to navigate Web pages. Before looking further at Internet information, take a few minutes to familiarize yourself with the Internet Explorer screen by following this To Do item:

To Do: Managing the Internet Explorer Screen

1. Study Figure 11.2 to learn the parts of the Internet Explorer screen. The figure shows the Search Companion, available by clicking the toolbar's Search button. Internet Explorer displays your home page and lists its address in the address area. Your screen might differ slightly depending on your Internet Explorer configuration. Internet Explorer is fully customizable. For example, you can hide a toolbar to make more room for the Web page content.

The Search Companion, the window pane to the left of Figure 11.2's browser's Web page, is just one option available for this section of your Web browser. The general name for the window pane on the left is the *Explorer Bar*. By selecting from the View, Explorer Bar menu, you can select one of several items to place on the Explorer Bar.

You probably recognize most of Internet Explorer's toolbar buttons. Windows intentionally puts similar buttons throughout all its windows so that you can navigate the Web from Windows Explorer, My Computer, and other locations. You can display labels under each toolbar button by right-clicking over a blank area on the toolbar and selecting Customize. Select the option labeled Show text labels from the Text options list box to display the toolbar button captions.

▼

FIGURE 11.2

Learn the Internet Explorer screen so that you can utilize its many features when surfing the Web.

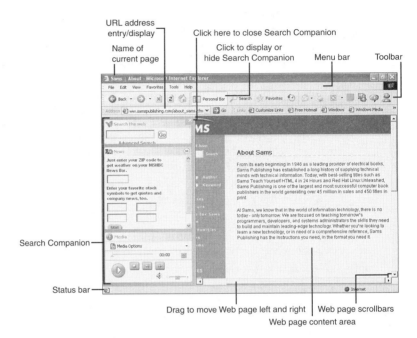

2. Some Web site addresses are lengthy. Drag the Links label to the right of the Address box left to shrink the Address Bar and see links to other Web pages. If you cannot drag the Links area left, your toolbars are locked into place; select View, Toolbars, Lock the Toolbars to unlock the toolbar positions and allow for the dragging of toolbar widths left and right. The more room you give the Address text box, the less room the other toolbar buttons have.

3. Click the down arrow at the right of the address entry to open a list of recently traversed site addresses. If this is the first time you or anyone has used your computer's Internet Explorer, you might not see sites other than the current start page sites. The toolbar's History button switches from whatever you had in the window's left pane to the History Bar. Click the History button to see the History Explorer bar, such as the one in Figure 11.3 that enables you to return to sites you've gone to in past Internet visits. If you click any of the sites (click any date name to open its list of sites), the display area at the right of the screen updates to show that site. You can return to a full-page view by clicking the Explorer Bar's Close button.

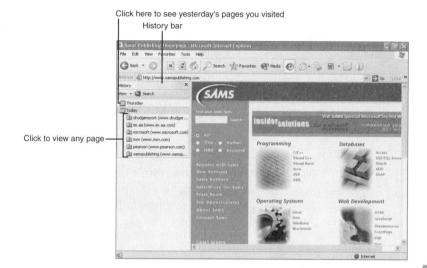

FIGURE 11.3

Internet Explorer uses the Explorer Bar for various Internet-traversal functions such as this history list.

Click here to see yesterday's pages you visited

History bar

Click to view any page

4. Click the scrollbar to see more of the page. Most Web pages take more room than will fit on one screen.

5. Select View, Full Screen (or press the F11 shortcut key) to dedicate your entire screen, except for part of your toolbar at the top, to the Web page.

6. To return from the full screen view, press F11 once again.

Familiarize yourself with Internet Explorer's screen elements. As you traverse the Internet, Internet Explorer will aid you—as you will see throughout the rest of this hour.

Surfing the Internet

Remember that the Web is a collection of interconnected Web pages. Almost every Web page contains links to other sites. These links (also called *hot links*, *hypertext links*, and *hyperlinks*) are often underlined. You can locate these links by moving your mouse cursor over the underlined description. If the mouse cursor changes to a hand, you can click the hand to move to that page. After a brief pause, your Web browser displays the page.

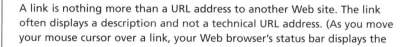

A link is nothing more than a URL address to another Web site. The link often displays a description and not a technical URL address. (As you move your mouse cursor over a link, your Web browser's status bar displays the actual URL address to the link.) Therefore, you can traverse related Web pages without worrying about addresses; just click link descriptions to move to those sites.

Suppose that you view the home page of your financial broker. The page might include links to other related pages, such as stock quotation pages, company financial informational pages, and order-entry pages in which you can enter your own stock purchase requests.

One of the most useful features of Internet Explorer and every other Web browser is the browser's capability to return to sites you've visited, both in the current session and in former sessions. The toolbar's Back button returns you to a site you just visited, and you can keep clicking the Back button to return to pages you've visited during this session. The Forward toolbar button returns you to pages from which you've backed up.

Keep in mind that you can click the Address drop-down list box to see a list of URL addresses you've visited. In the History bar, you'll find addresses from the current as well as previous Internet Explorer Web sessions.

If you know the address of a Web site you want to view, you can type the site's address directly in the Address text box. When you press Enter or click Go, Internet Explorer takes you to that site and displays the Web page. In addition, you can select File, Open to display a URL dialog box and type an address in the dialog box. When you click OK, Internet Explorer displays the page associated with that address. From the Start menu, you can even enter a URL in the Run dialog box to see any page on the Web. If you want to return to your original home page, click the toolbar's Home button.

As discussed previously, Internet Explorer more fully integrates into Windows XP and Windows applications than any previous Windows version. Most of the Microsoft Office products, for example, include an Internet Explorer-like interface in many areas, and they link directly to Internet Explorer when you perform certain Internet-related tasks from within an Office product. From Internet Explorer's File, Open dialog box, instead of entering a URL address, you can type a disk, pathname, and filename. If Internet Explorer recognizes the file's registered type as it will for common files such as Office data files, the file's contents appear inside your Internet Explorer browser. You then can traverse back and forth between files on your disk and Web pages without ever leaving your browser.

If you find a location you really like and want to return to, save that location in Internet Explorer's Favorites list. For example, perhaps you run across a site that discusses your favorite television show and you want to return to that site again quickly. Just click the Favorites toolbar button to display the Favorites bar, click the Add button, enter a description, and click OK to add the site to your Favorites list. The Favorites bar differs from your History bar in that the History bar updates over time as you visit Web sites, keeping at most three weeks' worth of visited site addresses. Your Favorites bar keeps track of any Web site you store there until you change the Favorites list. That means you can return to a favorite page years after you stored the page's address in your Favorites bar.

You can practice moving among Web pages by using the Internet Explorer browser. After you visit a site, you can return to that site very simply. The following To Do item demonstrates how you traverse the Web using Internet Explorer.

To Do: Moving Between Pages

1. If you have not started Internet Explorer, start it and log on to the Internet.
2. Click the Address list box to highlight your Start page's URL address.
3. Type the following Web page address: **http://www.firstgov.com**. A Government Web page appears, as shown in Figure 11.4. (Depending on the changes that have been made to the site recently, the site might not match Figure 11.4 exactly.)

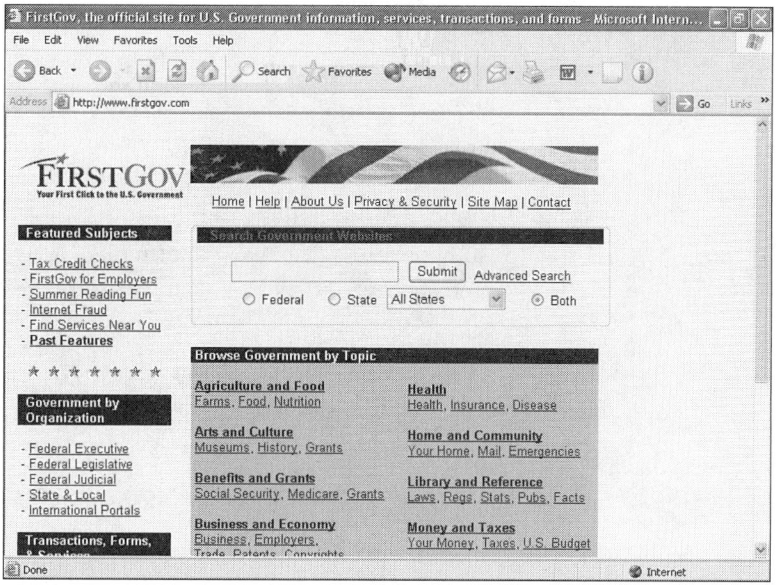

FIGURE 11.4

www.firstgov.com *provides links to all the Government's Web pages.*

Often, you see Web addresses prefaced with the text http://. This prefix enables you and your browser to both know that the address to the right of the second slash is a Web page's URL address. Internet Explorer does not require the http:// prefix before URLs. Be sure to type forward slashes and not the MS-DOS backslashes you might be used to typing on PCs.

Most Web addresses begin with www and end with com, although many other Web site suffixes exist, such as gov and edu. Knowing that com is the most common, Microsoft added a time-saving feature to the Address list box: Type the *middle* portion of any Web site that follows the general format http://www.*sitename*.com, such as firstgov, and then press Ctrl+Enter. Internet Explorer surrounds your entry with the needed http://www and com to complete the address.

4. Click any link on the page (indicated by a hand mouse pointer or a text color change when you move the mouse over a link's hot spot). After a brief pause, you see the linked Web page.

5. Click the toolbar's Back button. Almost instantly, the first page appears.

6. After you're back at the original page, practice building a favorite site list by clicking the Favorites toolbar button.

7. Instead of using the toolbar's Favorites button, select the Favorites, Add to Favorites menu option. Internet Explorer displays the Add to Favorites dialog box.

8. Type a description for the page such as **Government Link Page**. Instead of typing a new description, you can always keep the default title that appears; often, this title is rather lengthy for a Favorites list.

9. Click the Create In button to display a list of folders in which you can store the page. (You can create new folders by clicking the New Folder button and entering a folder name.)

10. Click OK.

11. Click the Favorites toolbar button to display the Favorites bar once again. You'll see the new entry in its folder. When you select that favorite entry, Internet Explorer looks up the entry's stored URL address and goes to that Web page.

If you add too many favorites, your Favorites list might become unmanageable. Utilize the Folders option to organize your Web content. By setting up a series of folders named by subjects, you can group your favorite Web sites by subject.

Internet Explorer makes your Favorites list available in three places:

- The Windows Start menu
- The Favorites toolbar button in Internet Explorer and other Windows XP menus that display the toolbar, such as the My Computer window
- The Internet Explorer Favorites menu option

Windows XP does not automatically display your Favorites list, but you can request that Windows XP do this as an option on the Start menu. Open your Control Panel's Taskbar and Start menu window. Click the Customize button, click the Advanced tab, and click the Favorites menu option under the list labeled Show These Items on the Start Menu. (See Figure 11.5.) After adding your favorite Web sites to your Start menu, you can open any of those Web pages by selecting the page from your Windows Start menu without first having to start Internet Explorer. As soon as you select a Web page, Windows automatically starts Windows Explorer and loads the Web page.

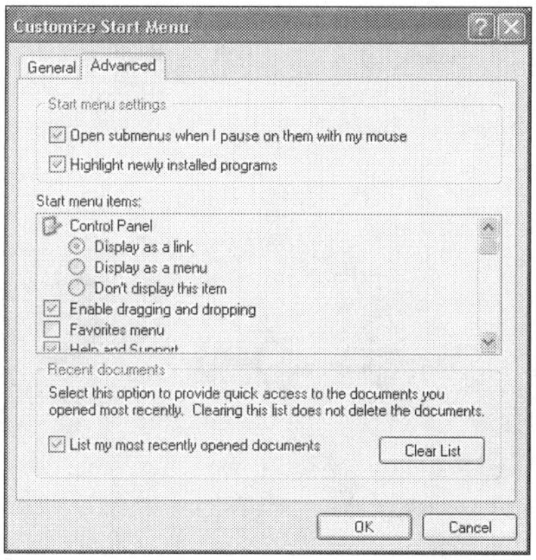

11

FIGURE 11.5

You can display your list of favorite Web pages from your Windows Start menu.

As with all the Windows XP menus, the Internet Explorer menus are personalized to display only your most recent selections. By providing only the most recently accessed sites, the sites you are most likely to look for again, Internet Explorer keeps you moving quickly to the information you want to access. If you've turned off the Windows XP personalized menus on the Start menu's Settings, Taskbar and Start Menu option, Internet Explorer always displays all your favorites when you select from the Favorites menu option.

Locating Information

When you want to find something on the Internet, just turn to the tools you already know: the Windows Search Companion feature. You learned how Windows XP searches for data in all kinds of places in Hour 9, "Finding Files, Folders, and Friends." Internet Explorer displays the same search window as Windows displays when you click the Internet Explorer toolbar's Search button. The Search Companion window appears when you click the toolbar's Search button, as shown in Figure 11.6. You specify the search criteria in the Search bar and the results appear in the right window. When you finish with the search pane, click its Close button and your browser window returns to its normal appearance.

FIGURE 11.6

Internet Explorer offers the same search window options as Windows XP.

Most of the search engines are case sensitive; that is, you need to type words and phrases exactly as you expect them to appear if you want the search to match your search case exactly. Otherwise, if you enter a search

> criteria in all lowercase letters, the search engines generally do not base the match on case. Therefore, if you want to locate the city named Flint in Michigan, enter Flint. Entering the name in all lowercase letters will result in the search engine searching both for the city name as well as the rock.

Most of the time, to use the Search companion, you'll simply type a question and click Search. The Search Companion will search the Web and return a list of possible Web pages that match your question's goals. For example, if you type **What is C++?**, the Search Companion will return a list of several Web sites devoted to teaching the C++ programming language. These results will appear in the large right windowpane. You can click any of these C++ links to access the pages that explain C++.

Helpful Browsing Tools

Internet Explorer provides several features that help you accomplish your Web-browsing job. You will use these tools to speed your online access as you browse the Internet.

Keeping Links Handy

If you want your most important Web sites located even closer than the Favorites list, add the site to your toolbar's Links list. You can right-click the top of Internet Explorer taskbar and click the Links option to display a series of links to Web sites. Although the links consume a row of Internet Explorer browser content space, they provide yet another quick way to access your frequent Web sites. Figure 11.7 shows the links at the top of the browser window.

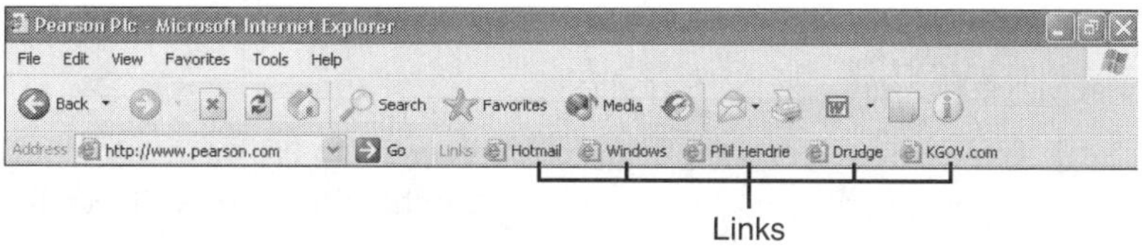

FIGURE 11.7
Your links are ready for one-click access.

Links

Internet Explorer comes pre-installed with a set of links to get you started, but you can add your own and remove those that are already there. To remove or change a link, right-click over the link and select the appropriate menu item from the pop-up menu. To add a link, drag its Web site icon from the Internet Explorer Address text box to the Links bar. You can rearrange links by dragging them one at a time to a different location. To see the links that don't fit on the Links bar, click the arrow at the far right of the Links bar.

Using Shortcut Keys

Internet Explorer supports these two shortcut keys that will save you time:

- F4—Opens the Web address's drop-down list box so that you can quickly jump to a site you have visited recently.
- F6 (and Alt+D)—Places the text cursor in the Web address list box so that you can type a Web address to display.

Open Multiple Browser Windows

You can open multiple Web pages from within Internet Explorer. Suppose that you have been viewing a Web page with links to another page. You want to read both pages, perhaps to compare notes in resized windows. You can open a second Internet Explorer browser window by right-clicking over the hyperlink and selecting Open in New Window from the pop-up menu that appears. In addition, you can hold the Shift key while clicking on that hyperlink to open the page in the second window.

When you open a second window, the browser window opens with your Web site shown there. Your original browser window will still be open, displaying the Web site you started from. By judiciously opening new Web sites in additional windows, you can view several Web pages at the same time without having to browse between them each time you go back to one.

Summary

This hour introduced you to the Internet, a vast collection of interrelated computers all around the world. You can browse the Internet as long as you have access through an Internet Service Provider. Although Internet information appears in many forms, the most useful information often appears on Web pages that contain text, graphics, sound, and video.

Windows supports the Internet Explorer Web browser with which you can view Web pages. Internet Explorer includes searching tools as well as a history system that keeps track of recent Web pages. Not only can you view Web pages with Internet Explorer, but you can also view other kinds of files on your computer. As the Internet becomes better organized and as Internet access becomes faster and cheaper, you will make the Web browser a greater part of your daily computing routine. One day, you might find that you do most of your work with Web browsing software such as Internet Explorer.

Q&A

Q **I've clicked the Windows XP Internet icon, but I don't see Web pages. What do I have to do to get on the Internet?**

A Do you have Internet access from Microsoft Network or from another Internet service provider? Generally, unless you work for a company that offers Internet access to its employees, you must sign up for Internet access, get the access phone number, pay a monthly fee, and set up your browser to access that provider.

Q **How do I know whether I'm viewing a Web page from the memory buffer or from the actual site?**

A If the page appears almost instantly after you enter the address, the chances are great that you are looking at the page from your browser's memory called the *buffer*. In most cases, the memory's page will match the actual Web site. Nevertheless, if you want to make sure that you're viewing the latest and greatest version of the Web page, click the Refresh toolbar button or press F5. Refresh forces Internet Explorer to reload the page from the actual site's address.

Workshop

The quiz and exercise questions are designed to test your knowledge of the material covered in this hour. The answers are in Appendix C, "Answers to Quizzes."

Quiz

1. Where is the central Internet computer located?
2. What is a URL?
3. What is the purpose of the ISP?
4. How do hypertext links help you maneuver around the Web?
5. How does Internet Explorer make searching for data familiar to you?

Exercises

1. If you've never tried the Internet, sign up with an ISP. If you don't like your ISP, you can usually change with no penalty unless you sign up with a long-term contract. (Don't do that!) Browse the Web and see the fun you've been missing. It's not so difficult, is it?

2. Go to the Microsoft home page at `http://www.Microsoft.com/` and, from that page, open four separate windows from four separate hyperlinks that you find there. Notice that you cannot return to a page in a different window; when you open a new window, your Back key does not return you to the previous window. To move between separate browser windows, you must use the same techniques that you use to move between Windows XP windows, such as closing or resizing a window to see another window underneath.

HOUR **12**

Tying Windows into the Web

With Windows XP, Internet Explorer supports several features not previously found, such as an integrated media player for listening to audio Web content while you view Web pages. In addition, you can customize the Explorer bar to display information that interests you, such as your local weather and news.

Those of you who want to communicate with other users will appreciate the MSN Messenger feature that Microsoft has now integrated into Internet Explorer. By signing up for a Passport account, which is free, you can access Microsoft's free e-mail and chat service.

Of course, in today's world of interconnected communications, you must be careful to protect your connection from unauthorized access. Windows XP provides security features with which you can help keep others from accessing your computer through your Internet connection.

In this hour, you will

- Customize Internet Explorer's Personal bar
- Listen to Internet audio
- Set up a Microsoft Passport
- Communicate with others using the instant messaging feature of MSN Messenger
- Set up a firewall to protect your Internet connection

Listening to Audio Content

Data is no longer limited to numbers and characters. Data consists of numbers and characters, but also audio, video, and graphics. Windows XP and the Internet both work well with all these types of data. As Internet access speed called *bandwidth* increases, more audio and video content will be delivered over the Internet to the user's browser.

You could listen to audio content from the Internet before Windows XP came along. With Windows XP, however, Internet Explorer's latest version now supports the playback and control of Internet audio from within Internet Explorer. Before Internet Explorer 6, the version supplied with Windows XP, if you clicked a link that produced audio, a separate program window would open and you would control the playback, pause, and volume level of that Internet content from the separate program window. Therefore, to hear audio, you'd have to control two windows: the browser window and the audio playback software.

The audio controls appear at the bottom of your browser's Personal bar as the following To Do item shows.

To Do: Listening to Internet Audio

1. Select Internet Explorer.
2. Go to www.WindowsMedia.com, and you'll see several entertainment items and pictures that describe content currently available. The WindowsMedia page contains both audio and video. For this task, you need to be sure you select an audio link.
3. Click the Music link at the left of the page. Several items appear.
4. Locate any item on the page with a speaker icon as opposed to a film icon that would represent a video clip. If you have a bandwidth choice, such as 28k, 56k, or 300k, click on the speed that most closely matches your Internet connection. Most modem users will click 56k, whereas most DSL and cable modem users will click

▼ 300k. The audio clip will begin after a brief pause, after opening the Media box at the left of the Internet Explorer window, as shown in Figure 12.1. Another window might open to display information about the artist. You can close the extra window by clicking its Close button.

FIGURE 12.1

Internet Explorer now allows you to control audio content directly from within the browser.

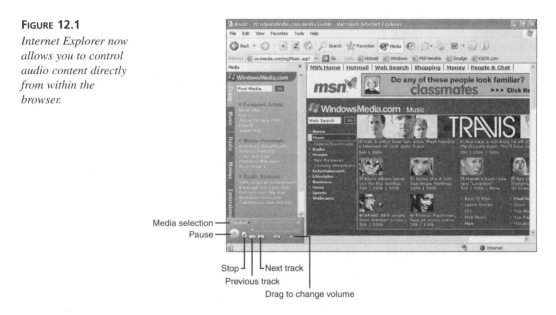

Media selection
Pause

Stop
Previous track
Next track
Drag to change volume

5. Press the Pause and Play buttons to stop and start the playback.

6. Adjust the volume of the sound.

> Click the Undock player button to the right of the Media box to place the Media box in a separate window that you can move and resize independently of the Internet Explorer window.

7. Close the media player window clicking the toolbar's Media button. The audio continues to play. When you click the media button again, the media player reappears and the media controls also reappear.

▲ 8. Click the Stop button to stop the playback.

12

Customizing the Explorer Bar

Keep in mind that you can display several different items to the left of the Internet Explorer window. The left windowpane is generically called the *Explorer bar*, although you can select specific bars such as the Personal bar to place inside the Explorer bar's area.

Select View, Explorer Bar and you'll see a list of items you can display inside your Explorer bar. These include a Search box, a Favorites list, a Media box, a History box, contacts from Microsoft Outlook if you have it installed, and folders on your computer so you can manage and display files from within Internet Explorer just as you can do inside Windows Explorer.

Instant Messaging with MSN Messenger

One extremely popular aspect of the Internet that is growing in popularity all the time is *instant messaging*. Instant messaging is the ability for you to communicate with other instant messaging users. Windows XP supports *MSN Messenger*, Microsoft's version of instant messaging software. Microsoft is developing a complete Internet-based programming and user environment called *.NET*. Windows Messenger will be critical to using .NET when .NET is eventually released. Even if you don't plan to program computers, Microsoft tells the computer community that .NET will be integral to the way users use computers soon. Although the veil of .NET has not fully been lifted, you should get ready to use Messenger now so you'll have it when you need it.

You can access MSN Messenger from within Internet Explorer. As long as you and someone else are both signed up for a *Microsoft Passport*, a holder of contact information you supply so that Microsoft-based Web sites and services will know who you are, you can communicate with anybody in the world by typing messages back and forth. You just both have to be online at the same time. Even better than typing, you can actually talk to them as long as you have the proper hardware and a fast enough Internet connection speed.

The following To Do item explains how to sign up for a Microsoft Passport account.

To Do: Signing Up for a Microsoft Passport

1. Click the taskbar's Notification Area labeled Windows Messenger to open the Messenger window.
2. Click the option labeled Click here to sign in. A window opens asking for your Microsoft Passport Sign-in name and password.

▼   3. Click the option labeled `Get a .NET Passport` to open the .NET Passport Wizard window shown in Figure 12.2, where you can enter information for your own Microsoft Passport.

FIGURE 12.2

Sign up for a Microsoft Passport to use Messenger.

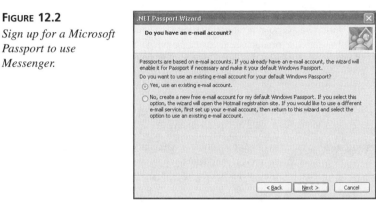

4. Follow the wizard's prompts to enter all the information you want to supply and click Sign Up. Please remember your Hotmail Sign-In Name field's value because you will use this as both your Hotmail e-mail address and your Passport sign-in name. You might not use Hotmail if you already have an e-mail service, but you still need the account to generate a Microsoft Passport account that will also give
▲   you access to MSN Messenger.

No two Microsoft Passport users can have the same sign-in name. If you use a name that is already taken, the Microsoft Passport screen will let you know and will request that you enter a different name.

12

Using Messenger

After you set up your Microsoft Passport, you can use MSN Messenger to send instant messages to other users. The following To Do item explores some of the ways you can use MSN Messenger while you're online.

To Do: Using MSN Messenger

1. Click the Messenger toolbar button to open the Messenger window.

2. Click the sign-in link.

3. Complete the sign-in window with your Microsoft Passport sign-in name and password.

▼   4. Click OK to sign in to MSN Messenger and display the MSN Messenger window.

> If you have e-mail waiting in your Hotmail account, a message pops up from
> your Windows XP taskbar's notification area to let you know. You can click
> the pop-up message to go directly to Hotmail and read your e-mail, or you
> can ignore the pop-up message and continue with your instant messaging
> session. After a brief pause, the pop-up e-mail message disappears.

5. The first task you'll want to do is enter the e-mail address of other users with
   whom to communicate. Click the toolbar's Add button. You can add a friend with
   whom to communicate by entering your friend's e-mail address or by requesting
   that MSN Messenger search for the friend using Hotmail's internal databases or
   your own Windows XP address book. MSN Messenger works only with people
   who have a Passport and Hotmail account. You'll have a better chance at connecting to your friend if you know the Hotmail address or their Passport sign-in name
   instead of trying to search for their information.

6. Assuming you know your friend's Hotmail address or Passport sign-in name, click
   Next and enter your friend's Hotmail address or sign-in name. If the friend whose
   e-mail account you enter does not have an associated Passport sign-in name, you
   cannot communicate with the person using MSN Messenger. MSN Messenger
   offers to send your friend an e-mail telling him that you want to communicate with
   him and explaining how to get a Passport account.

7. Click Finish, close the window, and return to your MSN Messenger window. After
   you add one or more friends, your MSN Messenger window will look something
   like the one in Figure 12.3 showing which of your friends are and are not online.

8. The MSN Messenger window shows that some of your contacts might be online
   while others are not. You can send an instant message to one of your online friends
   by double-clicking his name. An Instant Message window opens.

9. You'll type messages, one at a time, at the bottom of the Instant Message window,
   and you'll see your message and the response from your friend in the larger
   window. Figure 12.4 shows an Instant Message session. You don't have to wait for
▼   your friend to respond to each message before you send another.

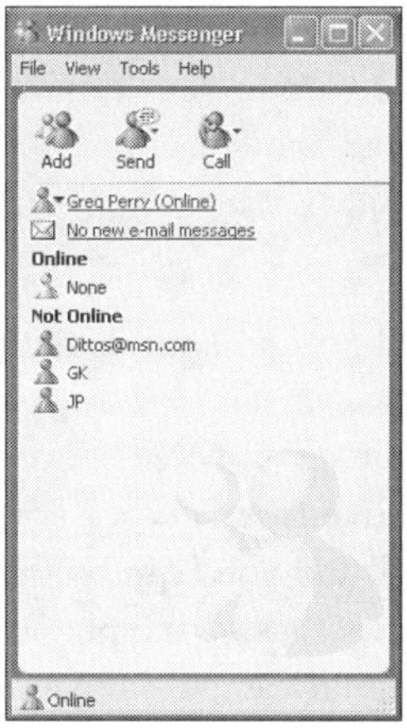

FIGURE 12.3

You can now interact with your friends across the Internet.

An emoticon

FIGURE 12.4

Communicate instantly with anyone else on the Internet.

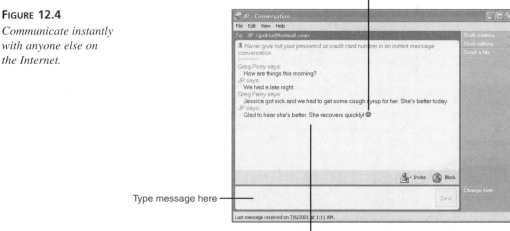

Type message here

Both sides of your conversation appear here

12

An *emoticon* is a popular combination of punctuation that represent happy faces and sad faces, such as :) and : (. When you type an emoticon, MSN Messenger converts your punctuation-based symbols to their actual happy face and sad face equivalents. If your punctuation does not convert, select Edit, Show Emoticons from MSN Messenger's menu.

10. You are not limited to a two-way conversation. Invite others to join in by clicking the Invite button and selecting To Join This Conversation. You can also keep two or more Instant Message sessions going with multiple people, each conversation remaining in a separate window. Just return to your original MSN Messenger window, which will still be open, and select another online contact.

11. To close one or more of your Instant Message sessions, simply click the window's Close button.

12. If both you and your friend have speakers and a microphone connected to your computers, click the Start talking button. Instant Message sends a note to your friend asking if he or she is willing to begin a voice conversation through MSN Messenger. If your friend agrees to move from a typed conversation to a voice conversation, your friend will press Alt+T and you both will be connected by voice just as you would be if you called each other on the phone (but without the long-distance charges). If you both have digital cameras attached, you can use two-way video to communicate also.

If either you or your friend is using a dial-up modem to communicate with the Internet, your voice conversations will be marginal at best. A DSL connection or cable modem connection is really the minimum bandwidth to adequately perform voice communications.

13. When you're finished talking, simply click the Stop talking link to close the Instant Message window.

MSN Messenger Is Flexible

MSN Messenger is more than just an instant messaging service. You'll find many uses for it. Your friends don't always have to be online at the time you are for you to route messages to them. Simply send them an instant message and they'll get it when they sign into MSN Messenger.

Introducing the Internet Connection Firewall

Hackers are people who utilize online connections to connect remotely to computers and to program computers remotely. *Crackers* generally have hacking skills, but they often use their skills in a devious, harmful way, perhaps to erase a remote computer's hard disk. Some people don't distinguish between the two groups, especially the media, but the hacking community likes the distinction. Crackers scan the Internet looking for ways to snoop into other computers. Sometimes hackers are malicious and they want to damage files. Other times, they are just curious or they find that accessing another computer through an Internet connection is challenging.

You can limit the danger of others getting access to your files while you're online by setting up a *firewall*. A firewall is a hardware or software device that monitors your Internet connection looking for unauthorized use. Dial-up users are prone to cracking at times, but due to the nature of always-on connections such as DSL or cable modems, if you have an always-on connection, your risk is even greater than that of dial-up users at becoming a victim of a cracker.

Windows XP comes with a software-based firewall solution called *Internet Connection Firewall (ICF)*. With ICF, you can specify exactly how information is to communicate between your computer or computer network and the outside world through your Internet connection. Your goal should be to allow all users on your computer's side of the Internet connection to access the Internet freely, while blocking what can occur from the other side of the Internet connection.

Setting Up a Firewall Is Not a One-Time Process

Setting up a firewall can be tricky. Some outside access to your computer is needed for you to use many Web sites properly. For example, often a Web site will send your computer a Java program along with a Web page. The Java program allows you to interact with the Web site in a more timely manner than would otherwise be possible. Other kinds of programs can come to your computer through your Internet connection and often, these programs should have access to do what they're intended to do.

ICF is relatively intelligent. As you access Web sites, ICF builds a table. If a Web site attempts to respond in a manner that is more than simple Web pages coming back to your machine, the ICF checks to see if you had been at the sending site and possibly requested information. If so, ICF lets the information come to your computer. If not, ICF blocks the information.

Sometimes, ICF makes an incorrect decision and blocks information that you want. As you use ICF and the Internet more, you will locate trouble spots and be able to grant permission to those sites that should have access to your machine.

12

The following To Do item explains how to initially set up your Internet Connection Firewall and what things to look for and modify as you continue to use the ICF.

To Do: Using the Windows XP Firewall

1. Open your Control Panel and select Network and Internet Connections.

2. Click the link labeled Network Connections.

3. Right-click your Internet connection icon. The icon will be a dial-up icon if you have a modem, or a high-speed Internet icon if you have a higher-speed Internet access along with a shared Internet connection. Then display the Properties window from the pop-up menu.

4. Click the Advanced tab. The Internet Connection Firewall window appears.

5. Click the ICF option to check it.

6. Click the Settings button to display the customizable firewall settings shown in Figure 12.5 that you can control.

FIGURE 12.5

Set up a firewall to protect your online sessions.

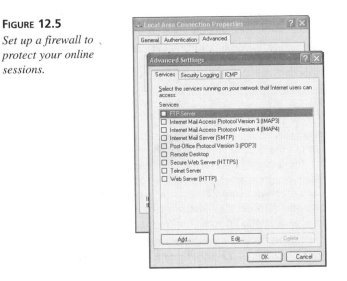

7. Now the real work begins. You must go through the Services listed in the window, as well as the services on the other tabs, checking all the items you normally use. The problem is, many of the settings are advanced and difficult to understand. By their very nature, firewall settings are difficult. For example, you want to allow e-mail to flow freely, back and forth between your computer and others on the Internet. The window in Figure 12.5 shows two e-mail options, Internet Mail Access Protocol Version 3 (IMAP3) and Internet Mail Access Protocol Version 4 (IMAP4). Which conforms to your e-mail system? Your e-mail service will have to let you know.

▼

Unless you have strong skills in networking and online protocol, you may have to make a few guesses when setting up your firewall for the first time or two and see what happens. This might not be comforting news to you, but the effort is worth your time if you stop attacks on your system. For example, you might want to check all the e-mail options you think will apply to your computer and then check your e-mail for a while to see if e-mail is getting through properly and being sent from you properly. Of course, your e-mail's intended recipients will have to tell you if they are not receiving e-mail that you tell them to expect.

Many of the options, such as `FTP Server`, might be unfamiliar to you; in those cases, leave those options unchecked. As you use the Internet, you might find that you have to return to these settings periodically to tweak one or more options for normal Internet use.

▲

Using a firewall adds a layer of protection, but with that protection comes a layer of complexity. Fortunately, in most cases, after you set up your firewall and get it working smoothly, you will have little need to return to the firewall settings unless you add new networking or online hardware in the future or change the way you access the Internet.

Summary

This hour explored ways to utilize your browser to set up personalized content that makes your sessions go more smoothly. You can access local weather, check stock quotes, and customize other kinds of information in your Explorer bar; that information shows up while you surf the Web in the larger, right window pane of Internet Explorer.

Communicate instantly with friends by signing up with an MSN Passport. You can send instant messages back and forth and even communicate by voice, free of charge, to your MSN Messenger contacts. For a fee, you can initialize a conversation between your computer and any phone in the world.

While online, protect yourself from unauthorized hacker attempts by utilizing Windows XP's firewall. The Internet Connection Firewall, or ICF, will monitor your connection and help eliminate unwanted attempts to get to your computer through the Internet connection.

12

Q&A

Q Do I need a Microsoft Passport to use MSN Messenger?

A Yes. By signing up for a free Microsoft Passport, you gain access to a free Hotmail account, instant messaging with MSN Messenger, and even computer-to-telephone communications. (Hour 14, "Managing E-mail and Newsgroups with Outlook Express," explains how to send and retrieve your Hotmail e-mail without using Internet Explorer so that you can more easily manage your messages.) Microsoft hopes to use Passport accounts in other ways as well. In the future, if you want to purchase a product directly from Microsoft or any other Passport-enabled vendor, you will be able to give the vendor your Passport sign-in name without having to type your mailing information because the Passport, with your permission, will supply it.

Q What is a firewall?

A A firewall helps guard your Internet connection from unauthorized access. Firewalls are not perfect, but for always-on Internet connections, they greatly hinder hacker attacks. The settings can be tedious, but you can fine-tune them so that, over time, you provide a customized interface between your computer and the rest of the world. That way, your computer has full access to others, but others do not have full access to your computer.

Workshop

The quiz and exercise questions are designed to test your knowledge of the material covered in this hour. The answers are in Appendix C, "Answers to Quizzes."

Quiz

1. What can appear on the Explorer bar?
2. *True or false*: You can control audio playback directly from within Internet Explorer.
3. What is the difference between a Microsoft Passport, MSN Messenger, and Microsoft Hotmail.com?
4. What is an emoticon?
5. Which is more critical: limiting access from your side of the Internet connection to the world, or limiting the world's side of your Internet connection to you?

Exercises

1. Sign up for a Microsoft Passport if you don't already have one. Ask a friend to do the same. If you know someone with a Hotmail account, they already have a Passport sign-in name. You can use either their sign-in name or Hotmail e-mail address to add them to your MSN Messenger contacts. Set up an instant messaging session with them. Notice that when you finish, the MSN Messenger icon still appears at the bottom-right of your Windows taskbar. When you want to contact that friend or check e-mail from your Hotmail account, you can right-click the MSN Messenger icon and select the option.

2. Set up a firewall on your computer using the Windows XP Internet Connection Firewall. At first, don't check any options on the setup window and see what you can do on the Internet. Send and receive e-mail. As you use your computer more, you will find areas that you have to modify in the ICF setup to gain access.

12

Hour **13**

Networking with Windows XP

This hour shows you ways to combine Windows XP and multiple PCs to develop a cost-effective, efficient, networked system in the small office or home office environment. The low prices and high power of today's PCs means that anyone can automate many areas of a small business, which was not possible just a few years ago.

The material in this lesson focuses as much on computer hardware as Windows XP's networking interface. The nature of networking makes the understanding of hardware as important as the understanding of software. New technology makes PC networks an inexpensive way to pull the power of multiple PCs together into a single system. Whether in a home or small office, networked PCs help ensure file integrity and enable you and people around you to share PC resources.

In this hour, you will

- Learn what it takes to network
- See your network hardware options

- Understand network speed options
- Master peer-to-peer networking
- Connect multiple networked computers to a single Internet connection

Networking Your Environment

Many homes and offices have more than one PC. Perhaps you use a laptop on the road and a desktop at work. Perhaps you replaced an older PC with a more modern one and the older PC is relegated to the kids' room. The victims of today's low-priced, high-powered PCs are yesterday's PCs. Older PCs are too expensive to throw out, they aren't powerful enough to use as a serious business tool, and you've depreciated their costs so you cannot donate them for a tax break.

You can now begin to use that second, slower PC in your home office. Such PCs used to be discarded, but new advances in simple networking technology enable the home and small office user to take advantage of every computer. Although the slower machine might not be your primary computer, you can use it to access the other PC's files when you are in another room, putting the slower machine back into operation once again.

The primary reasons why you will network PCs are to share a single printer, files, and possibly a high-speed Internet connection between them. Your office PC can be connected to a laser printer and the kitchen PC can, through the network, print documents to the laser upstairs. Of course, the printer must be turned on for the documents to print, but if it's not, Windows will hold the output until you can get there to turn on the printer.

Although the printer does not have to be on, your printer's PC must be connected and turned on to accept print commands from the network. Therefore, the machine that you designate as the file and printer server must be on or the network's PCs will be no better than standalone PCs. Unlike larger, more powerful, more expensive networks, however, you don't have to designate a machine as a *network server* machine that nobody can sit at and use. In a home-based networking system described in this lesson, every PC on the network, including the file and printer servers, can also be used as additional PCs on the network. The networks described here are *peer-to-peer* networks, meaning that every machine is a usable machine and does not have to be designated as a reserved server for files and the printer.

Networking Hardware

A network used to require cabling between two or more computers. Most networks in use today still require cabling, but you have some new options that might eliminate the need to run cables. Right now, you can network PCs together using one or more of these three methods:

- Traditional wiring: Small wired networks are generally *ethernet*-based. Ethernet is a type of network that is simple to install and requires a *network hub* to which all network cables run to manage the traffic across the network (see Figure 13.1). The wiring, called *10BaseT wiring*, is similar to telephone cable, is flexible, and easy to run through walls and under carpet.

FIGURE 13.1

A hub routes network information to the proper destination.

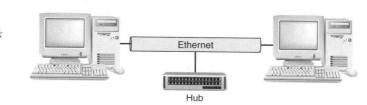

- RF (Radio Frequency) transmission: Each PC includes an RF transmitter that transmits and receives network signals from other PCs. RF-based networks are traditionally slower than wired Ethernet but provide the obvious advantage of being wireless. RF networks are now beginning to show Ethernet speed performance, but the units are higher priced than traditional wired Ethernet cards, costing as much as five times the equivalent Ethernet-based network. Nevertheless, when you count the cost hiring a professional electrician to run the wires in a wired network, the RF network is not so costly.

- Telephone and House Current networks: Low-cost, but slower-than-Ethernet networks, these networks exist that you plug into your home or office's telephone or AC wiring, and the PCs will be communicating as soon as you tell Windows to share files and printers. The obvious ease of installation and setup makes these two kinds of networks attractive. You already have the wiring throughout your home or office. Some don't even require a network interface card or a hub. The drawback is their speed and lack of standards. These are the slowest networks you can get and suffice for temporary office setups but have some speed issues to resolve before they become the clear winner in networking.

13

The telephone-based networks promise not to interfere, in any way, with phone calls, telephone options such as call-waiting, DSL, or dial-up modem connections. These networks use part of the wire's bandwidth left vacant by these other phone services so that your network will not conflict with anything happening on your telephone line.

When you install a network, each networked PC requires a *network interface card* (*NIC*) that you can insert into one of the empty PC slots. If you use a wire-based network, you'll run the wire from card-to-hub until all PCs are connected to the hub. Some modern network devices plug into the USB jack that many modern PCs have.

All the network options offer home-based packages that come with enough network interface cards, cables, and the hub if required to connect at least two PCs together right away. Computer stores also sell individual parts of the network so that you can add PCs to the network as needed. Buying a complete network has never been easier or less expensive; you can often come away with a two-machine network for less than $100.

If you opt for an Ethernet wire-based network, still the most commonly purchased network because of its ease of use, lost cost, and high speed, get one that's rated at *10/100* Mbps, meaning that the network can transmit 100 megabits per second over a 10BaseT wire. Although you can save a few dollars by purchasing a slower network, you won't save *much*, and the efficiency of the 10/100 speed is too much to sacrifice given today's multimedia environment.

If you use a laptop, you're not out of luck when it comes to networking hardware. All the hardware options are available to you because laptops have available a PC card-based network interface card that connects to networked PCs. When you work on the road and come back to your desktop, you only need to plug your laptop into its network cable and the laptop becomes another PC on the system. You will be able to transfer files back and forth without using floppy disks.

After you assemble two or more networked PCs, you can keep all your name and address contact information on a single machine. When anyone in your house adds or changes a name and address, every other PC will instantly reflect that change because each machine will be accessing the same file. Your kids will also appreciate the networked files because they'll be able to play those cool, multiplayer, multimachine games!

Windows XP Helps You Network

Just ten years ago, managing a network of any size required a *Network Administrator*, one who was responsible for maintaining the network connections, adding users to the network, and setting up security, giving access to certain files and printers. Networks were extremely cumbersome to maintain. Although larger network systems still require extensive training and procedures to operate, the home-based PC boom of the past few years has turned the smaller segment of the networking market into a consumer-oriented technology segment.

One of the reasons home-based networks don't require much know-how to operate is because of Windows. Beginning with Windows 3.11 (called *Windows for Workgroups*), peer-to-peer networking became a reality instead of a difficult-to-deliver promise. More importantly, Windows 3.11 (which continued throughout all the versions until Windows XP appeared) gave the industry a standard on which to build network hardware and write network software.

Each Windows network installation requires a slightly different setup. You'll have to read the documentation that comes with your network package, assuming that you purchased one of the all-in-one packages described in the previous section. These packages are designed to make the home or small office network as simple to install as possible, and you should have little trouble.

Keep in mind, however, that you will probably have to change some system settings although these settings should be described in your network's documentation. As an overview, the following To Do item explains the steps you can expect to take to get your network installed, set up, and running.

If you are following this hour's session to set up your network, read through the following To Do item's steps but do not follow them yet. The steps are useful for illustrating the process of networking setup, but Windows XP can do some of the work for you with a special networking wizard. Following this To Do item is another To Do item that explains how to get network setup help with the Windows XP Wizard. You'll probably use the wizard for your network setup, but after reading through the following non-wizard steps, you will better understand what the wizard is doing in the background and how the network operates.

13

To Do: Setting Up a Network Manually

1. Install the network interface card in your PC. Most are plug-and-play, and as long as you use Windows XP, your card should configure automatically the next time you start your PC and Windows begins. If you use a wireless network device that does not require a card slot, or if you use a USB-based device or PC network card in a laptop, you don't need to open your system unit to connect the device.

2. You might have to access your Start menu's Control Panel window to configure your network from the Network Connections icon that you open. Figure 13.2 shows the Network Connections window from which you might have to make settings. This To Do item cannot accurately describe the settings. The settings are technical and confusing and differ for virtually each network system that exists. Your network card's documentation will describe exactly which settings you must make.

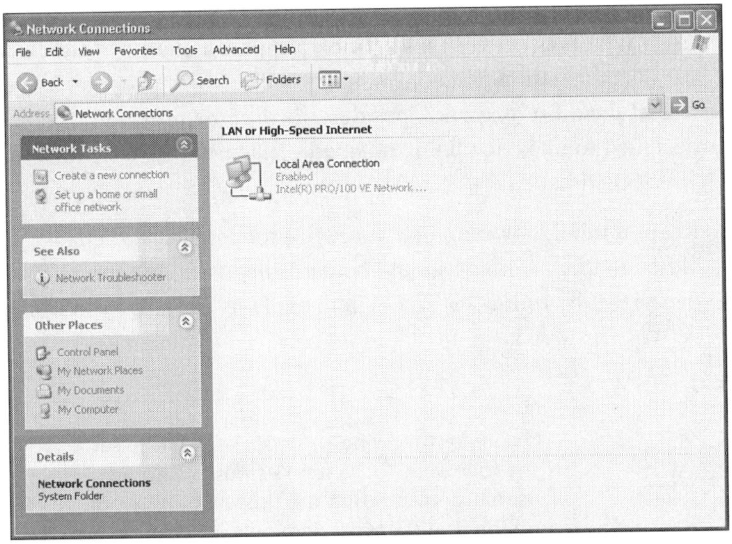

FIGURE **13.2**

You might have to make some adjustments to your Network window's settings.

3. Designate which disk drives on each PC will be shared. In many cases, you'll share all the PC files between the computers, but you can also designate only certain folders and printers to be shared if you don't want someone else to have access to a particular device. You must designate each PC's sharing capabilities from each individual machine.

   To share a folder on a particular disk drive, open the My Computer window, double-click the disk drive with the folder you want to share, and right-click the folder to display the pop-up menu. Select the Sharing option and check the option labeled `Share This folder on the Network`. Optionally, you can add a name that all networked computers will see for this shared folder. That name will appear to the other shared computers, but the folder's original name will remain intact on the owner's computer.

To share a printer, open the Control Panel's Printer and Faxes window. Right-click on the printer you want to share and click the Sharing tab. Select the Network Setup Wizard to start the Network Sharing Wizard shown in Figure 13.3. Run the wizard to turn printer sharing on.

FIGURE 13.3

Set up a printer for network sharing.

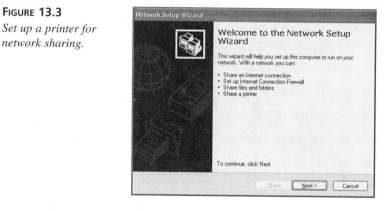

4. After you complete the final PC's file and printer sharing specifications, your network is ready to use. You must now make sure that other computers see your computer on the network.

When setting up your folders for sharing, you might want to allow networked users to change the folder's contents. When you select a folder for sharing and type its shared name, you can click the option labeled `Allow others to change my files`, giving others full read and write access to the folder. You can also give only read access so that others can use your files but not change them. If you turn sharing off altogether, nobody on the network can access your files in any way.

Making Your Network Connect All Your Computers

Windows XP includes a *Network Setup Wizard* that takes the drudgery out of setting up network connections. After you've installed the network cards and set up file and printer sharing on the computers, you are ready to run the Home Networking Wizard to guide you through the remaining setup.

13

To Do: Using the Network Setup Wizard to Share an Internet Connection

1. Install your networking hardware by following the hardware's instructions. This includes your cables and NIC cards.

2. Open the Control Panel.

3. Select the option labeled Network Connections.

4. Select the option labeled, Set up a home or small office network. The Network Setup Wizard begins.

5. Click Next to display the wizard's opening screen. You are reminded that all your network cards must be in place and that you should turn on all computers and printers that will comprise your network.

6. Click Next to display the Internet connection window. The wizard must know how your computer connects to the Internet. If you connect using a modem, select the first option. If you're running the wizard on the computer connected to a high-speed Internet connection or networked to an Internet connection, you would choose the second option. That option signals to the wizard that the other computers will use the network to share this computer's Internet connection. Another wizard, the Network Connection Wizard, will finalize the Internet connection sharing process. The Network Connection Wizard is described in more detail in the next section.

7. Click Next. You must type a description and name for your computer so that others on the network will know which computer yours is.

8. Click Next. Enter a workgroup name. A *workgroup* is a sub-group of networked computers. Suppose you have seven computers on your large home-based small-business network and two are related to one project, three are for another project, and two happen to be your children's computers. You might set up three work-groups so that those three groups of computers can share files and act as though they were part of three separate networks. The fact that they are actually one physical network allows you to monitor and manage all seven computers, but each user connects only to the computer within the matching workgroup.

9. Click Next to see a summary window, similar to that of Figure 13.4. Use the scroll-bar to read the entire summary.

FIGURE 13.4

The Network Setup Wizard summarizes your network settings.

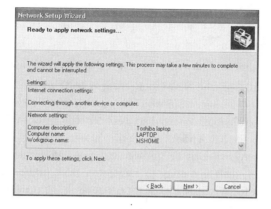

10. Click Next and the wizard will set up all the connections needed to make your computer available to others on the network.

11. When you click Finish to close the final screen, other computers on your network will be able to recognize yours once you've run the Home Networking wizard on them also.

Before Windows XP, sharing files and printers over a network comprised of different network hardware was difficult. For example, if your office connected through a combination of Ethernet, wireless, and FireWire connections, a single network view was difficult to achieve. You often had to set up different networks for each type of device. Windows XP acts as a single bridge between all these otherwise disparate devices. By acting as a network bridge, computers recognize each other as though your entire system is connected via a single, uniform network.

Sharing an Internet Connection

After the network is working, you might want to share an Internet connection across the network. In doing so, only one computer needs to be set up to access the Internet directly; the other computers on the network will use the network to tap into the one computer's network connection. The following To Do item explains how to share your Internet connection.

13

To Do: Using the Network Connection Wizard to Share an Internet Connection

1. From the Windows XP Control Panel, go to the network area and open the Network Connections window.

2. Select Create a new connection. The New Connection Wizard will begin.

3. Click Next to display the New Connection Wizard window shown in Figure 13.5. You have several options from which to choose. The first option allows users over your network to share an Internet connection. The rest of this To Do item will explain how to do that. The second option allows a process called *tunneling*, or *Virtual Private Networking (VPN)* whereby you can dial into a network from a remote location, such as dialing to your office from home. The third option enables you to connect to an existing network (as done in the previous section). The last option sets up your computer so that you can access it from a second computer connected by a parallel or serial cable. The third option is less stable and slower than a true network connection that you would have from an Ethernet or similar connection; however, if you want to transfer files on a one-time basis, connecting by a parallel cable is sometimes more cost-effective than buying network cards. Hour 15, "Exploring Your Hardware Interface," describes this process of direct-cable connection.

FIGURE 13.5
Windows XP makes sharing an Internet connection simple.

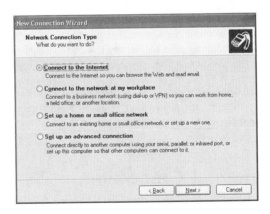

4. Click Next to continue the wizard. Choose whether to connect by a broadband or a dial-up connection.

5. Click Next. Enter a service name for the Internet connection. For users with multiple Internet connections such as DSL and a dial-up connection as a backup, you'll type a name to the connection you're sharing, such as **Family DSL Connection**.

▼ 6. Click Next. Although you'll typically select the top option that will connect the networked user to the Internet connection's default name and password, you can specify an alternative login name and password for this connection. When a networked computer accesses this Internet account, the name and password you specify will be used.

7. Click Next to display the naming screen where you will name this online networked connection and determine how the shared connection will appear on the ▲ primary computer.

Working with a Network

Using a network is no different from using a standalone PC except that, instead of selecting a printer connected to your PC when you print, or a disk in your system unit when you access a file, you specify the printer or file on the other computer. When you select File, Open Any Windows Application, click the Look In drop-down list box to locate the networked disk drive you want to access. To print to a network printer, select File, Print as you normally do to prepare for printing and select the network printer from the Printer dialog box's Name list. Windows prompts you for a password if one is required to use the device.

> If you disconnect one or more of the PCs from the network, reverse the file- and printer-sharing settings so that the PC is no longer designated for the network; otherwise, the computer will run more slowly than it has to. Remove the network card altogether if you don't want to use it, and your computer will also speed up because it will not continue to poll the network card looking for other computers.

Summary

This hour introduced you to the world of networking. Network technology has come a long way in power increases and cost decreases. The true winner in the network advances has been the small office and home-based PC users. Just a couple of years ago, consumer computers did not even carry networking equipment because of the network's place in the corporate world. At that time, the network's place meant that the network technology was expensive, difficult to use, hard to install, and costly to maintain.

All that has changed. With the low-cost PCs that have flooded the PC market in the past few years, the demand for connecting PCs has increased as people buy second machines

13

and laptops. Networks are popular for two reasons: Users of multiple machines can share files and printers, and file integrity is maintained when only one disk keeps the data used by several PCs. Fortunately, Windows XP takes much of the mystery out of the software side to networking setup by providing you with the Home Networking Wizard.

Q&A

Q How does a network ensure file integrity?

A Consider what happens if you use the same program, such as Microsoft Outlook, on your kitchen PC as you use in your upstairs office. What if you record a new contact's name and phone number upstairs and then, two days later, you want to call from the downstairs PC? The second PC will not have the name. What do you do? You can walk upstairs to make the call, manually look up the name once again and type the information in the downstairs PC, or you can make a backup of your upstairs PC's PIM files and copy those files to your downstairs PC.

Neither of those solutions is adequate. As a matter of fact, they leave too much room for error. You might type the name and number incorrectly into one of the PCs. If you restore one file on the other PC, you might overwrite information someone had just typed in the second PC! Without a network, your files can lose integrity and contain different information.

By utilizing a shared, networked-based disk drive, both PCs will use the same data file. You'll install the program to the shared disk drive and any PC on the network will then be able to use that program and access the shared file's information. If you make a change from one PC and then walk to the other PC, that change will appear there as well.

Q If I build a new home, should I install network cabling if I think I'll network, or will high-speed wireless be here soon?

A By all means, install the wiring. It appears that wireless network technology is getting better, faster, and less expensive every day, but the king of networks is the hard-wired system. As wireless speeds get better, wired speeds do too, so you still win if you have the wire.

Wire-based networks don't allow for as much freedom of machine placement as the wireless devices allow. Nevertheless, the low-cost of hard-wired networks makes them attractive alternatives for many years to come. When you install the wiring at the time you build your home, the added cost of the installation is negligible compared to the cost of having the cabling installed in an existing structure where sheetrock might have to be patched. Therefore, if you have any reason to believe you'll network your home, install the wire when the walls are still exposed.

Workshop

The quiz and exercise questions are designed to test your knowledge of the material covered in this hour. The answers are in Appendix C, "Answers to Quizzes."

Quiz

1. What is the difference between a local network and the Internet?

2. Which kind of physical network connection is the easiest to install?

3. Which network connection generally provides the fastest connection speed?

4. *True or false*: If you have an Internet connection, all of the computers on the network can share the Internet connection.

5. What is tunneling?

Exercises

1. Do you have multiple computers in your home or small office but still transfer files via *sneakernet*? (Sneakernet is the process of copying a file to a disk or CD-ROM and walking the file to the computer on which you want to copy that file.) Go to your local computer store and look at the networking options available. Many are all-in-one solutions for a small networking system. For example, you can typically find all the hardware and cabling needed for a two-computer network system for less than $100. Why are you waiting to network?

2. After you install your network hardware, run the Home Networking Wizard to set up the network's sharing of devices. After that is installed on all of your networked computers, go to Windows Explorer and look at the drives available there. If you don't see a network drive, select My Network Places and you'll see the network drives there. You can reference those other computers' drives by name any time you open or save a file just as you reference your own computer's disk drives by name when you open or save files to them.

13

Hour **14**

Managing E-mail and Newsgroups with Outlook Express

The Internet Explorer portion of Windows XP includes a program called *Outlook Express* that manages both e-mail and newsgroup information. By combining a newsgroup reader with e-mail capabilities, you can manage more information easier than before.

E-mail plays as bigger role in today's communications than regular mail. E-mail's paperless aspect keeps your desk less cluttered, and e-mail generally arrives at its destination within a few minutes to a few hours. Newsgroups offer a different kind of messaging center for messages you want to communicate publicly on a topic. You can post newsgroup topics, answers, and questions, as well as read responses from others interested in the same subject.

In this hour, you will

- Discover how Outlook Express enables you to view and send e-mail messages
- Attach files to e-mail messages you send
- Post and read newsgroup messages
- Set up Outlook Express for multiple accounts

The E-mail World

It is common for computer users to access more than one online service. Perhaps you work on the Internet but have two Internet accounts, one for personal use and one for business. Each morning you might log on to your business Internet account on your laptop to get incoming messages and send your outgoing Internet messages. The burden of managing e-mail grows as more people sign up for more online services.

Wouldn't it be nice to tell your computer to send and receive all your e-mail without any intervention on your part? The computer could store all received mail in a central location; you could then manage, sort, print, respond to, or delete from there. Outlook Express provides the one-stop answer.

Don't confuse Outlook Express with Microsoft Outlook that comes with Microsoft Office. Outlook Express is not the same program as Microsoft Outlook. Microsoft Outlook has more features than Outlook Express but Outlook does not support newsgroups.

Managing E-mail with Outlook Express

Outlook Express offers benefits for e-mail users. Outlook Express supports several formats within an e-mail message. You can send and receive text data, *binary data* (compressed data such as programs and graphics), sound files, and video as e-mail. In addition, Outlook Express enables you to store HTML code inside your message so that you can customize the look of your message. A message you send might look like a Web page. You can even send complete Web pages as e-mail inside Outlook Express. If you embed a URL inside an e-mail message, the recipient can click that URL and go straight to that site on the Web (as long as the recipient uses Outlook Express or some other e-mail package that converts URLs to hyperlinks automatically).

Here are some of the additional features of Outlook Express's e-mail capabilities:

- Send or receive e-mail in plain, unformatted text to speed performance at the loss of seeing formatted messages.

- Attach files to your messages.

- Provide full support for Hotmail.com users so they can send and receive e-mail messages as well as chat online with other MSN Messenger users. (Hour 12, "Tying Windows into the Web," explains Hotmail.com and MSN Messenger, as well as the Passport that makes both easier to use.)

- Check spelling before you send a message.

- Reply to messages and forward messages to other recipients.

- Connect to Web-based e-mail address search engines to find people's addresses. (See Hour 9, "Finding Files, Folders, and Friends," for more information on Web searching.)

- Send and receive mail to and from multiple Internet accounts.

Setting Up Outlook Express

The following To Do item explains how to set up Outlook Express for use within Internet Explorer.

If the wizard begins when you start Outlook Express the first time, you need to answer the wizard's prompts to set up your e-mail account. Most of the online services automatically set up Outlook Express, but if you see the wizard, you might need to contact your ISP to determine which settings are needed for Outlook Express to recognize your ISP-based e-mail account.

To Do: Using Outlook Express and Internet Explorer Together

1. Start Internet Explorer and sign in to your Internet account.

2. Select Tools, Internet Options and click the Programs tab to display the Internet Options dialog box, as shown in Figure 14.1.

3. Select Outlook Express from the second and third options labeled E-mail and Newsgroups.

4. Click OK to close the Internet Options dialog box. When you send or receive mail, Internet Explorer will now use Outlook Express as your e-mail program.

14

FIGURE 14.1

Make sure that Internet Explorer knows about Outlook Express.

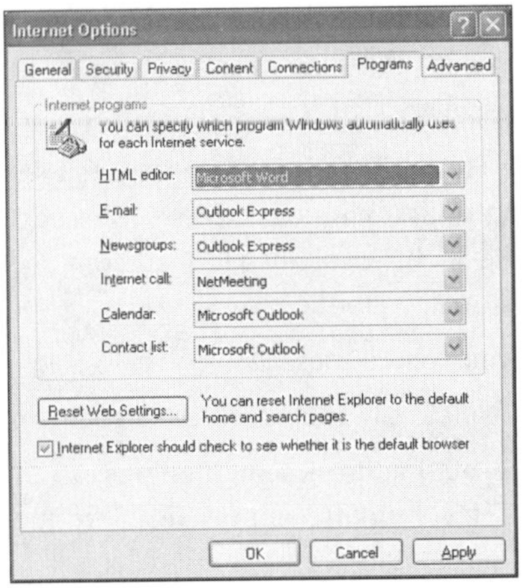

▲

> Outlook Express is smart and recognizes whether you've already set up another e-mail program before installing Windows XP. If you see an Import dialog box the first time you use Outlook Express to send or receive a message, Outlook Express offers to use your previous e-mail program's messages and addresses, so you don't have to re-enter them. Follow the wizard to load any or all of your previous program's options.

After you've told Internet Explorer that you want to use Outlook Express as your e-mail program, Internet Explorer remembers your setup and uses Outlook Express every time you send or receive e-mail.

Storing E-mail Contacts

To improve your e-mail productivity, you'll want to store many e-mail addresses in Outlook Express's address book. By storing e-mail addresses of people with whom you regularly communicate, called *contacts*, you subsequently only need to select the recipient by name when you want to send an e-mail instead of typing the e-mail address for each e-mail message that you send.

The following To Do item explains how to build your e-mail contact list in Outlook Express. Outlook Express makes adding names and e-mail addresses easy and, as you will see, Outlook Express enables you to add new contacts in several ways.

To Do: Adding Names and E-mail Addresses to Outlook Express

▲ To Do

1. Start Outlook Express.

2. If you have signed up for MSN Messenger (see Hour 12), your Messenger contacts will automatically appear in the Contacts windowpane. You will not need to add these again because Outlook Express retrieves these contacts from the Web.

3. Click the Addresses toolbar button to display your Address Book, shown in Figure 14.2.

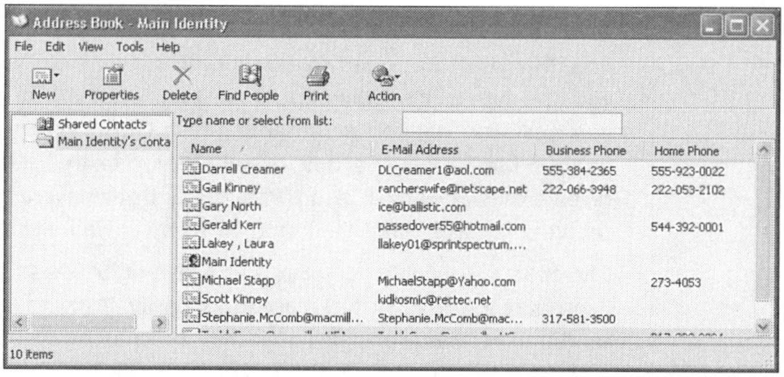

FIGURE 14.2

Your Address Book contains a list of your e-mail contacts.

4. Click the New button, then select New Contact from the dropdown list that appears, to open a new Properties window with a blank set of fields. Each tab at the top of the window, such as Home, Business, and Personal, provides a means by which you can enter as much or as little information about your contact as you want. At a minimum, you should enter your new contact's name and e-mail address.

> Notice the check box labeled Send E-mail Using Plain Text Only, at the bottom of your contact's Properties window. If you check this box, Outlook Express will convert all of your e-mail messages to text, except for pictures, video, and sound, so that the recipient receives no formatting in the e-mail that you send. You'll want to check this box for all recipients who are unable to receive formatted e-mail properly. You might have to send a sample e-mail, if you regularly send formatted e-mail to this contact, to see if the contact is capable of receiving formatted e-mail properly and then check this option if the formatting didn't arrive properly. All subsequent e-mail will arrive in the text format.

14

▼   5. Click the OK button to save your contact's information.

6. When you receive e-mail, you can quickly save the sender's contact information by clicking Tools, Add Sender to Address Book from Outlook Express's menu. Outlook Express adds the contact's name and e-mail address. You can then right-click over the contact's name in the Contacts windowpane, select Properties, and

▲   enter any additional information that you want to add.

> **Chat with Messenger**
>
> Given that both Outlook Express and MSN Messenger are Microsoft products, Microsoft designed Outlook Express to work well with Messenger. If you and one of your Messenger contacts are both online at the same time, you can click that contact's name in the Outlook Express Contacts list and begin a Messenger chat session where you both, interactively, send and receive messages back and forth. If you both have a microphone and headset, you can even chat back and forth by voice by clicking the Talk button.
>
> Microsoft's Hotmail.com users and Messenger users find that Outlook Express recognizes Hotmail accounts easily. You can use Outlook Express to send and receive Hotmail e-mail without having to go to the Web browser and access Hotmail from the Hotmail site. Select Tools, Accounts, click Mail, and enter your Hotmail name and account information. If you don't have a Hotmail account, you can sign up for one without ever leaving Outlook Express by selecting Tools, New Account Signup, Hotmail.

Sending Mail with Outlook Express

The following To Do item explains how to send various forms of e-mail to recipients. Outlook Express has many options, but you can send e-mail messages and files to others very easily without worrying too much about what else is under Outlook Express's hood.

To Do: Sending E-mail from Outlook Express

1. Start Internet Explorer and sign in to your Internet account.

2. Click the toolbar's Mail button and select New Message from the menu that drops down. (You can also click the Taskbar's Outlook Express icon if you've displayed the Quick Launch toolbar or select Outlook Express from the Start menu.) The New Message dialog box opens, as shown in Figure 14.3.

3. Type your recipient's e-mail address in the To field or click the To button to select
▼   the recipient if you've saved the name in your Outlook Express address list.

FIGURE 14.3

You can now send a message to one or more recipients.

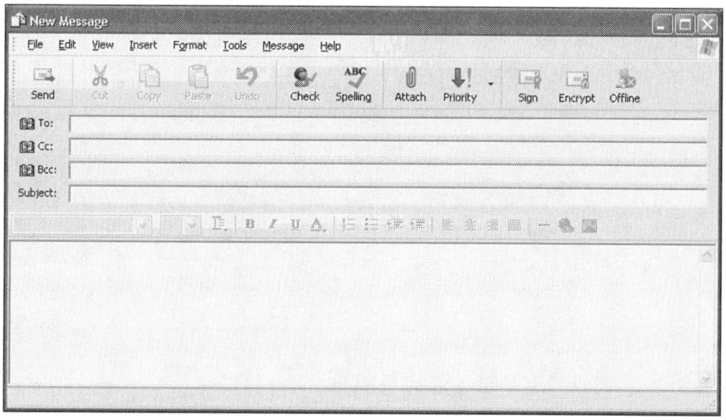

4. Use the Cc (Carbon copy) field to send copies of your message to another recipient. The recipient will know that the message was copied to him. If you enter an e-mail address in the Bcc (Blind carbon copy) field, the To and Cc recipients will not know that the Bcc recipients got copies of the message. If you do not see the Bcc box, select View, All Headers, and the Bcc field will appear beneath your carbon copy field.

5. Enter a subject line. Get in the habit of entering a subject so that your recipients can file your messages by subject.

6. Press the Tab or Shift+Tab key to move from field to field. When you type the message in the message area, a scrollbar appears to enable you to scroll through messages that don't fit inside the window completely. Use the formatting toolbar above the message area to apply formatting, color, and even numbered and bulleted lists to your message. You must be careful, however, to make sure that your recipients have an e-mail program capable of reading all the formatting that Outlook Express can produce. Unless you send plain text messages, your recipient might not be able to read your message clearly without Outlook Express or a fully compatible e-mail program.

7. If you want to attach one or more files to your message, click the Attach toolbar button (the one with the paper clip) and select your file from the Insert Attachment dialog box that appears. (The Insert, File Attachment menu option also includes attachments.)

8. To send the message, click the Send button and the message goes on its way toward the recipients.

14

Sending e-mail messages and files requires only that you know the person's e-mail address or that you've stored the address in your Outlook Express addresses. This address collection becomes your Windows Address Book, available for you to use in other programs as well. Attach files of any type to your message and the recipient will receive the message and the files.

> When in Outlook Express, you can quickly start a new message to one of your contacts by double-clicking over the contact's name from within the Contacts window pane. Outlook Express will then open a New Message window with your contact's e-mail information already entered for you.

Sending Web Pages as E-mail

You can send entire Web pages or any file composed of the Web page's HTML code by following the next To Do item.

To Do: Sending Web Pages Inside E-mail

1. Start Internet Explorer and sign in to your Internet account.

2. Display the Web page that you want to send to somebody. (You can send the page to your own e-mail account for a test.)

3. Click the toolbar's Mail button.

4. Select Send Page. If the Web page is complicated, it might be considered a read-only Web page that cannot be edited. If so, Internet Explorer displays a message telling you that your recipient might receive the message as an attached file or as a read-only file. In this case, if you are sending the page to yourself or to someone you know has Internet Explorer, send the page as a read-only page.

5. The e-mail window opens so that you can select a recipient and add copies to others if you like. You can see the Web page at the bottom of the window as shown in Figure 14.4. Now *that's* quite a fancy e-mail message!

6. Click the Send button to send the Web page.

FIGURE 14.4

The recipient will see the Web page when viewing this e-mail.

Emailing: www.we-travel.htm

File Edit View Insert Format Tools Message Help

Send | Cut Copy Paste Undo | Check Spelling | Attach Priority | Sign Encrypt Offline

To:
Cc:
Bcc:
Subject: Emailing: www.we-travel.htm

Interests
Photo Album
Favorites
Home

we-travel.com.

the wide world on the web ™

For those whom travel is not an option
Vol. 2002, Issue 1

Destination: **Manhattan, New York**

Nicknames: *The Big Apple, New York City, NYC*

Remember that your recipient must also use an e-mail program, such as Outlook Express, that can display formatted e-mail as Web-based HTML code; otherwise, the recipient will get garbage in the message. Your recipient will still be able to read the mail's text, but the e-mail will be messed up because of all the HTML formatting codes that the recipient will see that are normally hidden. You can convert HTML pages to straight text from the Format menu. Also, if you've told Outlook Express to send this particular recipient only text-based messages, the recipient contact will receive only the text from the Web page, without all the fancy graphics.

Receiving E-mail

You can receive and organize the e-mail that people send to you by following this To Do item.

14

To Do: Receiving and Managing E-mail in Outlook Express

To Do

1. Start Outlook Express. Click the Inbox icon in the Folders windowpane if the Inbox icon is not selected. You will see any existing e-mail and contacts, as Figure 14.5 shows.

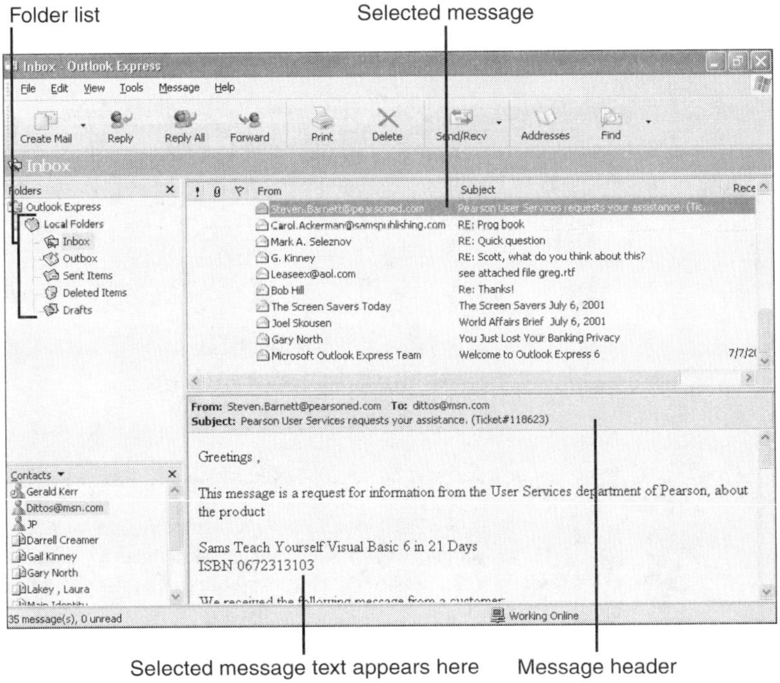

FIGURE 14.5

Check your e-mail from this window.

Folder list   Selected message

Selected message text appears here   Message header

2. E-mail comes to your *Inbox* (the preview area) at regular intervals, but Outlook Express does not constantly check for new mail because your Internet connection would slow down because of the mail check. At any time, you can manually check for new mail and send any that has yet to be sent by clicking the toolbar's Send/Receive button or by selecting from the Tools, Send and Receive menu option. You don't have to be signed on to the Internet to create or read e-mail after the e-mail arrives in your Inbox.

3. The Outbox area (you can click on the Folder list to see your Outbox contents) holds items that you've readied to send but that have not actually gone out yet. When your Outbox contains unsent mail, the Outbox icon changes to show that mail is still there unsent.

4. As you click on the headers in the Inbox, a preview appears for that message in the lower pane. (Drag the center bar up or down to make more or less room for the headers.) If you double-click on an Inbox item, a window opens so that you can view the message from a larger window without the other screen elements getting in the way.

5. Delete mail you do not want by selecting one or more message headers and dragging them to the Deleted Items icon. Deleted Items acts like the Windows Recycle Bin. Mail does not really go away until you delete items from the Deleted Items area by clicking on the Deleted Items icon and removing unwanted mail. You can also delete mail by clicking the mail item and pressing Delete.

6. You can easily reply to a message's author, or to the entire group if you are one of several who was sent mail, by clicking the Reply or Reply All toolbar button. In addition, when reading e-mail, you can compose a new message by clicking on the toolbar's Compose Message button.

7. Create new folders to store e-mail that you want to keep for future reference. Right-click over the Local Folders icon and select New Folder. Type a name for the folder and press Enter to see the new folder. You could create a folder for business correspondence and one for personal correspondence that you've received and want to keep. When an e-mail comes in to your Inbox that you want to save, drag that e-mail's icon from the Inbox window to its appropriate folder.

> When you're in Outlook Express, click the Folder list's icon labeled Outlook Express to see the one-click Outlook Express window shown in Figure 14.6. From this window, you can easily read and compose e-mail, modify your Microsoft Address Book entries, locate people, and check newsgroups. (The next section describes newsgroup access.)

14

FIGURE **14.6**

The Outlook Express folder shows this one-step usage screen.

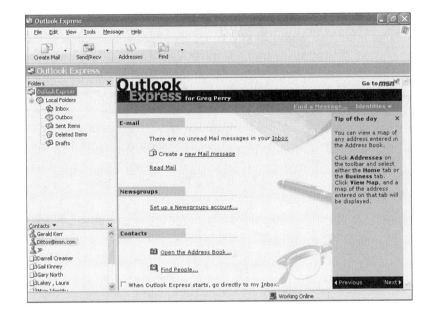

Using Newsgroups

In a way, a newsgroup acts like a combination of a slow e-mail program and a community bulletin board. Newsgroups have little or nothing to do with the daily news. Newsgroups are thousands of lists, arranged by subject, that hold messages and files that you and others can post and read.

Suppose that you are interested in rollerblading and want to trade information you have with others who are interested in the sport. You could find one of the several newsgroups related to rollerblading and read the hundreds of messages and files posted to that newsgroup. Depending on the Internet service you use and the newsgroup filing rules, you might find messages months old or only from the past few days. Often, the larger newsgroups can keep only a limited number of days' worth of messages and files in the newsgroup.

This is how newsgroups act like slow e-mail services: If someone has posted a question for which you know the answer, you can post a reply. Your reply will be seen by all in the newsgroup who want to read the reply. It is not guaranteed that the person who submitted the question will ever go back to the newsgroup to read the answer, but the postings are for anybody and everybody who is interested.

Each ISP provides access to a different number of the thousands and thousands of newsgroups in existence. To see newsgroups available to your service, click Internet

Explorer's Mail button and select Read News. Although your ISP might give you access to thousands of newsgroups, subscribe just to those that interest you. The Internet Explorer Read News button displays the Newsgroups listing dialog box shown in Figure 14.7.

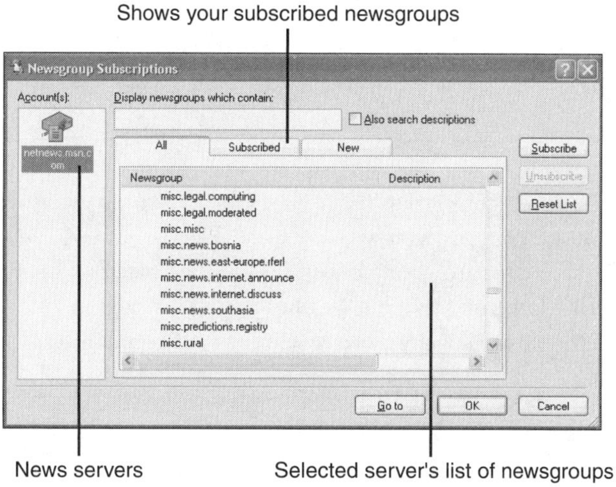

Figure 14.7

Select the newsgroups to which you want to subscribe.

Shows your subscribed newsgroups

News servers   Selected server's list of newsgroups

You might see one or more news servers in the left column. Each news server contains a different set of newsgroups. Your ISP determines the number of servers that appear in the news server column. When you click on a server, the list of newsgroups that reside on that server appears in the center of the window.

The newsgroups have strange names, such as `rec.pets.dogs` and `alt.algebra.help`. Table 14.1 describes what the more common newsgroup prefixes stand for. Somewhere else in the newsgroup name you can often glean more information about the newsgroup's primary topic; for example, a newsgroup named `rec.sport.skating.roller` would probably contain skating news, and `alt.autos.italian` would contain files and messages pertaining to Italian cars. (*i macchina l'italiani!*)

Table 14.1   Common Newsgroup Prefixes Describe the Nature of the Newsgroup

Prefix	Description
`alt`	Groups that allow informal content and are not necessarily as widely distributed as the other newsgroups
`biz`	Business-related newsgroups

14

TABLE 14.1 continued

Prefix	Description
comp	Computer-related newsgroups
misc	Random newsgroups
rec	Recreational and sporting newsgroups
sci	Scientific newsgroups
soc	Social issue-related newsgroups
talk	Debate newsgroups

Scroll through the newsgroup list to find the newsgroups you want to see. When you find one or more newsgroups you want to see, subscribe to those newsgroups by double-clicking on the newsgroup name (or highlight the name and click Subscribe). If you click the Subscribe tab, you see the list of newsgroups to which you've subscribed. Click the OK button to close the Newsgroups window and prepare to read the news.

> Enter a search topic in the text box at the top of the Newsgroups window to display newsgroups that contain that topic. As you type more of the topic for which to search, the list below the text box shrinks to include only those newsgroups that include the text you enter.

The following To Do item describes how you would read newsgroup messages and post new messages to the newsgroups. Keep in mind that a message might be a short note or an entire file. As with e-mail, if a news posting contains a file, the file will come as an attachment to the message.

To Do: Reading Newsgroups

1. Start Internet Explorer and sign in to your Internet account.
2. Click the toolbar's Mail button.
3. Select Read News. A list of your subscribed newsgroups appears, as shown in Figure 14.8.
4. To read messages in a newsgroup, double-click that newsgroup name. Figure 14.9 appears showing the newsgroups in the upper window and the text for the selected newsgroup in the lower window. Some long messages take a while to arrive, and you won't see any of the message until the entire message downloads to your PC.

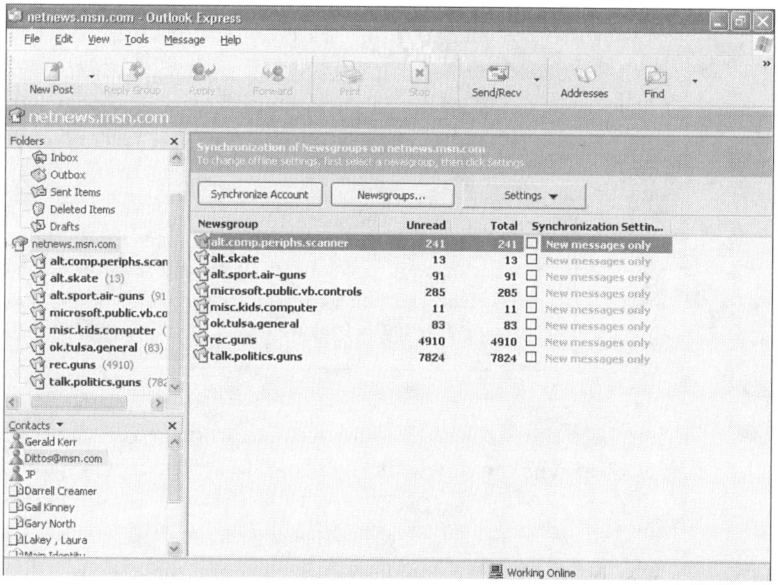

FIGURE 14.8

Your subscribed news-group messages appear when you first request newsgroup access.

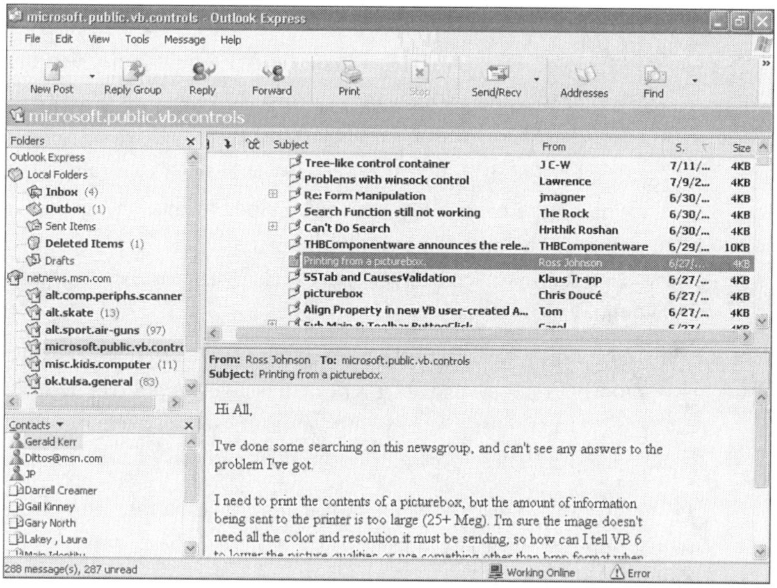

FIGURE 14.9

Scroll through the news message headers and see detail in the lower window.

14

If a message has a plus sign next to it, click the plus sign to open all related messages. The messages form a *thread*, meaning that they are related to each other. If
someone posts a question, for example, and several people reply to that posting, all
those related messages group under the first question's message, and you can see
the replies only after you click the plus sign. The plus sign becomes a minus sign
when you expand the newsgroup item so that you can collapse the item again.

> Some newsgroups are moderated better than others. You'll often find unre-
> lated messages throughout all newsgroups that don't belong within that
> newsgroup. Some newsgroups are moderated by a staff who monitors and
> removes messages that do not pertain to the newsgroup subject.

5. Check the Size column to determine whether you can read the message in the
    lower window or whether you should open a new window to view the message. If
    a message is more than 2 or 3 kilobytes, you should probably double-click the
    message header to view the message inside a scrollable window. The window con-
    tains a menu that enables you to save the message in a file on your disk for later
    retrieval. If a message has an attachment, you must open the message in a separate
    window to save the attachment as a file on your disk.

    After you read a message inside the preview pane, you can click another message
    header to view another message. If you view a message in a separate window, you
    can close the window to view a different message.

6. If you want to reply to a message, you have two options: reply to the group, in
    which case everybody who subscribes to the newsgroup can read your reply; or
    reply to the author privately via e-mail. The Reply Group and Reply toolbar but-
    tons accomplish these purposes. Each copies the original message at the bottom of
    your reply.

    You don't have to reply to existing messages if you want to start a new message
    topic. You can also start a new message thread (related postings) by clicking the
    New Post button and typing a new message. Your message appears in the news-
    group as a new post and not part of a chain of previous postings.

Probably the biggest problem with newsgroups is the time you waste in them! You
might hop over to a newsgroup to see whether the group contains an answer you need,
and two hours later you're still reading the postings there. Newsgroups can provide a
wealth of information on thousands and thousands of topics. Although the Web is great
for organizing information into collections of pages, newsgroups are useful for the
straight messages and files that people want to share with each other.

Summary

This hour explained how to use Outlook Express, Internet Explorer's e-mail program and newsgroup manager. E-mail is a major part of the Internet user's life these days, and you'll appreciate Outlook Express's advanced support and e-mail management simplicity.

If you want detailed information on a subject, you can search the Web for all kinds of data, but remember to look for related newsgroups as well. Whereas some Web sites are often consumer-related collections of merchandise and hype, newsgroups often contain thousands of messages from people such as you who have questions and answers for others with the same interest.

Q&A

Q How can I get e-mail from my multiple Internet accounts?

A If you subscribe to multiple online services or to multiple ISPs, you can set up Outlook Express to send and retrieve e-mail from all your Internet accounts. Select Tools, Accounts to display the Internet Accounts dialog box. Select Add, Mail and follow the wizard to add your accounts to the e-mail. You will almost surely have to contact your ISP to get the wizard's requested information. After you set up the accounts, Outlook Express will check each one when you request new mail.

Q I read a newsgroup message last month that I can no longer find in the newsgroup. How can I see old messages?

A Often you cannot. Each news server holds a limited number of messages. (Your news server has only so much disk space!) Often, Outlook Express downloads, at most, 300 messages at any one time. Sometimes, the server will have more than 300 messages available. To request that Outlook Express retrieve additional messages, select Tools, Get Next 300 Headers. If more than 300 messages are available, Outlook Express will download up to 300 more. By the way, you can change the number of messages that Outlook Express downloads, from 1 to 1,000, by changing the number from the Tools, Options menu item on the Read tab page in the News section.

Workshop

The quiz and exercise questions are designed to test your knowledge of the material covered in this hour. The answers are in Appendix C, "Answers to Quizzes."

14

Quiz

1. *True or false*: Outlook Express supports only a single e-mail account.
2. What is the purpose of the Bcc field?
3. How do you attach files to an e-mail letter?
4. Where does your incoming e-mail reside?
5. What is a newsgroup?

Exercises

1. Locate a Web page you want to send to a friend and send the page using the Outlook Express HTML support described in this hour. Also, send a blind carbon copy of the page to yourself. You might have to add the Bcc button to your New Message window before you see a Bcc field.

2. What is your favorite hobby? Log onto the Internet, start Outlook Express, click on one of the newsgroup servers, and type your hobby name in the newsgroup list to see if any matching newsgroups appear. If so, read through the messages and make new friends with a similar interest to yours.

PART V

An Evening with Advanced Windows

Hour

Hour 15

Exploring Your Hardware Interface

Microsoft designed Windows XP so that you could take advantage of the latest hardware advances. Windows XP recognizes most devices currently in use and is designed with future devices and expandability in mind. This hour shows how the Windows interface utilizes your hardware. Windows supports *Plug and Play*, a term that describes automatic installation of new hardware you add to your PC. Prior to Plug and Play, you had to set jumper switches and make operating system settings. Often, hardware and software conflicts would occur, creating many hours of debugging headaches. With Plug and Play, you simply plug new hardware components such as memory, disk drives, CD-ROM drives, and expansion boards into your computer, and Windows immediately recognizes the change and sets up everything properly.

Plug and Play requires almost no thought when installing new hardware to your system. At least that's the theory. In reality, you might still encounter problems, as this hour explains. If Plug and Play does not perform as expected, Windows provides a hardware setup wizard that you can use to walk you through the new hardware's proper installation.

Windows has not only made it easier to change hardware on one system, but it also contains a program that aids you in changing entire machines. Many people work on multiple PCs. Perhaps you have a laptop as well as a desktop computer. Perhaps you work both at home and at the office. Whatever your situation, Windows XP's direct cable connection helps you transfer document files between machines without a network connection.

In this hour, you will

- Discover what Plug and Play is all about
- Learn which components must be in place for Plug and Play to work
- Learn how Plug and Play benefits both you and hardware companies
- Use the Hardware Wizard to add special hardware that requires more than Plug and Play
- Implement direct cable connection to make connecting two computers virtually trouble-free

Plug and Play

Despite the industry hype over Plug and Play, it does not always work. If you attempt to install an older board into your computer, Windows might not recognize the board, and you could have all kinds of hardware problems that take time to correct. Generally, devices currently billed as Plug and Play are fairly stable and install well.

New USB (*USB* stands for *Universal Serial Bus*) and FireWire, also called *IEEE 1394*, hardware generally works as well or better than the plug and play installations described here. The advantage to USB and FireWire is that you don't have to power-off your computer to install new devices. Simply plug the device's connector into your computer's USB or FireWire port and Windows recognizes the device, prompts you for installation software if any is required, and you are ready to use the device. In spite of the advantages to these connections, plug and play devices are still needed, such as graphics adapters that must plug directly into your computer's motherboard.

 Windows prior to Windows XP did not support FireWire well. FireWire provides a high-speed connection for video input and output. Many digital cameras and video devices now connect to computers through a FireWire port.

Things do not always go as planned when installing non–plug-and-play hardware. New hardware that supports Plug and Play often has a seal with *PnP* on the box indicating its compatibility. You often have to set certain hardware switches correctly. You might also have to move certain jumpers so that electrical lines on your new hardware flow properly to work with your specific computer. The new hardware can conflict with existing hardware in your machine. Most hardware devices, such as video and sound boards, often require new software support contained in small files called drivers that you must install and test.

Hardware designed before the invention of plug and play specifications is called *legacy hardware*.

Before Plug and Play can work in Windows, these two plug-and-play items must be in place:

- A Basic Input Output System called the *BIOS* in your computer's system unit that is compatible with plug and play. The computer manual's technical specifications or technical support should tell you whether the BIOS is compatible with Plug and Play. Fortunately, virtually all PCs sold since early 1996 have supported Plug and Play.
- A device to install that is compatible with Plug and Play

You are running Windows XP, which is compatible with Plug and Play. If you do not have the Plug and Play BIOS inside your computer (most computers made before 1994 have no form of plug and play compatibility at all), you have to help Windows with the installation process by answering some questions posed by a new hardware setup wizard. When you purchase new hardware in the future, try to purchase only hardware rated for plug-and-play compatibility.

One key in knowing whether the hardware is designed for Plug and Play is to make sure that the Windows logo appears on the new hardware's box or instructions. Before a hardware vendor can sell a product with the Windows logo, that product must offer some level of plug-and-play compatibility. If you have older hardware already installed under a version of Windows when you install Windows, you will not have to reinstall this hardware.

If you run Windows, own a computer with a Plug and Play BIOS, and purchase only plug-and-play hardware, the most you usually have to do is turn off the computer, install the hardware, and turn the computer back on. Everything should work fine after that.

> Although most hardware sold today supports Plug and Play, some notable exceptions do not. For example, the Iomega Jaz and some internal Zip high-capacity drives require several non–plug-and-play steps that you must go through to install these devices. The parallel port versions are simpler but are slower in their operation. When possible, purchase USB or FireWire versions of products such as these. However, if you already have an inventory of such devices, you can certainly make them work with Windows XP in almost every case.

Plug and Play works both for newly installed hardware and for removed hardware. If you remove a sound card that you no longer want, or remove memory and replace that memory with a higher capacity memory, Plug and Play should recognize the removal and reconfigure the computer and operating system automatically. Again, Plug and Play is not always perfect and does not always operate as expected, but as long as you run a Plug-and-Play BIOS and install plug-and-play hardware, you should have little trouble with installation.

Windows Offers Hardware Help

If you install hardware and find that Windows does not properly recognize the change, double-click the Add Hardware icon in the Control Panel window. You might have to click the option labeled Switch to Classic View to see the Add Hardware icon. Windows starts the Add Hardware Wizard, shown in Figure 15.1, which helps walk you through the installation process.

The wizard goes through a series of tests and attempts to detect the newly added hardware. Remember that Windows recognizes most plug-and-play hardware; that is, when you install a new graphics card, for example, and then restart Windows, Windows often recognizes the graphics card and configures itself for use with your new card. Nevertheless, Windows cannot automatically recognize all plug-and-play hardware.

After the Add Hardware Wizard searches for plug-and-play hardware, you can have it search for non–plug-and-play hardware, or you can select the hardware from the list of vendors and products that Windows offers. Of course, if your hardware is newer than Windows, Windows will not list your specific hardware.

FIGURE 15.1

The Add Hardware Wizard helps you install non–plug-and-play hardware.

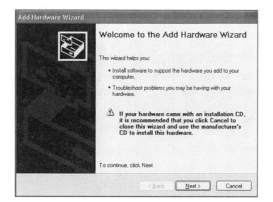

15

You can let the Add Hardware Wizard search for the new hardware, and if the wizard does not recognize the hardware, you can select from the list of devices.

Be sure to read your new hardware's installation documentation thoroughly before you begin the installation. Often the new hardware comes with updated drivers that fix minor bugs and add features to drivers that Windows already includes. Therefore, instead of letting the wizard search for the new device, and instead of selecting from the list of supported devices shown in Figure 15.2, you use a disk or CD-ROM that comes with the new hardware to add the latest hardware support for the device to Windows. Therefore, you have to click the dialog box's Have Disk button and select the hardware's disk or CD-ROM location to complete the installation.

FIGURE 15.2

Select from the list of known hardware or use your hardware's own installation disk.

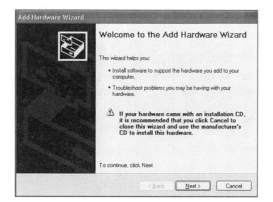

If you add a new modem to a serial port or a printer to a parallel port, you should not run the Add Hardware Wizard. The wizard works only for hardware you physically connect to the system unit, such as a disk drive or graphics card. If you plug a modem into an existing serial port, that serial port will already be installed, so you don't need to run Add Hardware. You will, however, have to double-click the Control Panel's Modems icon and select your modem from the list of modems displayed if the modem does not automatically install.

If you have a laptop or desktop with a PC card (PC cards are sometimes called *PCMCIA cards*), you can plug it directly into the laptop, changing a PC card hard disk to a PC card modem, and Windows will adjust itself automatically. Hour 17, "Using Windows on the Road," explains more about mobile computing and the hardware issues you'll encounter.

Additional Hardware Support

Windows uses a Registry and hardware tree to keep track of the current and changeable hardware configuration. The Registry is a central repository of all possible hardware information for your computer. The hardware tree is a collection of hardware configurations, taken from part or the entire Registry, for your computer. In addition, your Registry holds software settings.

Luckily, you don't have to know anything about the Registry because Windows keeps track of the details for you. If, however, you want to look at the hardware tree currently in place on your computer, you can display the Control Panel, double-click the System icon, and click the Device Manager button on the Hardware page to display the Device Manager page shown in Figure 15.3. This hardware tree shows the devices currently in use.

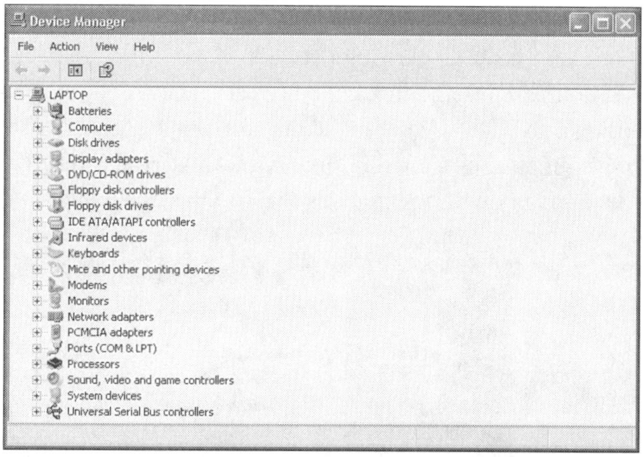

FIGURE 15.3

Analyze and change your computer's hardware settings from the Device Manager window.

15

Setting Up a Second PC

When you purchase a second PC, such as a laptop or a second home PC, you'll probably want to transfer files from your current PC to the new one. For example, you might have data files on the current PC that you want to place on the new one. The best way to transfer files is through a network. Hour 13, "Networking with Windows XP," explains how to put together and configure a network. Nevertheless, some people do not want to install networking hardware to transfer a lot of files from one computer to another. Perhaps you're setting up a new laptop and don't want to purchase a network card for the laptop.

Windows supports a feature called *direct cable connection* that lets you transfer files between computers without the need of a network and without moving data between the PCs via disk. The cable must be a *DirectParallel cable*, a special cable that connects one PC's parallel port to another's, or a *null modem cable* connected between the two computer serial ports. If both computers have an infrared eye, as most laptops have, you don't even need a cable; the infrared links serve as the "cable" between the two machines.

If you attach such a cable between two computers, or if they both have infrared ports, those computers can share files and printer resources with one another. This is a simple replacement for a more expensive and extensive network system. The direct cable connection is useful if you have the need only for two computers to share resources.

You'll access the direct cable connection option from your Network Connections window even if you don't have an existing network of any kind connected to your computer. When you double-click the link called Create a new connection, the Network Connection Wizard (the same wizard you read about in Hour 13 that also sets up an Internet sharing connection) initiates, as shown in Figure 15.4. After answering the wizard's prompts, your two computers will be linked as the To Do steps explain next.

FIGURE **15.4**

The Network Connection Wizard helps you connect two computers via a cable or infrared port.

New Connection Wizard

Welcome to the New Connection Wizard

This wizard helps you:

* Connect to the Internet.

* Connect to a private network, such as your workplace network.

* Set up a home or small office network.

To continue, click Next.

[< Back] [Next >] [Cancel]

To Do: Making a Direct Cable Connection

1. Connect your two computers' parallel or serial ports with the cable. If both computers have infrared ports, point one infrared port to the other.

2. Select the Network Connection Wizard.

3. Click Next to select the connection type. Choose the last option labeled Set up an advanced connection to let the wizard know that you want to connect your computer to another by a direct cable connection.

4. Click Next and select the option labeled Connect directly to another computer.

5. Click Next. You will select one PC as the *host* and one as the *guest* by clicking the appropriate options on the wizard's screen. The host is the PC from which you'll transfer the file or files, and the guest receives those files. After you designate a host and guest, you cannot send information in the other direction without restarting the wizard on both computers.

6. Click the Next button to select the port on which you've connected the computers from the dialog box that appears in Figure 15.5. You'll have to select the port used on each PC.

FIGURE 15.5

Tell the wizard to which port the cable connects.

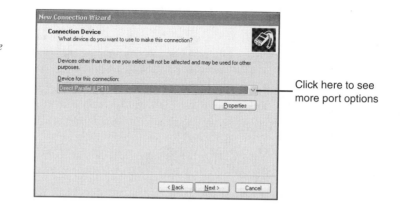

Click here to see more port options

15

7. Click Next to display the permission screen where you designate which of the computer's users can connect to the computer through the direct cable connection. The permissions determine whether the connecting user must have a password to connect to your computer.

8. Click Next to assign a name to the direct cable connection so that the other computer will recognize the connection option by its name. You can set up multiple direct cable connections, each with its own name and with different user permissions.

9. Click Finish to make the connection. After you've followed the wizard on the connecting PC, the two should be able to communicate with each other. If they do not both recognize the connection, you might have to check cable connections and rerun the wizard to ensure that all the options are set correctly. For example, you'll want to make sure that both PCs are not set as host or both as guest.

    The guest's Windows Explorer or My Computer window now holds an icon for the host PC, and you can transfer files from the host as easily as you can transfer from one of your disks to another. In addition, the guest's application programs can now print to the host printer because the host printer will be available from all File, Print dialog boxes.

The direct cable connection provides a way for you to connect two computers to use the files and printer on one (the host) by the other (the guest). The direct cable connection enables the guest computer to share the host's file and printer resources without requiring expensive and elaborate networking hardware and software.

After you set up a host or guest PC, your subsequent use of the direct cable connection is easier. You then have to specify the dialog box settings only if you change computers or if you decide to change directions and switch between the host and guest when transferring files.

Summary

This hour got fairly technical during the discussion of hardware. An operating system must run through several operations before it can recognize and work with new hardware. Fortunately, the plug-and-play process makes such work slightly easier and sometimes trouble free.

If you do not use 100% plug-and-play or USB or FireWire hardware, the Add Hardware Wizard will walk you through each installation and make the hardware easier to install. Suppose, for example, you add an internal modem, but you cannot communicate with it. The Add Hardware Wizard might realize that you have a new internal modem after running through its series of tests, but might not be able to determine exactly what kind of internal modem you have. You and the wizard together should be able to determine the proper configuration.

The direct cable connection wizard means that you'll be connecting more computers than ever before. You'll be able to transfer files and share printers easily from one to the other by attaching a cable between the parallel ports of each machine.

Q&A

Q How do I know whether I have Plug and Play?

A You have Windows XP, which means that installing hardware should be easier than with previous operating systems and earlier versions of Windows. Perhaps the best way to see whether you have Plug and Play is to plug the next device you get for your computer into the computer, power on your machine, and see what happens. Of course, you should read the new hardware's installation instructions to learn the correct way to install the device.

If you turn on your computer and the computer responds to the new device properly, you have, for all intents and purposes, all the plug-and-play compatibility you need. You have Plug and Play, at least, for that one device. Just because Windows and your BIOS are compatible with Plug and Play, however, does not mean that the hardware you install will also be compatible with Plug and Play.

Q I don't want to buy and install a network in my house, but how do I easily connect my laptop to my desktop to share files between them?

A Use Windows XP's direct cable connection. Connect a parallel cable to both parallel ports. Your laptop will be able to access the desktop's shared files. As simple as the direct cable connection is, if your laptop contains an infrared port, you'll learn in Hour 18 how to share files between the laptop and another device without cables.

Workshop

The quiz and exercise questions are designed to test your knowledge of the material covered in this hour. The answers are in Appendix C, "Answers to Quizzes."

Quiz

1. What is a legacy device?
2. What advantage does Plug and Play offer over legacy?
3. What further advantage does a Plug and Play USB device provide you?
4. What is a PC or PCMCIA card?
5. What kind of port, serial or parallel or infrared, do you need to use for the direct cable connection feature?

Exercises

1. Open your Control Panel, display all the icons there, and open the System window. Click the Device Manager tab and look at all your installed hardware devices. Don't change anything unless you know exactly what to do. Close the System window when you're finished. You can learn a lot about your computer from the Control Panel's System window.

2. If you have a laptop, create a direct cable connection between your desktop computer and your laptop. Open Windows Explorer to see the connection and to transfer files between the two computers.

15

HOUR 16

Understanding Printing and Fonts

This hour explains the printing options available to you as a Windows XP user. The printer is one of those devices that you don't want to think much about; you want to print a document and a few moments later, grab the resulting printed output from the printer. You can better manage your printer's output with this hour's information.

When you work with documents, the availability of fonts is important so that you have the richness that fonts provide. This hour explains how to work with fonts inside Windows. With ample fonts, you can view more documents accurately.

In this hour, you will

- Use the Add Printer Wizard to set up new printers
- Work with Print dialog boxes to route output to a printer
- Manage the Print job window's list of printed documents
- Master the Fonts window
- Add and remove fonts in Windows

Introduction to Spooled Printing

When you print documents, Windows automatically starts the printer *subsystem*, a program within Windows that handles printing requests. The printer subsystem controls all printing from within Windows. Windows *spools* output through the printer subsystem. When spooled, the print job first goes to a disk file, managed by the printer subsystem, before being sent directly to the printer.

By routing printed output to a spooled disk file instead of sending the output directly to the printer, you can intercept it before that output goes to paper. That gives you more control over how the output appears on the printer. You also can select which printer receives the output in case more than one printer is connected to your computer.

Setting Up a Printer

If you add a printer to your system, remove a printer from your system, or set up Windows to use a printer for the first time, you'll have to inform Windows. But that's not always a problem because Windows supports Plug and Play as well as gives you the Add Printer Wizard to help you each step of the way.

Turn off your PC before you plug a new printer into your PC's parallel printer port. If you have a USB-based printer, you don't have to do this. After plugging in the printer and Windows XP restarting, Windows XP will often recognize, through Plug and Play, that you've added a new printer and perform one of the following tasks:

- Automatically recognize the printer and install the drivers for you
- Recognize that you've changed the hardware and start the Add Printer Wizard so that you can select the new printer
- Not realize that you added a printer, requiring you to run the Add Printer Wizard yourself

A special Printers and Other Hardware category appears on the Start menu's Control Panel. This category provides information about your computer's printer hardware. If you haven't set up your printer, and Plug and Play failed to install it, you will have to open the Printers and Other Hardware category window and walk through the Add Printer Wizard so that Windows knows exactly which printer to use.

Windows needs to know how to format the printed output that you want. Almost every printer supports different combinations of print functions, and almost every printer requires unique *print codes* that determine how the printer interprets specific characters and character-formatting options. The Add Printer Wizard configures the necessary details and asks you appropriate questions that determine how printed output eventually appears. The next To Do item shows you how to add a printer.

If you use a network and you need to set up a network printer in Windows, use the Network and Internet Connections category in the Control Panel window to open the network printer; you can browse the network to find the printer. Then set up the printer following the instructions that appear onscreen.

16

To Do: Using the Add Printer Wizard

1. Connect your printer to your computer using a printer cable. Most printers connect to the computer's parallel port or USB port.

2. Click the Start button to display the Start menu.

3. Select Control Panel, Printers and Other Hardware, and then click the option labeled, View installed printers or fax printers. The Printers and Faxes window shown in Figure 16.1 opens.

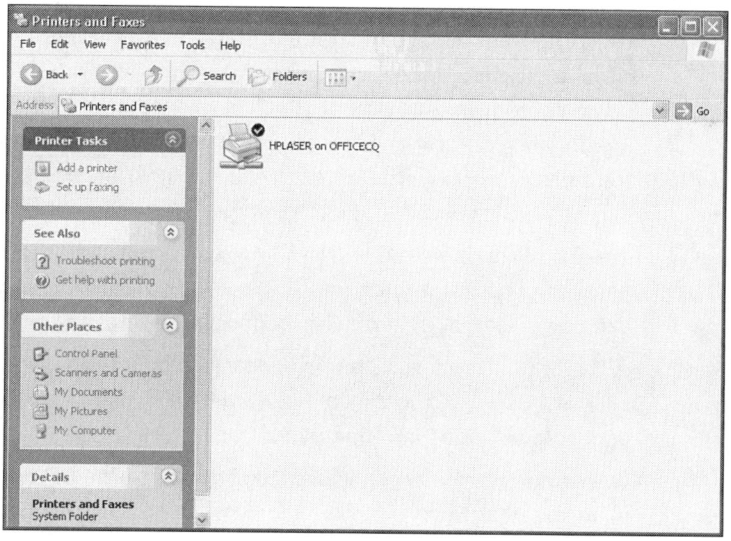

FIGURE 16.1

The Printers and Faxes window controls the setup and operation of printers and any online faxing software you might have.

If you have not set up a printer, you will see only the Add Printer icon in the Printers and Faxes window.

▼   The Printers and Faxes window provides access to all your printer subsystem capa-
     bilities. It is from the Printers window that you can manage and rearrange print
     jobs you've started from Windows applications.

4.   Click the link labeled, Add a printer, to start the Add Printer Wizard. If you haven't
     set up a printer, select the Add Printer icon now. When you select it, you will see
     the first screen of the Add Printer Wizard shown in Figure 16.2.

5.   Click the Next command button to start the Add Printer Wizard's operation. Select
     either the Local printer or the Network printer option. (If you want to set up your
     computer to print to a printer attached to another PC on your network, select the
     option labeled Printer Connection before clicking Next.) The wizard will look
     for a plug-and-play printer and install it if possible. If no plug-and-play printer
     exists, you'll proceed to the next step.

6.   The Add Printer wizard will ask how you connect your printer to your computer. If
     you use a parallel printer, you'll select the default option, LPT1:. Doing so informs
     Windows XP that the printer is connected to your PC's printer port.

7.   A list of printer manufacturers appears in the left scrolling window. When you
     choose a manufacturer, such as *Epson* or *HP*, that manufacturer's printer models
     appear in the right scrolling window.

     Over time, printer manufacturers update their printers and offer new models. There
     is no way that Microsoft can predict what a printer manufacturer will do next.
     Therefore, you might buy a printer that's made after Windows was written. If so,
     the printer should come with a disk that you can use to add the printer to
     Windows. If this is the case, click the Have Disk button and follow the instructions
▼   on the screen.

▼   If your printer *is* in the list, find your printer's model on the right, highlight the model, and click the Next button.

8. When you see the screen shown in Figure 16.3, you can enter the name you want to use for the printer when selecting among printers within Windows. If you like the default name, don't change it. If you want a different name, such as Joe's Printer (in case you're setting up a network printer that others will use), type the new name. If this is the only printer you are setting up, select Yes when the wizard asks about this being the default printer. (If this is the first printer you've installed, Windows makes it the default printer.) Windows will then use the printer automatically every time you print something. If you are setting up a secondary printer, select No.

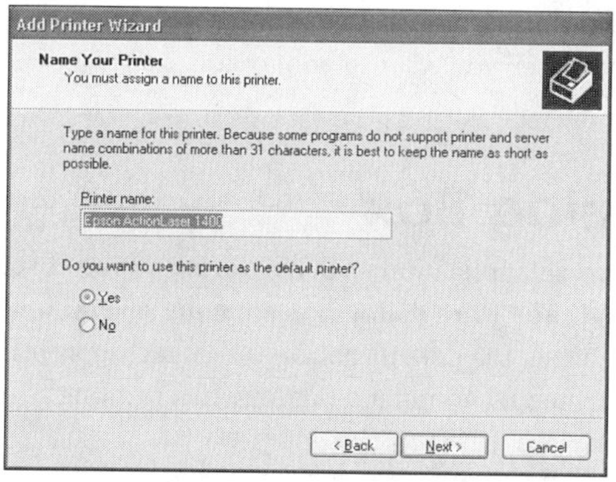

16

FIGURE 16.3

You must tell Windows how to refer to the printer.

9. Click the Next command button to move to the next wizard screen. If you are going to allow others to use this computer over the network, indicate that you want to share this printer. Click Next.

10. Use the Location and Comment fields that appear to enter a brief description of the printer's location and, optionally, a comment about its use (such as a note telling the users to check the printer's ink weekly). On a large network, such descriptions help ensure that users route printing to the proper printer.

11. If you click Yes on the next wizard screen, Windows will print a test page on the printer. (Be sure that your printer is turned on and that it has paper.) By printing a test page, you ensure that Windows properly recognizes the printer. Click the Finish command button to complete the wizard.

12. After Windows completes the printer setup, a new icon with your printer's name appears in the Printers window.

▲

When running the Add Printer Wizard, you specify which printer Windows should use for the default printer. (The default printer might appear with a check mark next to it in the Printers and Faxes window.) Of course, any time you print documents, you can select a printer that differs from the default printer if you want the output to go to a secondary printer source. You can also change the default printer by right-clicking over the printer you want to set as the default printer and selecting the Set As Default command from the menu.

> If you use your computer for accounting or personal finance, you might have a laser printer for reports and a color ink-jet printer for color banners. The default printer should be the printer that you print to most often. If your laser printer is the default printer, you'll have to route output, using the Print dialog box explained in the next section, back to the default check printer when you want to print checks.

The Print Dialog Box

When you print from an application such as WordPad, you'll see the Print dialog box shown in Figure 16.4. The Print dialog box contains several options from which you can choose. Most of the time, the default option values are appropriate, so you'll simply press Enter to select the OK command button when printing.

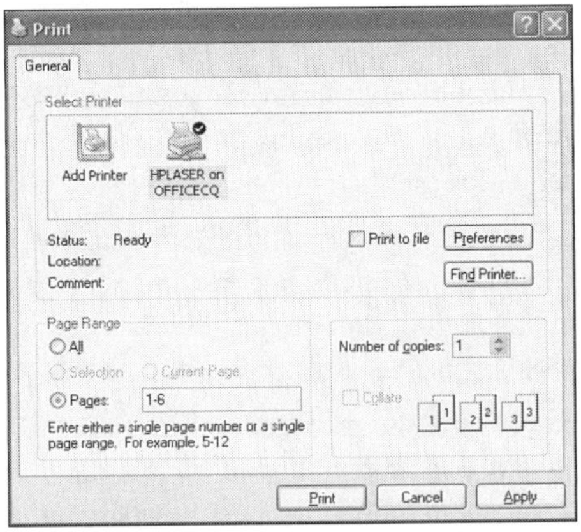

FIGURE **16.4**

The Print dialog box controls the way a print job is routed.

The Print dialog box contains a drop-down list box of every printer you've added to Windows. The default printer will be the printer you've chosen using the Add Printer Wizard's final screen. To change the default printer to another printer so that Windows automatically routes output to it when you print (unless you select another printer at printing time), right-click the printer's icon from within the Printers dialog box in My Computer and choose Set as Default.

> You can route the printer's output to a file by clicking the Print-to-File option. If you want output to go to a physical printer as soon as possible, as is most often the case, leave this option unchecked. By printing to the file, you can print the file at a later time.

16

The Print range will be All if you want to print all pages. For example, if you are printing 20 pages from a word processor, the All option sends all 20 pages to the printer. If you select the Pages option, you can enter a starting page number and ending page number to print only a portion of the document.

The Copies section determines how many copies you want to print. The default is one copy, but you can request an additional number of copies. If you enter a number greater than 1, check the Collate option if you want the pages collated (you usually do). If you highlight part of the text before beginning the print process, you can click the Selection option button to print only the selected text.

For special print jobs, you can click the Properties command button to display a printer Properties dialog box. Each printer model supports a different set of options so each printer's Properties dialog box contains different options. In the Properties dialog box, you specify the type of paper in the printer's paper tray, the *orientation* (the direction the printed output appears on the paper), and the printer resolution (the higher the printer resolution, the better your output looks, but the longer the printer takes to print a single page), among other options that your printer might support.

Keep in mind that the output goes to the print spooler and *not* directly to the printer. The next section explains how you can manage the print spooler.

> Some print jobs take a while to send their output to the spool file and, subsequently, to the printer. The taskbar displays a printer icon to the left of the clock during the printing process. If you rest the cursor over the printer icon, Windows displays a roving help box that describes how many jobs are in line to print. If you open the print icon, Windows displays the list of all print jobs (the next section describes the window of print jobs). If you right-click over the icon, Windows gives you the choice of displaying a window containing a list of all print jobs or the print jobs for specific printers that are queued up waiting for printed output.

Explorer and Open dialog boxes all display documents, as you've seen throughout this book. If you want to print a document, such as a bitmap graphics document file, a text document file, or a word processing document file, the right-click menu contains a Print command that automatically prints the selected document (or documents) that you right-click over. The right-click does *not* produce the Print dialog box described in this section; rather, Windows automatically and instantly prints one copy of the document on the primary default printer.

There's one more way to print documents that works well in some situations. If you have the My Computer window open or if you are using Windows Explorer, you can print any printable document by dragging it to any printer icon inside the Printers window. Windows automatically begins printing the document that you drag to the printer icon.

Managing Print Jobs

When you print documents, Windows formats the output into the format required by the default printer and then sends that output to a spool file. When the output completes, the printer subsystem routes the output to the actual printer, as long as it is connected and turned on.

Suppose that you want to print several documents to your printer in succession. Although today's printers are fairly fast, the computer's disk drives and memory are much faster than the relative speed of printers. Therefore, you can end up sending several documents to the printer before the first document even finishes printing on paper.

After printing one or more documents, open your Printers and Faxes window and double-click the Printer icon that represents the printer you printed to. A scrolling list of print jobs, such as the one shown in Figure 16.5, appears inside the window.

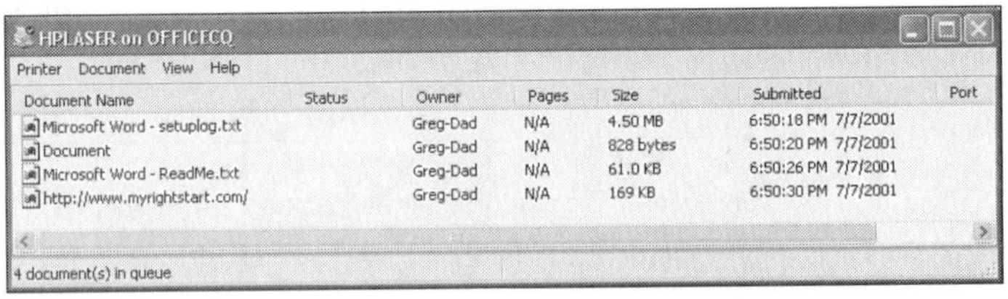

FIGURE 16.5

You can see all the print jobs spooled up, waiting to print.

Each line in the window describes one print job. If you've printed three documents, all three documents appear inside the window. The Status column shows how far along your print job is by telling you how many pages of the print job have completed. The remaining print jobs on the list are awaiting their turn to print.

If you want to change the order of the print jobs in the *queue* (another name for the list of print jobs), you can drag a print job to the top or bottom. Dragging a print job around in the list changes priority for that print job. For example, your boss might be waiting over your shoulder for a report. If you had several jobs you had sent to print before your boss showed up, you could move the boss's print job to the top of the list so that it would print next.

Right-clicking over a print job gives you the option of pausing a print job (putting it on hold until you resume the job) or canceling the print job altogether.

16

Deferred Printing

Sometimes you'll print documents but *not* want those documents to appear on a printer. Often people carry a laptop with them but not a printer. Even if you don't have a printer with you, you might create expense reports and other documents that you want to print as soon as you get back to your office.

Instead of keeping track of each document you want to print later, you can go ahead and issue a *deferred printing* request. When you do this, Windows spools the document or documents to a file on your disk drive. The printer subsystem will not attempt to send the spooled data to a printer just yet. When you later attach a printer to your PC, you can release the deferred printing request and Windows begins printing the saved print jobs.

Ordinarily, if you were to print a document to a printer but you had no printer attached to your computer, Windows would issue a taskbar error message, shown in Figure 16.6. Although Windows can spool the output properly and set up a print job for the output, Windows cannot finish the job because of a lack of a printer. The dialog box lets you know about the problem.

FIGURE 16.6

Windows cannot print if a printer is not attached to your PC.

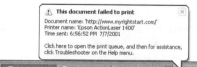

If you do have a printer attached to your computer but you get the error dialog box shown in Figure 16.6, you probably forgot to turn on the printer or put the printer *online* so that it can accept output. You can correct the problem and click Retry to restart the printing. If you do not click Retry, Windows will automatically retry printing every five seconds.

If you want to defer printing for another time, open the Printers folder and right-click over the icon that matches the printer for which you want to store print jobs. After you right-click, select Use Printer Offline. When you return to your office or plug a printer into the printer port, you can repeat this process to deselect the Use Printer Offline option. As soon as you set the printer icon back to its normal online status, Windows XP will begin printing to that printer.

Fonts Have Style

Because of the design of documents, the way that Windows displays documents is critical to your viewing of them. The documents must be easy to read. If Windows doesn't automatically display a document in a format that is easy to read, you'll have to change the way the document appears. Perhaps the simplest way to make a document easier to read, no matter what tool you use to view those documents, is by changing the document's font. A font is the typeface Windows uses to display a character. If you see two letter A's on the screen and one is larger, more slanted, bolder, fancier, or more scripted, you are looking at two different fonts.

Fonts from the same *font family* contain the same typeface (they look alike), but they come in standard formatting versions such as italicized, boldfaced, and underlined text. Therefore, an italicized font named *Courier* and a boldfaced font named *Courier* both belong to the same font family, even though they look different because of the italicized version of the one and the boldface version of the other. A font named *Algerian* and a font named *Symbol*, however, would belong to two different font families; not only do they look different, but they also come in various styles.

Fonts and Typefaces

Before computers were invented, printer experts stored collections of typefaces in their shops. Each typeface contained every letter, number, and special character the printer would need for printed documents. Therefore, the printer might have 50 typefaces in his inventory with each of those typefaces containing the same letters, numbers, and special characters but each having a different appearance or size.

Windows also contains a collection of typefaces, and those typefaces are stored as fonts on the hard disk. If you want to use a special typeface for a title, you must make sure that Windows contains the typeface in its font collection. If not, you will have to purchase the font and add that font to your system. Software dealers sell numerous font collections. Several fonts come with Windows and with the programs that you use, so you might not even need additional fonts.

The Control Panel's Classic View (available when you select Switch to Classic View from the Control Panel window) contains an icon labeled Fonts from which you can manage, add, and delete fonts from Windows XP's collection. When you open the Control Panel window's Fonts icon, Windows opens the Fonts window shown in Figure 16.7. The following To Do item explains how to manage fonts from the Fonts window.

FIGURE 16.7
The Fonts window displays your fonts.

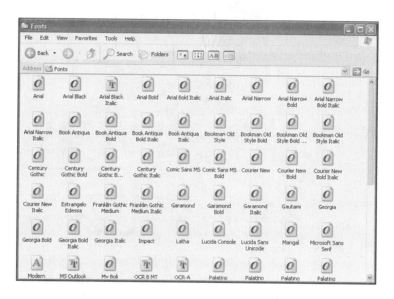

16

To Do: Working in the Fonts Window

1. Open the Control Panel window.
2. Click Switch to Classic View if you see the Control Panel categories listed.
3. Open the Fonts icon. Windows opens the Fonts window.

   Each icon inside the Fonts window contains information about one specific font on your system. Some fonts are *scaleable,* which means that Windows can display the fonts in one of several different sizes.

> Font sizes are measured in *points*. A font that is 12 points high is 1/6 inch high, and a font that is 72 points is one inch high.

4. Open any of the icons inside the Fonts window, and Windows immediately displays a preview of that font, as shown in Figure 16.8. When you want to create a special letter or flier with a fancy font, you can preview all of the fonts by opening

▼

each one until you find one you like. When you find a font, you can select it from your word processor to enter the text using that font.

Many fancy fonts are available to you. Don't go overboard, though. Your message is always more important than the font you use. Make your font's style fit the message, and don't mix more than two or three fonts on a single page. Too many different fonts on a single page make the page look cluttered.

5. If you click the Print command button, Windows prints the preview of the font. If you click Done (do so now), Windows closes the font's preview window.

6. Another way to gather information about certain kinds of fonts is to right-click over a font and select Properties from the menu that appears. The Font Properties dialog box will appear.

    The font icons with a green, rounded *O* symbol are *TrueType* fonts (you can verify that a font is a TrueType font from its Properties window. A TrueType font is a scaleable font that Windows prints using 32-bit technology so it will look as close to typeset characters as possible. The remaining fonts, with the letter A or another icon, refer to screen and printer fonts of more limited size ranges than TrueType fonts normally can provide.

▼

▼

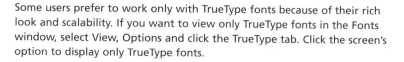

Some users prefer to work only with TrueType fonts because of their rich look and scalability. If you want to view only TrueType fonts in the Fonts window, select View, Options and click the TrueType tab. Click the screen's option to display only TrueType fonts.

16

7. Click the Similarity toolbar button. Windows searches through your fonts looking for all other fonts that are similar to the font you choose from the drop-down list box and displays the result of that search.

8. Click Large Icons to return to the icon view.

9. Check or uncheck View, Hide Variations (Bold, Italic, and so on) depending on whether you want to see variations within font families. If the box is unchecked, Windows displays a different icon for each font variation within the same family.

10. When you purchase new fonts, you cannot simply copy those fonts to a directory and expect Windows to know that the fonts are there. When you want to add fonts, you'll probably obtain those fonts on a CD, disk, or from the Internet. Insert the disk or CD (or make sure that you know where the file is located on your hard disk if you downloaded it from the Internet) and select File, Install New Font. Windows displays the Add Fonts dialog box.

Select the drive with the new fonts inside the Drives list box, and Windows displays a list of fonts from that drive in the upper window. Click on the font you want to install (hold Ctrl and click more than one font if you want to install several fonts) and click the OK command button to install the font to the Windows folder named Fonts.

▲ 11. Close the Fonts window.

After you install fonts, they will immediately be available to all your Windows applications.

Windows provides a single location, the Fonts window, where you can view and manage all the fonts on your system. Because of the graphical and document-centered design of Windows, your collection and selection of fonts is vital to making your documents as easy to read as possible.

Removing Fonts

Fonts take up a lot of disk space and slow down the startup of Windows. If your disk space is a premium and if you have lots of fonts you rarely or never use, you can follow the steps in this To Do item to remove some of them. Often, today's word processing and desktop publishing programs add more fonts to your system than you'll ever use.

To Do: Removing Fonts from Windows

1. Open the Control Panel window.
2. Open the Fonts icon.
3. Scroll to the font you want to delete.
4. Click the font you want to delete; Windows highlights the font. If you hold the Ctrl key while you click, you can select more than one font to delete. By selecting several at once, you can remove the fonts with one task instead of removing each one individually.
5. Right-click over any highlighted font to display the menu.
6. Select Delete.
7. Click the Yes button to confirm the removal.

Remove unwanted fonts if you want to save disk space and make your fonts more manageable. The Control Panel window's Fonts entry lets you easily select and remove fonts.

Summary

This hour explored the printer options you have with Windows. Before using a printer for the first time, you must set up the printer using the Add Printer Wizard available inside the Printers folder. Windows supports several hundred makes and models of printers, so you stand a good chance of finding your printer on the list.

The Fonts window contains a centralized location from which you can manage all the fonts used by Windows. When you purchase new fonts, you'll add those fonts using the Fonts window.

Q&A

Q Aren't all printers sold today Plug-and-Play? If so, why does Windows XP still support such old technology?

A All new printers are Plug-and-Play, but users are still using some printers that are not truly Plug-and-Play. Those printers won't die anytime soon. Not all computer users buy new printers with each new computer. Windows XP must make available support for virtually any printer that might still be in use.

Workshop

The quiz and exercise questions are designed to test your knowledge of the material covered in this hour. The answers are in Appendix C, "Answers to Quizzes."

Quiz

1. Where does Windows XP initially send all printed output?

2. If you plug in a new printer but Plug and Play does not properly detect the printer, what must you run to install the printer?

3. If you have two or more printers attached to your computer, how can you direct output to a specific one?

4. *True or false*: If you issue print commands to print ten documents in a row, you can change the order in which the documents print as long as you make the change to the documents that are still waiting to print.

5. What fonts are considered to be the best Windows fonts?

Exercises

1. Print a document that's at least ten pages. When the printer icon appears in your taskbar, double-click the icon. Watch how Windows updates the status of the print job as each page prints. If you leave this window open and print more documents, those documents will appear in the window.

2. Open your Fonts window and look through the fonts you have installed on your Windows system. Notice the variety. Print samples of both TrueType and non-TrueType fonts to see if you can tell the difference. On some systems, the non-TrueType fonts are similar, but often the TrueType fonts are superior to the non-TrueType fonts.

HOUR 17

Using Windows on the Road

This hour shows how Windows XP supports mobile computing environments. If you use a laptop, you'll appreciate the laptop-aware features that Microsoft included with Windows XP. Windows XP supports power management functions and recognizes when you change a laptop's configuration using a different type of Plug and Play, in which you're not required to turn off your laptop when making common hardware changes, such as docking the laptop into a docking bay.

Perhaps you use a laptop on the road and a desktop computer at the office or at home. If so, you need to transfer files easily between them and, at the same time, keep those files in synchronization so that you always work with the latest file version. Whatever your situation, the Windows *Briefcase* will help you synchronize your document files so they remain as current as possible.

The nature of laptop use is mobile computing. The cables you must plug in when connecting your laptop to a printer or to another PC make the laptop somewhat cumbersome when you want to communicate to another device. Fortunately, most of today's laptops come with infrared ports so that you can access other devices without cables.

In this hour, you will

- Learn why automatic configuration for mobile computing environments is so important
- Discover why the Briefcase feature is the most important icon for Windows XP users who work with both portable and desktop computers
- Watch as Windows detects common laptop hardware changes
- Use infrared connections to make communicating with peripherals and other computers simpler than using cables

Docking Your Laptop

The Microsoft programmers understood the need for mobile computing environments when they developed Windows XP. Mobile computing environments refer to those environments in which portable computers such as laptops are used. In the past few years, companies have begun developing *docking stations* for computer users who take a laptop with them on the road. Now they can come home and plug the laptop directly into a docking station. The docking station is a device that connects the laptop to a full-size color screen, printer, mouse, and keyboard. Therefore, the computer user uses the laptop on the road and then uses the laptop's system unit at home or in the office, with regular-size peripheral equipment.

Sitting at the Dock

Many devices known as docking stations are more accurately described as *port replicators* because they extend the laptop's expansion ports, such as the printer and serial port, to the docking station device on your desktop. Leaving all your peripherals plugged into the docking station is simpler than plugging each device into your laptop every time you arrive back at your desk. You only have to slide your laptop into the docking station to access those peripherals plugged into the docking station.

Be careful when plugging your laptop into your docking station. The connection pins are sometimes fragile and could easily break if you do not align the laptop correctly with the station.

Figure 17.1 shows a laptop connected to a docking station. Windows can detect whether a computer is docked and make appropriate adjustments instantly and accordingly. When undocked, Windows can use the laptop's screen, and when docked, Windows can immediately adjust the screen to a larger and higher-resolution monitor.

FIGURE 17.1

A docking station lets you utilize full-size desktop peripherals from your laptop.

Laptop docks here.

17

Windows XP can often recognize that a computer has been docked, but most hardware does not allow you to undock your PC without Windows knowing about the undocking. If Windows does not recognize the fact that you've undocked, you can select Eject PC from the Start menu, and Windows will know to reconfigure for the undocking and use the laptop's own configuration. For example, if your laptop contains an internal modem, the laptop, when undocked, will no longer be configured to use the docking station's modem.

When undocked, the Eject PC option does not appear on your Start menu.

Using PC Cards

For several years, laptops have supported PC cards, the small credit card–sized expansion peripherals that plug into the side of your laptop. These cards enable you to add a modem, memory, networking capabilities, and even another hard disk to your laptop.

Three card types exist:

- Type I: The original card that was replaced with Type II cards
- Type II: The most common PC card you can purchase today, primarily used for modems, memory, and networking
- Type III: A double-sized card used primarily for disk expansion. Several megabytes can fit into the size of a couple of credit cards.

Most laptops in use today support two Type II (or Type I) cards at once, or one Type III PC card, because of its double width.

Your taskbar's notification area includes an icon that represents your PC card (PCMCIA) slot. When you double-click this icon, Windows XP opens the PC card Safely Remove Hardware window shown in Figure 17.2.

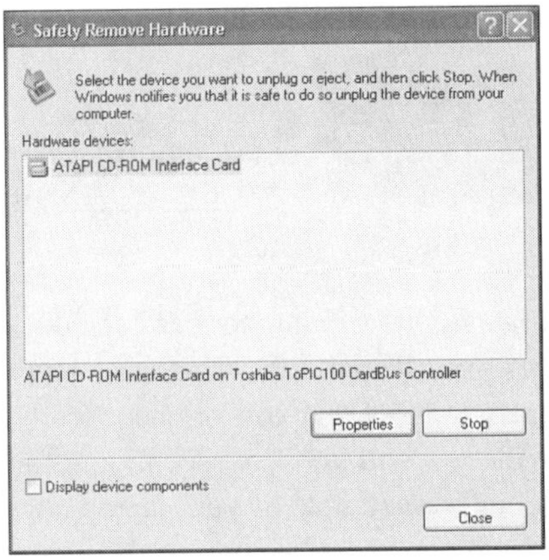

FIGURE **17.2**

The Safely Remove Hardware window enables you to control your PC card settings.

Figure 17.2 indicates that the laptop has one PC card socket (many have two) and that the socket has a D-Link PC card currently plugged in. The Safely Remove Hardware window also displays any USB devices you have installed, such as a laptop's USB-based floppy disk drive. Although you can insert and remove most PC cards during the operation of Windows without stopping the card first, if you use a PC card with a hard disk, you must stop the card *before* removing it to ensure that all unwritten data is on the card's disk.

To start any card, simply insert the card into the appropriate PC card slot. Your PC can be on or off for this operation; this is one of the only times you can modify PC hardware with the power on. Windows senses the change, installs the modem support through Plug and Play, and adds the card to the list in the PC card Properties dialog box that will no longer be empty. To remove the card, eject the PC card from its slot and Windows reconfigures itself accordingly.

To stop a PC card before you eject it, open the Safely Remove Hardware window, click the PC card device you want to stop, and click the Stop button. Windows then displays a dialog box telling you it's time to remove the card, and the PC Card icon is removed from your taskbar.

The Windows Briefcase

When on the road, you want to work with the most up-to-date data files possible. Therefore, users often copy the latest files from their desktops to portable PCs before leaving on a trip. The direct cable connection, described in Hour 15, "Exploring Your Hardware Interface," is a great way to copy those files, as is a networked system. Users can also use floppy disks and high-capacity disks, such as Zip disks, to transfer data between two computers.

When they return, those users often have to reverse the process and copy their latest laptop data files over the ones on the desktops to refresh the desktop's files so that both computers stay in synchronization with each other. Until Windows, the only way to ensure that you were working with the latest data files was to look at the file date and time values and work with only the latest. At best, trying to maintain the latest files was a hassle and often caused confusion and errors as well.

The Briefcase application, sometimes called *My Briefcase* because previous versions of Windows used that title beneath the application's icon, does all the nitty-gritty for you and synchronizes two computers that you have connected via a network or by cable. The Briefcase application is available from any window in which you view folders, such as the My Computer window or from Windows Explorer. You will create Briefcase files inside folders that you select for the purpose.

After you create a Briefcase item in a folder, a Briefcase icon appears in that folder. You can then drag files into the Briefcase from Explorer or from any Open dialog box.

Briefcase acts just like a briefcase that you take between your office and home. Before leaving in the morning, you put important papers in your briefcase. In the Windows XP environment, before going on the road with your laptop, you should drag all data files that you want to work with to the Briefcase.

After creating a Briefcase icon in a folder, you can click that icon to start the Briefcase application. Windows XP displays an introductory window, shown in Figure 17.3, when you first start the Briefcase program. The window provides an overview of the Briefcase operation.

17

Figure 17.3

*You'll see this intro-
ductory window when
you first start
Briefcase.*

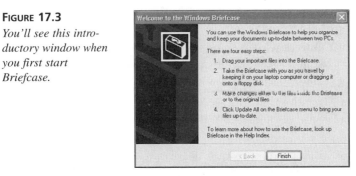

Suppose that you copy two files to the Briefcase icon by dragging the files from
Windows Explorer to the Briefcase icon you've created in a folder. Figure 17.4 shows
two files in the Briefcase window ready to be transferred to a laptop computer. Notice
that the Update All toolbar button is available.

Figure 17.4

*Two files are in the
Briefcase at the
moment.*

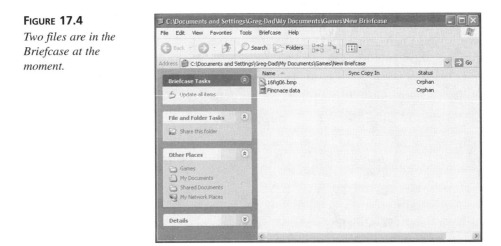

If you are using a floppy disk for the Briefcase intermediary storage media, move the
Briefcase icon to the floppy disk. Just click the Briefcase icon to highlight it. The Folder
Tasks in the right windowpane opens to display Copy This Folder. When you click the
link, Windows XP opens a Copy Items window where you can select your desktop's
disk drive to which to copy the folder. Alternatively, you could drag the Briefcase folder
to the disk drive from within any Windows Explorer window. You must have a formatted
disk in the drive before you copy the desktop's My Briefcase icon there.

After you copy the Briefcase folder to the floppy disk, insert the floppy disk into your laptop's disk drive and copy the Briefcase to your laptop. While on the road, you can work with those files in the Briefcase. If you save a Briefcase file to the laptop's hard disk, be sure to return the file to the laptop's Briefcase before you reconcile the files on your primary desktop computer later.

When you get back to the desktop, right-click the desktop's Briefcase folder and select Update All from the left window pane. (Alternatively, you can first select only those files you want to update, and then select Update Selection). Briefcase synchronizes the desktop's files by doing one of three things:

- If your desktop does not have one or more Briefcase files, the Briefcase application copies those files to the desktop computer.

- If your desktop already has those files on its disk, Briefcase transfers files from the Briefcase *only* if the Briefcase's files are newer than the desktop's.

- If your desktop already has one or more Briefcase files and the files are older than the Briefcase versions, the Briefcase application copies the newer versions over the old ones on the desktop.

As you can see from these options, the Windows XP Briefcase feature is smart enough to know when a file is already the same in both the Briefcase folder and your desktop and when the file needs to be updated.

If you want to update files using a direct cable connection, infrared connection (see the next section), or network instead of an intermediary floppy disk, make the physical connection first to the laptop with a direct cable or plug the laptop into your network. Then drag the files from the desktop computer to the laptop's Briefcase icon. This sends the files to the Briefcase on the laptop. While on the road, work with the files inside the Briefcase icon. When you reconnect to the desktop or network, you can select the Briefcase, Update All menu command to bring the desktop up-to-date.

Going Wireless with Infrared

In the 1980s, IBM introduced the PCJr, a PC designed for home use and one that used an *infrared port* for its keyboard. You cannot see infrared light, but infrared signals work well in remote-control devices such as television remotes. A wire on the keyboard did not encumber the user; the user could lean back in the chair and point the keyboard in the general direction of the PC to use the PCJr.

IBM was years ahead of its time and years behind the market. The PCJr's sales bombed.

Today, the home computer market has not only grown, but it has far surpassed anyone's expectations. With the integration of the television and PC, along with wireless keyboards and other peripherals, it is easy to see that part of the PCJr's demise was bad timing.

Windows XP fully supports infrared devices. At the time of the Windows XP release, the most common device that uses infrared technology is the laptop PC and printers. Infrared allows the laptop user to transfer files from one PC to another without networks or even cables. As you saw in Hour 15, "Exploring Your Hardware Interface," the direct cable connection for Windows XP makes transferring files simple; however, you can make it even simpler by using infrared transfer. Just point your laptop at another laptop or a desktop with an infrared transmitter, and Windows automatically senses the infrared devices and makes the connection you need.

Many manufacturers are adding infrared ports to peripherals such as printers and networks. Forget about cables—just point your PC in the direction of your printer to begin printing!

Most infrared devices are truly Plug and Play. Turn on your printer and Windows configures itself for the printer, emitting a sound telling you that the infrared ports are communicating.

As with many Windows features, including the PC card support described in the previous section, an infrared icon appears on your taskbar when your PC or laptop is ready for infrared communications. If you do not see the icon, you can add it to your taskbar.

You must enable your infrared port before you can use it. This To Do item shows you how to let Windows know that you want the port enabled for use.

To Do: Enabling Your Infrared Port

1. Open the Start, Settings, Control Panel window.
2. Click Switch to Classic View to display the full Control Panel window if you have only the category view showing.
3. Open the Wireless Link's window to display the Wireless Link dialog box. Figure 17.5 shows this dialog box.

FIGURE 17.5

Enable your infrared device from the Wireless Link dialog box.

4. The choices you make determine how the infrared, wireless link operates. Check the top option to display the wireless link's icon on the taskbar that will indicate when your laptop sends or receives infrared instructions. Check the second option if you want to transfer files to your laptop via the wireless link. The final option shows the status of a wireless transfer during the operation.

5. When you click OK, your taskbar will show the infrared icon during a wireless transmission.

When you enable your infrared port, the icon will appear on your taskbar and your PC will be ready to search for another infrared device. Your PC sends out a signal every time interval that you specify in the Wireless Link dialog box, and the icon will show a second icon if another device comes within range.

Connecting another infrared device to your laptop is simple. Windows does all the configuration as long as you bring the second device within wireless range. You will have no need to hook cables between two PCs with infrared devices or between a PC and an infrared printer. The infrared port is especially helpful for laptop users who want to use a wireless connection to transfer files between the PCs using the Direct Cable Connection Wizard.

A Word About Power

Depending on the support your laptop manufacture provides, you might have some or a lot of control over how much power your laptop consumes over time. Power consumption is an important issue for laptop users due to the limited storage of laptop batteries.

17

When you open your Control Panel and select Power Options, you'll see a window similar to the Power Options Properties window in Figure 17.6. From this window, you can select the power scheme that best suits the way you work. If you change the option to Always On, your laptop battery will be utilized to its fullest because Windows XP will always keep your monitor on and your hard disks spinning. By selecting other options, you can control how long your keyboard sits idle because Windows XP stops your hard disk and blanks out your monitor to save battery life. When you press any key, after one of these power-saving features starts, you will notice a pause while Windows XP brings the disk back to its full speed or powers the monitor once again.

FIGURE 17.6

Windows XP supports various power-management options.

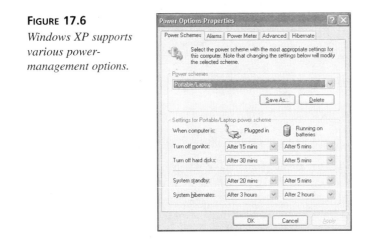

Other options that appear in your Power Options Properties window are determined by your laptop's abilities. For example, most laptops can go into a *hibernate mode* whereby your work session including all open windows and programs and loaded data are stored to your laptop's disk drive before the power goes off. You then can quickly return to the place you last were. The hibernate feature is useful when you need to stop using your laptop but then return to finish what you were doing before. By entering a hibernate mode instead of closing all your windows and then turning off your laptop, your laptop will power on back to the power where you turned it off; you won't have to restart any programs to return to your work.

Summary

This hour showed how laptop users can take advantage of the special mobile support features of Windows. Windows includes support for docked laptop computers, so the configuration changes whenever you dock and undock. In addition, infrared ports make communicating between two infrared devices simple and wireless.

The easy interconnection possible in Windows XP means that you'll be connecting more computers than ever before. With those connections comes confusion, however. A desktop and laptop computers' files can get out of synchronization. Generally, you want to work with the latest version of a file, but comparing dates and times is tedious and error-prone. The My Briefcase icon solves this problem by making the time and date comparisons for you and refreshing any laptop or desktop files which need it to make sure that both systems have the latest versions of document files.

Q&A

Q I often cross time zones and change my laptop accordingly. Will Briefcase be affected by the time changes?

A It is possible for Briefcase to make incorrect decisions when copying files using different time zones. You can do very little to make Briefcase happy when you move across time zones. The best thing you can do is resist the temptation to change the laptop's clock while on the road. Keep your laptop clock set the same as your desktop computer, so that when you return to the desktop, Briefcase will have no trouble reconciling your files.

Q I don't use a desktop PC, so do I need a docking station for my laptop?

A Actually, those without a desktop are the *best* candidates for a docking station. When on the road, you can use your laptop, and when you return to your desk, you can use the laptop's processor as your desktop PC. The docking station can connect to a full-screen monitor, keyboard, mouse, modem, and printer. To access these devices and to configure your laptop to use those devices, you only insert (*dock*) your laptop into the docking station, and Windows reconfigures itself for the new devices.

Workshop

The quiz and exercise questions are designed to test your knowledge of the material covered in this hour. The answers are in Appendix C, "Answers to Quizzes."

Quiz

1. Why would a laptop user need a docking station?

2. What common upgrade method, outside of using a docking station, do laptop users use to expand their laptop's options?

3. What utility program does Windows supply that helps you keep your laptop and desktop files in sync?

4. *True or false*: Users can use a floppy disk or a network to keep files up-to-date using the Briefcase feature.

5. *True or false*: Infrared signals are visible, but can only transmit for distances up to 1.2 miles.

Exercises

1. If you have a laptop with a PC card, close all programs but keep Windows XP running. Eject the PC card. Windows XP displays a message warning you that you should stop any device you are about to eject. By first stopping a device, using the taskbar's Unplug or Eject Hardware icon, you ensure that you don't lose any data during a PC card ejection.

2. Try transferring files between two laptop computers that support the infrared transmission of data. If you can't locate a second laptop, see if your printer has an infrared port as many do. If so, print to the printer using the infrared connection. You might have to adjust your printer property settings so that the printer knows to look for the wireless transmission.

HOUR 18

Giving Windows XP a Tune-Up

This hour shows you how Windows XP checks and updates itself. If you have Web access, you don't need to wait for a disk mailing or go to the store to get the latest Windows drivers and updates. You only click a menu option and Windows updates itself.

Not only can you be assured that you have the latest Windows support files, but you can also make sure that any new computer you purchase looks and acts just as your current computer does. A wizard helps you transfer all your data and system settings to a new computer when you purchase one.

In this hour, you will

- Learn how Windows XP informs you of system updates
- Learn how you can delay the update's installation process
- Learn when Windows downloads update files from the Internet
- Transfer your data files and customized settings to a new PC that you buy
- Print a listing of your computer's hardware and software settings

As long as you have Internet access, you can request that Windows XP check the Microsoft Internet sites and update any Windows files that have changed, have been added, or have had bugs which have been corrected. The update site gives you full control over the update. You can

- View a list of files that are needed by your system to run the latest versions
- Read a description of each update to help you decide whether you need the update
- Submit problem reports that you experience
- Keep track of the updates you apply to your system

The Windows Update program updates your Windows XP operating system files to ensure that you have the latest system files available. Windows Update can be automatic; you don't have to initiate Windows Update although you can if you want.

If you have an always-on Internet connection, you'll probably want to set up the Windows automatic update routine so your version of Windows XP stays as current as possible. The following To Do item explains how to set up the automatic Windows Update feature.

To Do: Setting Up Automatic Updates

1. Open your Control Panel window.
2. Click the Switch to Classic View link to see all Control Panel items.
3. Double-click the System icon.
4. Click the Automatic Update tab to display the Automatic Update page shown in Figure 18.1.

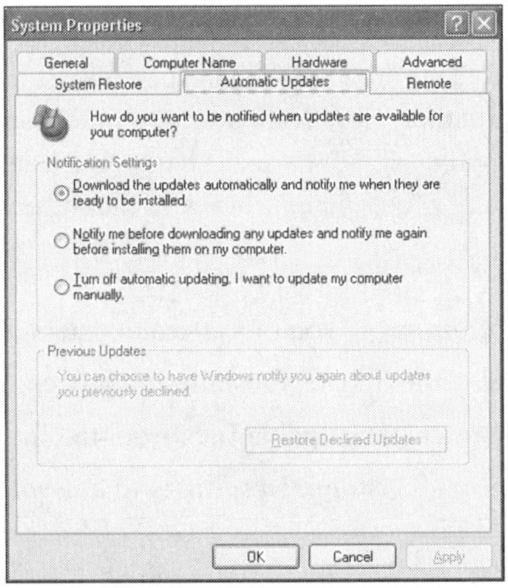

FIGURE **18.1**

Set up Windows automatic update so your operating system remains current.

▼   You have three ways to respond to automatic Windows XP updates. You can
     request that Windows XP automatically download any operating system updates
     when they become available, assuming you haven't already downloaded them, and
     notify you by a pop-up message from the taskbar's notification area when the
     update is downloaded to your PC and ready to be installed. You can also request
     that Windows XP notify you, via a message in your taskbar's notification area,
     before an update is downloaded to your PC. You can read about the update by
     clicking the notification area's message and decide if you want to take the time to
     make the update or ignore it for now. Finally, you have the option to turn off auto-
     matic updates so that you only update your Windows XP when you specifically
     select Windows Update from the Start menu.

▲   5. Make your selection and click OK.

Instead of installing an update that's available, you can click the Remind Me
Later button that appears in your notification area when an update is available. You can select the time frame from the list, such as Tomorrow, when
you want to be reminded to install the update.

18

How the Updates Work

Where do the updates come from? You got a hint of that from the previous To Do list if
you followed along. When you log on to the Internet, Windows XP, in the background,
goes to the Microsoft Web site and looks to see if any updates are required for your particular combination of operating system components. If an update is available, Windows
XP either downloads the update at that time and signals you with the taskbar's notification area message, or Windows XP tells you that the updates are available and asks if
you want to install them. Windows notifies you in one of these two ways depending on
how you set up Windows Update, not unlike the way you changed the settings in the
previous To Do steps.

Updating Windows Yourself

If you don't want Windows to do any updating or file-retrieval automatically in prepara-
tion for an update, you can request that Windows XP not update itself until you take the
action that directs Windows to locate updates that might be needed.

If you select the third option of the Automatic Updates dialog box, as you could have
done at the end of the previous To Do task list, Windows waits until you select the Start

menu's Windows Update option. Until then, Windows will not update your computer or download updates until you request them.

If you select the Windows Update option from the Start menu, Windows always goes to the Internet to see if a current update is available, even if an update has been recently downloaded but has not been installed.

If you want to trigger your own Windows Update and forego the automatic update process as you'll want to do if you use a slower, dial-up modem, select Windows Update from the Start menu. Figure 18.2 shows the Windows Update screen that will appear.

FIGURE 18.2

Select your own time for updating Windows.

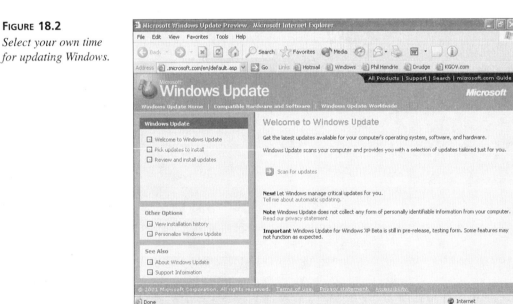

When you click the Scan for Updates option, Windows Update scans your system and compares what it finds to the updates available online. The available updates then appear and you can determine which, if any, you want to apply.

Windows Update attempts to locate these three types of updates:

- Critical Updates: These updates are important for bug fixes or security holes that Microsoft deems critical.
- Windows XP: These updates are new options and utilities that might be available for Windows XP but are not deemed critical or urgent.

- Driver Updates: Updates to specific hardware *drivers* (internal programs that enable your specific computer devices to work with Windows XP) to fix bugs or make your hardware work better with Windows XP.

> To view the updates you've applied in the past, click the option labeled View installation history. Windows XP displays the updates you've applied in the past, along with the dates on which you applied each of those updates.

Often, Windows must restart your computer to complete the update process. You should close all program windows before submitting to the system restart.

> If you've elected not to use Windows XP's automatic Windows Update feature, be sure to perform the update routinely to ensure that you have the latest and most correct system files possible.

Transferring Settings from One Computer to Another

18

When you purchase a new computer, one of the most time-consuming and difficult tasks in the past was transferring all your old computer's settings and files to the new one. You might have Windows set up a particular way, specific features set in Outlook Express, or perhaps have tasks that you've scheduled for automatic execution, such as a daily backup.

Windows XP supports a new feature called the Files and Settings Transfer Wizard that helps you mirror and transfer the settings from your current computer to a new one that you purchase.

Here are just some of the things the Files and Settings Transfer Wizard transfers to a new computer:

- Display property settings
- Dial-up settings
- Desktop settings such as colors and wallpaper
- Data files such as My Documents, My Pictures, and your shared documents
- E-mail settings

- Mouse and keyboard settings
- Regional settings, such as the time zone and country
- Sounds and other multimedia options
- Folder and taskbar options
- Internet Explorer browser settings

The following To Do item shows you how to use the Files and Settings Transfer Wizard.

To Do: Using the Files and Transfer Settings Wizard

1. Select the Start menu's All Programs, Accessories, System Tools, Files and Settings Transfer Wizard to open the introductory wizard window shown in Figure 18.3.

FIGURE **18.3**

The first Files and Settings Transfer Wizard window describes the wizard's operation.

2. Click Next to move to the next window in the wizard. You must tell the wizard whether you're moving your settings *from* the current computer or *to* the current computer. In other words, the wizard must know whether the computer you are on is receiving settings from another computer or is sending settings to another computer.

3. If you're working from the existing computer, when you click Next, Windows XP takes a few moments to analyze the current system to see what can be transferred to the machine.

4. Click Next to display the transfer method window shown in Figure 18.4. You must tell the wizard how you are going to get the settings from the existing computer to the new one. You can transfer the settings by disk or by network. If you are transferring via a networked drive, you must tell the wizard the location of the drive by specifying the pathname in the text box labeled `Folder or drive`.

FIGURE 18.4

Specify how you want to transfer the settings.

If you transfer data files along with your system settings, you'll need to transfer using a medium larger than a floppy disk. The easiest and fastest way to transfer is over a network connection if both your old computer and your new one are connected to the same network.

18

5. Click Next to display Figure 18.5's window where you specify exactly which files and settings you want to transfer.

FIGURE 18.5

Specify what you want to transfer.

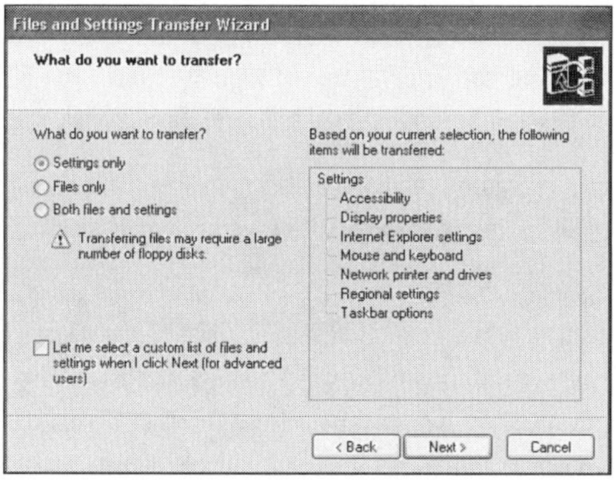

You must tell the wizard whether you want to transfer data files, settings, or both files and settings, from the older computer to the new one. Once you select your choice, Windows XP might take several minutes to gather the information and complete the process.

▼ As the wizard gathers the information to transfer, you'll be able to monitor the progress on the collection window shown in Figure 18.6.

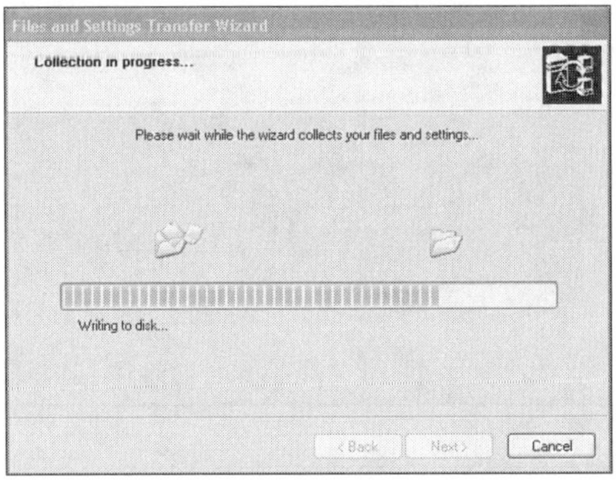

FIGURE **18.6**

The wizard is storing your current system's information and preparing to make the transfer.

6. After you complete the collection phase of the old computer, you now must start your new computer and run the Transfer Files and Settings Wizard on that computer. When you tell the wizard that you're on the new computer, the wizard will prompt you for the location of the other computer's settings and files, and you can

▲ make the transfer.

What's in Your System

Periodically, you might need to know specifics about your system, such as what hardware, memory, disk space, or other detail currently exists in case you want to upgrade your computer.

Windows XP supports a System Information window that displays all the details about your system. Figure 18.7 shows the results of running System Information on one computer.

Run System Information from your Start menu's Accessories, System Tools folder. Not only does the opening screen, shown in Figure 18.7, shows the details of your system, but you can get more specific information by selecting from the menus. For example, the Tools menu enables you to learn the specifics about your network connections.

FIGURE **18.7**

Run System Information to learn about your computer's contents.

System Information window

Item	Value
OS Name	Microsoft Windows XP Professional
Version	5.1.2502 Build 2502
OS Manufacturer	Microsoft Corporation
System Name	LAPTOP
System Manufacturer	TOSHIBA
System Model	Satellite Pro 4600
System Type	X86-based PC
Processor	X86 Family 6 Model 8 Stepping 10 GenuineIntel ~996 Mhz
BIOS Version/Date	TOSHIBA Version 2.40, 3/15/2001
SMBIOS Version	2.3
Windows Directory	C:\WINDOWS
System Directory	C:\WINDOWS\System32
Boot Device	\Device\HarddiskVolume1
Locale	United States
Hardware Abstraction Layer	Version = "5.1.2502.0 (main.010622-1750)"
User Name	LAPTOP\Greg-Dad
Time Zone	Central Daylight Time
Total Physical Memory	384.00 MB
Available Physical Memory	210.34 MB
Total Virtual Memory	1.27 GB
Available Virtual Memory	1,001.41 MB
Page File Space	922.49 MB
Page File	C:\pagefile.sys

Almost all the details from the System Information window are available elsewhere. For example, you can get network connection information from the Control Panel window. The System Information is the primary repository, however, of your system's every detail.

18

Much is available from the System Information window. You might want to look through the menu options to learn what is available. Perhaps the most important thing you can do right now is print a copy of your system information and save the printout in case you need to restore your system at a later time after a hardware failure of some kind. For example, if you later need to replace a faulty disk drive, you'll be glad you printed a copy of your system information so you can set up your replacement disk drives with the same system settings as the previous drive.

The System Information screen keeps track of the following details of your computer system:

- Your hardware and the internal resources each device uses
- Components such as the status of your USB ports and modem
- Software such as drivers and startup programs that automatically execute when Windows XP first starts
- Internet Explorer settings
- Office application settings (if you have installed Microsoft Office)

To print the system information, select File, Print and select All in the Print range field. Be warned, though, that this list can consume quite a lot of paper.

> Whenever you change or add hardware, be sure to print a fresh copy of your system information so you'll always have an up-to-date copy.

Summary

This hour described how you can keep Windows in top condition. The Windows Update manager makes sure that you have the latest Windows files on your system. To guard against possible application conflicts that sometimes occur with new Windows components, Windows Update enables you to restore from previous updates you made that might now be causing problems with older software you run. When you have the latest Windows files, you can transfer your settings to a new computer with the Files and Settings Transfer wizard. To make sure you can restore your system if a hardware failure occurs, keep a fresh copy of your system information on hand at all times.

Q&A

Q What if my new computer has different hardware from my old one but I attempt to transfer my Windows XP settings to the new one?

A The File and Settings Transfer wizard is smart and realizes that your new computer almost certainly is different from your old one. The wizard transfers your data files and system settings but not anything that is hardware specific. In other words, your new computer's monitor might be capable of a much higher resolution than your older computer's monitor, but the wizard goes ahead and keeps the old system's settings. You can also change the settings yourself to take advantage of your new computer's more modern capabilities. The wizard's job is to transfer any customization you've performed, such as the Auto-Hide feature of your taskbar, so that you can get up and running as quickly as possible on your new computer without having to reset and customize its settings.

Workshop

The quiz and exercise questions are designed to test your knowledge of the material covered in this hour. The answers are in Appendix C, "Answers to Quizzes."

Quiz

1. How does Windows know when an update is needed?

2. How can you keep Windows from updating automatically?

3. What wizard transfers your old computer's options to a new computer?

4. *True or false:* The File and Settings Transfer Wizard can transfer the My Documents folder from your old computer to your new one.

5. What Windows program must you run to see all your hardware and software details?

Exercises

1. If you have an Internet connection, perform a manual Windows Update now to make sure that you have the latest updates.

2. Print a fresh copy of your system information and store the printout in a safe place in case you need to reconfigure a new device in the future.

18

HOUR 19

Managing Your Hard Drives

Everybody seems to need more disk space no matter how much one has. This hour shows you how to get more disk space and use your disk more efficiently with the Windows disk-related system utilities.

Over time, your disk gets cluttered, not only with extra programs and Windows XP components that you don't need, but also with file *fragments*, small pieces of files that slow down the overall operation of your computer.

In this hour, you will

- Learn how to detect fragmentation problems
- Ensure that your disk is running efficiently by letting Disk Defragmenter clean up potential disk problems
- Use Disk Cleanup to better manage your disk drives
- Learn the importance of developing a backup regime
- Back up your files to protect them from a disk breakdown

Fill In the Holes

Disk Defragmenter fills empty gaps on your disks. As you add and delete files, the deleted space leaves free holes around the disk. Over time, your disk response time will slow down as you add or delete document files to and from the disk drive.

> **Pick Up the Pieces**
>
> Windows XP can store large files on a fragmented disk as long as there is enough free fragmented space to hold the file. Windows stores the files in linked chunks across the disk drive, filling in fragments and linking them.
>
> A large file is stored as one continuous file if enough space exists to do so. But often, Windows tries to reuse fragment space left over from a deleted file. Over time, the number of these file fragments can grow considerably and slow down your PC when you access a file that's fragmented.
>
> Disk access slows down on a fragmented disk drive because Windows must jump to each file fragment when retrieving a file. If you run Disk Defragmenter often enough (once or twice a month for the average user ought to be enough), Windows keeps the fragments to a minimum and, thus, increases the disk access speed.

The following To Do item walks you through an example that demonstrates how to defragment a disk drive. As you'll learn in this task, Disk Defragmenter not only closes empty disk gaps but also rearranges your disk drive so that often-used programs run more quickly.

To Do: Correcting Disk Fragmentation

▲ To Do ▼

1. Display the Start menu and select All Programs, Accessories, System Tools, Disk Defragmenter. Windows displays an opening window, like the one shown in Figure 19.1, which displays size and usage numbers about your computer's hard disks.

2. Select a disk drive to analyze.

3. Click the Analyze button. Disk Defragmenter checks the disk drive to see if fragmentation is a problem. Disk Defragmenter displays a message window such as the one in Figure 19.2, which suggests whether or not you need to defragment the drive.

4. Click the View Report button to see details about the disk drive. The report will show how much fragmentation has occurred as a percentage of your disk drive. Just because Defragmenter doesn't recommend that you defragment does not mean that you cannot or should not. If you regularly defragment, your computer will

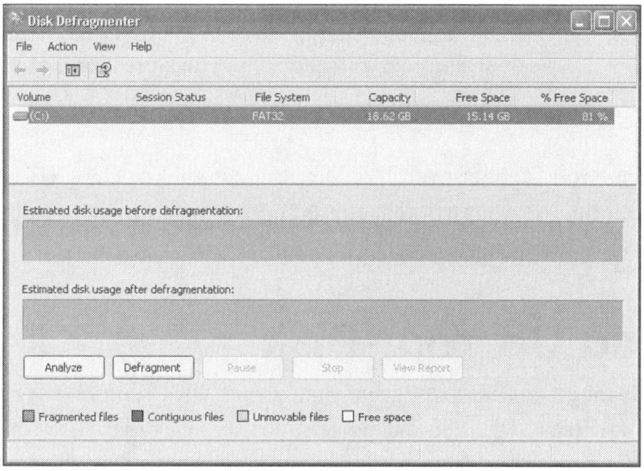

FIGURE 19.1

Disk Defragmenter shows details of all your system's disk drives.

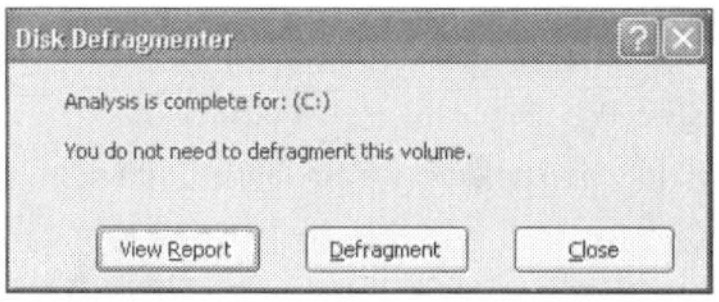

Disk Defragmenter

File   Action   View   Help

Volume	Session Status	File System	Capacity	Free Space	% Free Space
(C:)		FAT32	18.62 GB	15.14 GB	81 %

Estimated disk usage before defragmentation:

Estimated disk usage after defragmentation:

Analyze   Defragment   Pause   Stop   View Report

■ Fragmented files ■ Contiguous files □ Unmovable files □ Free space

FIGURE 19.2

Disk Defragmenter recommends that this drive not be defragmented.

Disk Defragmenter

Analysis is complete for: (C:)

You do not need to defragment this volume.

View Report   Defragment   Close

never get to the point of needing the defragmentation, and your hard disk will remain at its optimum performance.

5. To start the defragmentation, click the Defragment button. Disk Defragmenter will begin consolidating the free space on your disk and defragment the drive. Disk Defragmenter shows a graphical display of the process, color-coding fragmented pieces of your drive, during the process.

> Although you know that you should shut down Window XP properly before turning off your computer, nowhere is that advice more important than during a disk defragmentation process. Never turn off your computer while you are defragmenting a drive or you could very well lose information, and possibly destroy so much of the drive's contents that you'll have to reformat the disk drive and recover all its contents from a backup (if you have a backup).

6. When complete, Disk Defragmenter will tell you that the defragment process is finished. You then can select another disk drive or close the Disk Defragmenter window.

19

If you work in another open window while defragmenting your disk drive, Disk Defragmenter might not be able to defragment your disk, and will keep attempting a restart, until you close all other running programs.

Unlike previous versions of Disk Defragmenter, Windows XP's version is lenient about defragmenting on a networked, shared disk drive. You can often defragment a networked disk drive, without turning off the sharing mode of the drive.

Cleaning Up Your Disk

Disk Cleanup is a utility program that comes with Windows XP that enables you to free your disk drives of clutter and make more space available. Over time, your disk drives fill with temporary files and other information that you don't need to retain. Disk Cleanup can keep your free space at a maximum.

When combined with a regular use of Disk Defragmenter, Disk Cleanup ensures that your disk drives will perform at their optimal level and that you'll always have as much disk space as possible for your data.

The following To Do item explains how to use Disk Cleanup to remove clutter from your drive.

To Do: Using Disk Cleanup

1. Display the Start menu and select All Programs, Accessories, System Tools, Disk Cleanup. The Disk Cleanup window shown in Figure 19.3 appears.

2. Often, your Recycle Bin holds files that you no longer want. Disk Cleanup offers to delete all the files from your Recycle Bin. First, you can click the View Files button to open your Recycle Bin window and review everything there.

3. If you want to delete the files from your Recycle Bin, click the check mark next to the Disk Cleanup's Recycle Bin option.

4. Windows XP includes an indexing feature that operates when you search for data. Old searches might include indexes created but never deleted. If you have index files still left on your computer after searching for data recently, you can check that option as well from the Disk Cleanup window to remove the index files.

FIGURE 19.3

Determine the kinds of files you want to clean.

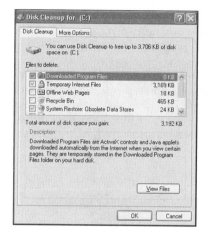

5. Before starting the Disk Cleanup process, click the More Options tab to display the Disk Cleanup options window shown in Figure 19.4.

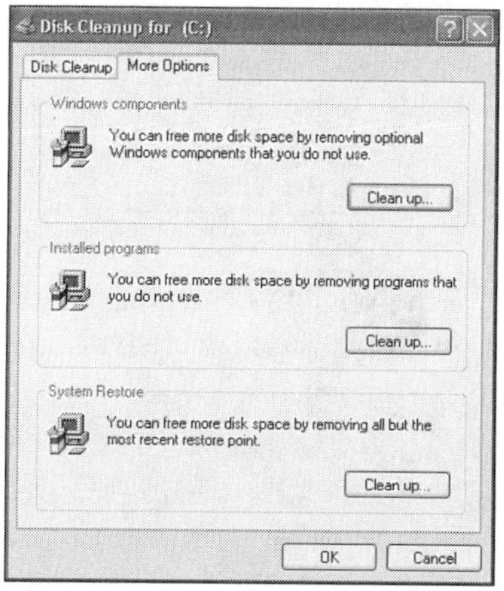

FIGURE 19.4

Disk Cleanup offers to clean up several areas of your disk drive.

19

6. The Windows components section of the Disk Cleanup window enables you to remove parts of your Windows XP installation to gain more disk storage. Although such a move only buys time temporarily (see the following tip), you might have installed Windows components that you rarely use. Click the Clean Up button to see the Windows Components Wizard window shown in Figure 19.5.

If you're running extremely low on disk space, Windows XP and your applications will begin operating at a sluggish rate. Programs require ample disk space to store temporary files, and Windows XP requires ample disk space to function. Although you should run Disk Cleanup regularly, if you are low on space, your sluggish computer will let you know. Given the relatively low cost of an additional disk drive today, if you find yourself needing to run Disk Cleanup more and more often, consider purchasing a second disk drive. You'll gain a tremendous amount of storage and your computing experience will be much better.

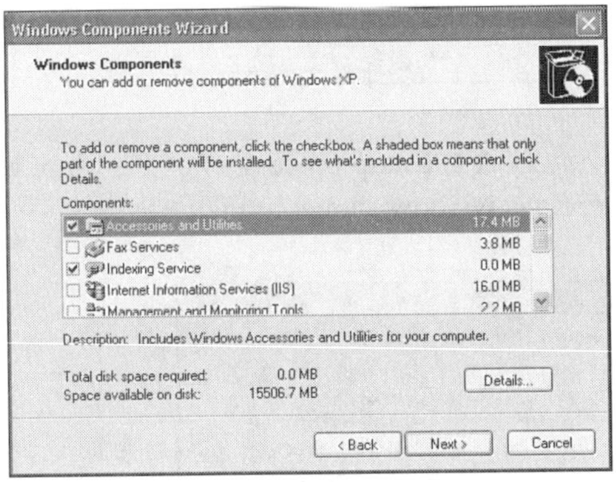

FIGURE 19.5

You might be able to remove some Windows XP components to gain disk space.

A check mark next to any of the Windows components indicates that the option is installed. You can click on an option and then click the Details button to read more about several of the Windows components.

7. If you decide to remove a Windows XP component that you do not need, such as the games installed with Windows XP (found in the Details section of the Accessories and Utilities section), uncheck that option. You can continue looking through the list of installed Windows XP components, unchecking all the options you don't need. When you click Next, Windows XP will remove those items from your system and free the disk space before returning to the Disk Cleanup window.

8. The Installed Programs section of the Disk Cleanup window offers to remove programs you no longer need that you previously installed. Clicking the Clean Up button in the Installed Programs section produces the Add or Remove Programs window, such as the one shown in Figure 19.6.

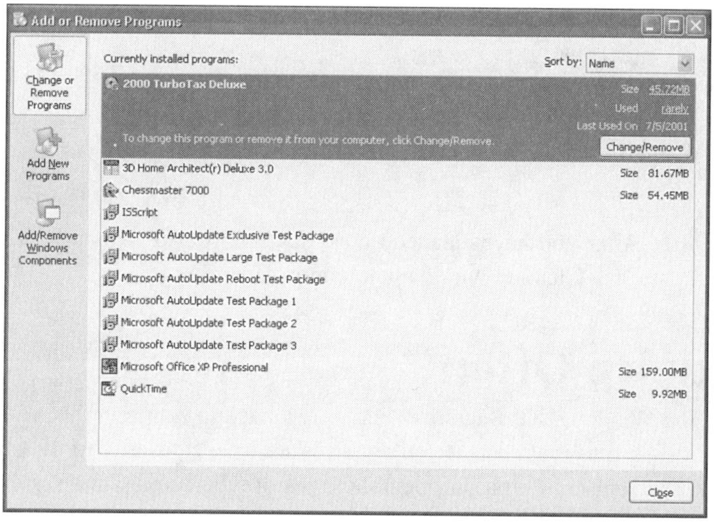

FIGURE 19.6

You might be able to remove some application programs that you no longer use to gain disk space.

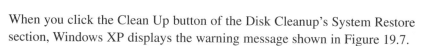

To remove a program, click to highlight that program's entry in the window and click the Add/Remove button that appears. The program's uninstall process will begin and remove the application from your system. (Hour 8, "Installing Programs with Windows XP," explains in more detail the benefits and pitfalls of application installation and removal.) After the application is removed, you'll be returned to the Disk Cleanup window.

9. The System Restore section of the Disk Cleanup window enables you to remove your most recent system restore point. As Hour 20, "Tinkering with the Advanced System Tools," explains, you can take a snapshot of your Windows XP system before installing new hardware and software and return to that former state if the installation goes awry and causes other problems to occur. If you want to forego the ability to restore your system to a previously working state, you can remove all the stored system restore states except for the most recent state.

Unless you've installed several new hardware devices recently and are having trouble with your system, you often can safely remove all but the most recent restoration point.

When you click the Clean Up button of the Disk Cleanup's System Restore section, Windows XP displays the warning message shown in Figure 19.7.

19

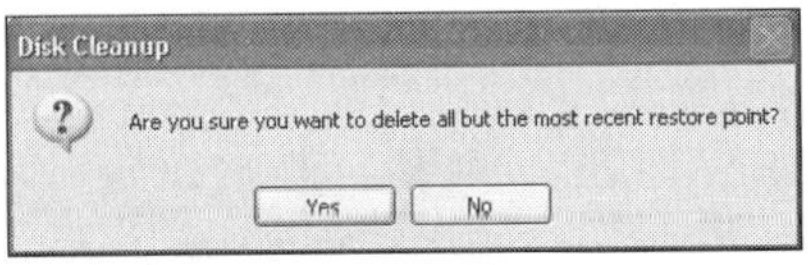

FIGURE **19.7**
Disk Cleanup ensures that you want to remove all but the most recent system restoration points.

10. After you have cleaned up as much of your disk as possible, you can close the Disk Cleanup window and continue working.

Back Up Often

The Windows XP Backup program is a backup program that you can use to save copies of disk files that protect you against data loss. If your hard disk breaks down, once you fix or replace it, you will be able to restore the backup and resume your work. You may have to install Windows XP first if the disk was your C: drive. Without Backup, you would have to try to recreate the entire disk drive, which is often impossible, because you will not have a copy of every transaction and document that you've created.

> The Windows XP Backup program both creates and restores backups.

The first time you back up, back up your entire disk drive. Once you back up the entire disk, you then can make subsequent daily or weekly backups of only those files that you've added or changed since the most recent backup.

Backup can compress files while backing them up so that you can back up large disk drives to other disks or tapes that would not normally be able to hold all the data. With compression, the backup should take less time and make the backups easier to do.

Backup lets you select which files you want to back up so that you can make a special backup of a few selected files. Backup can create a full backup of your entire disk drive or an *incremental backup*, which backs up only the files that have changed since the most recent backup. Backup also lets you direct restored files to a different drive or directory from where they originated.

Take your home backup files with you to work every day and bring your work's backup files home each night. If a terrible disaster happens at home or at work, such as a fire, you will be able to restore your data, because the backups would not be destroyed.

You must decide which medium you want to store the backup to. Backup creates back-ups on the following medium:

- Network storage, hard disks, and floppy disks
- High-density disks such as Zip drives
- QIC 40, 80, 3010 and other kinds of backup tapes

Today most people will back up regularly to higher-capacity non-diskette devices. The following To Do task explains how to use Windows XP Backup.

To Do: Using Microsoft Backup

1. Select the Start menu's All Programs, Accessories, System Tools, Backup. You'll see Figure 19.8's opening window.

FIGURE 19.8

Get ready to back up your files.

The Backup or Restore wizard walks you through the process of backing up or restoring from a backup.

2. Click Next and select the first option, Back up files and settings.

3. Click Next. Select what you want to back up. If you keep all your data files in the My Documents folder, you may want to select the first option to backup only these files and your user account's settings. If, instead, you want to back up multiple disk

▼   locations, select the option labeled, Let me choose what to back up. The rest of this task assumes you want to back up just your My Documents folder and system settings for your user account.

4. Select Next. The backup program needs to know where you want to back up to. Select a disk drive, tape drive, or network storage option, and then type a name for the backup.

5. When you click Next, you'll see a window such as the one in Figure 19.9 that reviews the backup you have just specified. To start the backup process, simply ▲   click Finish.

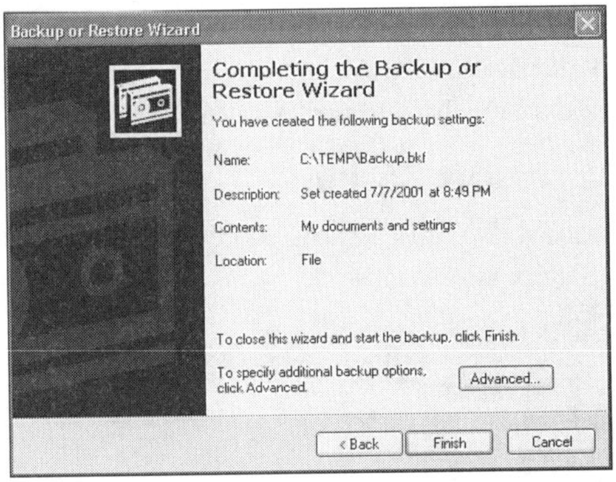

Figure 19.9
You have now specified the backup settings.

Backup or Restore Wizard

Completing the Backup or Restore Wizard

You have created the following backup settings:

Name: C:\TEMP\Backup.bkf

Description: Set created 7/7/2001 at 8:49 PM

Contents: My documents and settings

Location: File

To close this wizard and start the backup, click Finish.

To specify additional backup options, click Advanced.   [Advanced...]

[< Back] [Finish] [Cancel]

> When you want to restore from a backup, start the Backup program and select `Restore files and settings`. Backup asks where the backup files reside that you want to restore before restoring the backup.

Backup contains a complete set of backup, restore, and comparison features. The backup jobs make backing up regularly easy to do, because you can create backup jobs that describe different backup settings and open whatever backup job you want to use.

Summary

This hour described two of Windows XP's disk utilities: Disk Defragmenter and Disk Cleanup. Both work to make your disk drives operate faster and with more disk space. If your disk drive begins to slow down, run Windows XP's Disk Defragmenter to eliminate the empty holes in your drive so that your disk access runs at top-notch performance. If you find yourself needing more free disk space than you currently have, run Disk Cleanup to see if you can remove some unwanted clutter.

Take it upon yourself to be responsible for your applications and data. Computers often work reliably for years but you're still a possible victim at any unexpected moment of a disk drive failure. A copy of your files means the difference between returning to your regular routine quickly or spending hours, days, and weeks trying to restore your system to its original state.

Q&A

Q How often should I defragment my hard disk?

A You should defragment every week or so. Depending on the amount of file accessing you do, you might need to defragment more or less often. If you notice your disk speed slowing down a bit, you'll find that defragmenting speeds the access process somewhat.

Q Which kind of backup, a full or differential backup, should I perform?

A The first time you back up you should make a full backup. After you make one full backup, you can make subsequent differential backups of only those files that have changed. Be sure that you save the full backup, however, so that you can restore everything if you need to. If you have a disk failure, you'll restore the entire full backup and then restore each differential backup set of files.

After you've made several differential backups, you might want to make a full backup once again. By making a full backup every once in a while, you will be able to reuse your differential tapes or disks.

19

Workshop

The quiz and exercise questions are designed to test your knowledge of the material covered in this hour. The answers are in Appendix C, "Answers to Quizzes."

Quiz

1. What is the difference between Disk Defragmenter and Disk Cleanup?

2. *True or false*: Disk Defragmenter can remove unneeded files from your disk.

3. *True or false*: If you run Disk Cleanup regularly, you'll never have to defragment your disk.

4. Why does your hard disk access speed improve when you regularly use Disk Defragmenter?

5. What is the difference between a full backup and an incremental backup?

Exercises

1. Run Disk Defragmenter on all your computer's disk drives and defragment any drive that Windows XP deems requires it.

2. Run Disk Cleanup on your PC. Click the More Options tab to inspect areas of your disk drive that might need to be cleaned up.

Hour **20**

Tinkering with the Advanced System Tools

Windows XP works well but, like a well-made automobile, it sometimes gets overloaded with work, gets confused, and slows down. When your operating system slows down, your entire computer system slows down because the operating system controls everything else that happens. Windows provides system programs that enable you to monitor Windows XP's performance and determine where bottlenecks reside.

Periodically, you can schedule Windows programs to keep your system running smoothly even when you're not at the PC. By monitoring your system files, properly analyzing problems that occur, and scheduling system checking programs to run when you're away, you can help ensure that your system runs in top condition and that you don't have to remember to run important tasks.

In this hour, you will

- Adjust your system to run at its peak performance
- Learn how technical support technicians can use your system snapshot to correct problems

- Monitor your system's usage from the Task Manager window
- Schedule tasks to run when you're away from your PC
- Manage your scheduled tasks
- Use System Restore to return your system to a previous state

Check Your System

You can ensure that Windows XP runs at its peak performance by adjusting the operating system to match the way you use your computer. The System Properties window enables you to adjust the following system attributes:

- Visual effects: The movement and efficiency of icons and other screen elements that Windows XP uses
- Processor scheduling: The method by which your *CPU* (*Central Processing Unit*), the chip inside your computer that processes data and follows instructions, assigns priorities
- Memory usage: The utilization of your computer's memory during program execution
- Virtual memory: An area of disk space set aside for Windows XP's scratchpad use

You adjust these settings from the System Properties window as the following To Do item explains.

To Do: Making System Adjustments

1. Display the Control Panel.
2. Click Switch to Classic View if the Control Panel displays its options as categories instead of individual icons.
3. Select System.
4. Click the Advanced tab to display the advanced System Properties window shown in Figure 20.1.
5. Click the Settings button in the Performance section to display the Performance Options window shown in Figure 20.2.
6. Look through the scrolling list of items and you'll see all the visual features available in Windows XP that occur as you use your computer. For example, you can request that Windows XP animate the opening and closing of windows. Instead of instantly opening and closing them, the windows seem to open out of the taskbar when you maximize them, coming up and going together before your eyes in a cartoon-like (but quick) fashion. Other effects are available such as shadows that

FIGURE 20.1

You can adjust operating system performance from the System Properties window.

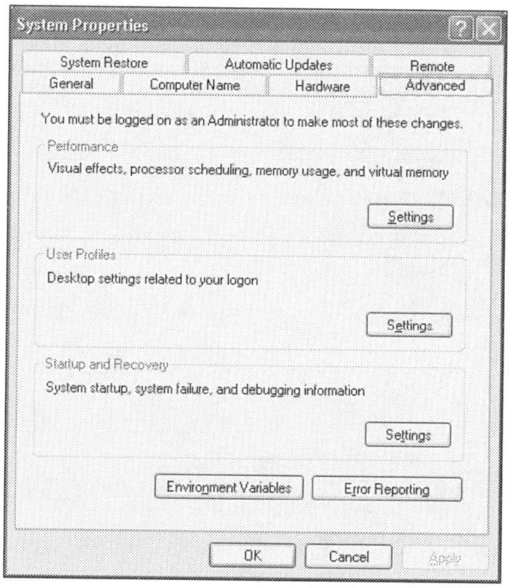

FIGURE 20.2

The Performance Options determine how your computer performs visually.

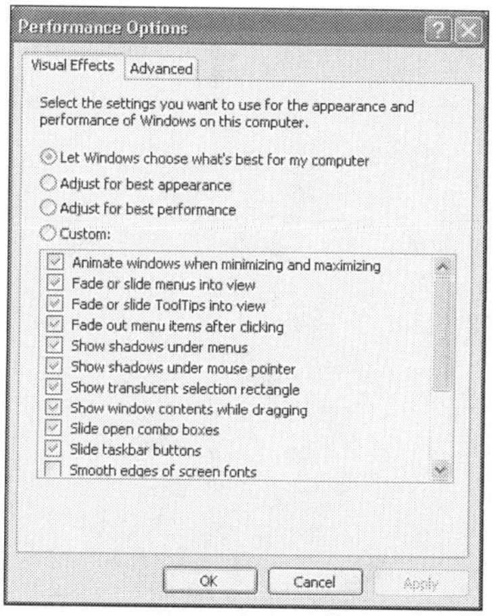

20

can appear beneath open menus and the mouse pointer, window contents that move with a window when you drag the window, and list boxes that slide open instead of dropping down instantly.

You can quickly check all these visual options by clicking the Adjust for best appearance button. Be warned, though, that if you do, your Windows XP performance will not be optimized. Each of these visual effects add up to make Windows XP work extra hard every time something happens on the screen. If you turn all these options off, as you can quickly do by pressing the Adjust for best performance

▼

button, you gain better use of your system because all the special visual effects go away. The downside is that you lose some of the friendlier aspects of the operating system.

7. To make your system perform at a good rate and to maintain some of the visual effects you prefer, you'll have to scroll through the list and check and uncheck the options you want and don't want. Over time, you'll return to this window to make further adjustments as you get used to Windows XP's visual effects.

> To return to Windows XP's default settings, click the Restore Defaults button.

8. You can adjust further performance options by clicking the Advanced tab in the Performance Options dialog box. This displays the advanced performance options shown in Figure 20.3.

FIGURE 20.3

You can control more advanced system options.

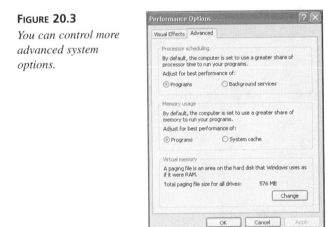

9. The Processor scheduling section determines how Windows performs when you run multiple programs simultaneously. Only one program can run in the *foreground* at one time, and that's the program that is active and whose window's title bar is blue and top-most on your screen. The other programs, running in the *background*, still run but with fewer CPU cycles. The general idea is that the program in which you're actively working in, the foreground program, is the program you want to give the most processor attention to. If you want to more equally share computer-processing time between both foreground and background programs, click the Background services option.

▼

▼

10. The Memory usage section determines how memory is doled out to foreground and background programs. By default, the foreground programs are given a larger slice of memory in which to run more freely. If you want to devote more attention to a program you're running in a background window, check the option labeled System cache.

11. The Virtual memory section determines how Windows XP utilizes the virtual memory area of your disk drive. Virtual memory is disk memory that Windows XP sometimes offloads work to as a temporary holding place. When you click the Change button to change the amount of memory given to the system's virtual memory, the Virtual Memory dialog box shown in Figure 20.4 opens. Keep in mind that the default setting for the virtual memory size is generally the best setting to keep so you'll rarely, if ever, have to change your virtual memory setting.

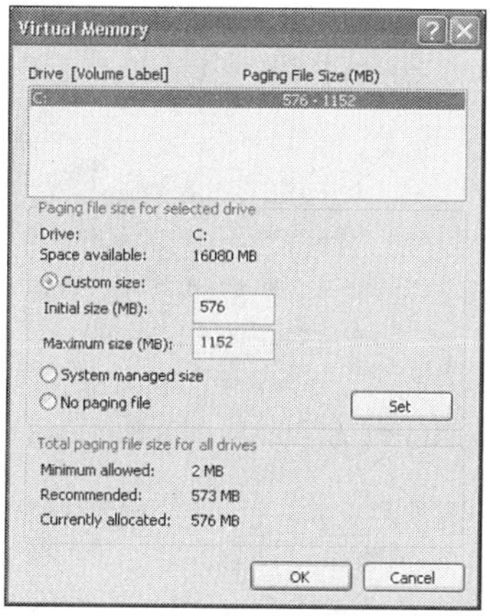

FIGURE 20.4

Virtual memory determines how much disk space Windows XP can utilize for a work area.

Generally, the recommended memory, shown at the bottom of the Virtual Memory window, is the value you should keep. Nevertheless, if you have ample disk space and want to devote more space to the system's virtual memory, you can adjust the top value of the virtual memory range in the Maximum size text box. If you are running out of disk space, you can lower this and the Initial size values.

▲

20

Generally, you should leave your Virtual Memory settings alone. If you're so low on disk space that you must lower your virtual memory usage, you will notice a dramatic system degradation and Windows will often slow to a crawl—if Windows even continues to work. If you ever make a change to your virtual memory settings, it's best to change the maximum values to allow Windows XP more room to work. But even too much virtual memory can cause Windows to slow down because so much time is spent managing all the virtual memory. The optimum value is almost always best to keep unless you read of a technical reason why a different value might make a difference in your performance.

Dr. Watson, Come Right Away

Although you won't find it on the Windows XP menus, a program called Dr. Watson can help you trace severe problems that occur when you run some programs. When you start the Dr. Watson system utility program, the program sits in the background (a new taskbar icon appears) and waits for a problem.

Although Windows XP is far more stable than previous Windows versions, problems can still occur. If your system freezes and you've started Dr. Watson, Dr. Watson will record all pertinent system information right before the error occurred. In other words, if your system freezes or displays a serious system error, you can restart your PC and read the log file that Dr. Watson will have created right before the problem occurred. Dr. Watson is not foolproof; some systems crash and freeze and Dr. Watson cannot always catch the problem.

Dr. Watson's log file will describe the error and often will suggest corrected action you can use to keep the problem from reappearing. If you cannot fix the problem, you can contact Microsoft's Technical Support staff on its Web site (www.microsoft.com), sending your Dr. Watson log file. The support staff can use Dr. Watson's log to diagnose and correct the problem.

Unlike most programs on your computer, Dr. Watson does not appear on the Windows XP menu. Therefore, you must start Dr. Watson from the Start menu's Run command as the following To Do item illustrates.

To Do: Running Dr. Watson

1. Display the Start menu's Run command.

2. At the Run prompt, type **Drwtsn32** and click OK to start the system program. After a brief pause, the Dr. Watson for Windows dialog box appears, as shown in Figure 20.5.

FIGURE 20.5

Dr. Watson helps you detect system problems.

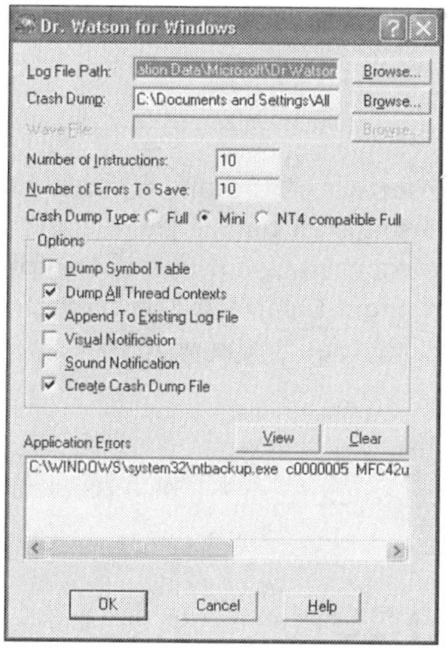

3. After starting Dr. Watson, you can start your other programs and continue working. At any time, you can click over the Dr. Watson taskbar icon to display the Dr. Watson window and adjust settings there. Be warned, however, that generally only computer technicians will know what to request other than the default Dr. Watson values. If you are familiar with routine program debugging, you will be better acquainted with Dr. Watson's options.

   After you start Dr. Watson, it saves a snapshot log of your computer's memory and other settings when a system error or application error occurs. The log is created based on the system information available at the time of the problem.

> Dr. Watson creates a listing of your PC's system information at a single instance in time—hence the term *snapshot*. Dr. Watson's log shows up to ten of the most recent system snapshots taken automatically due to errors or in response to your request.

20

4. To view the Dr. Watson log, you can use the WordPad text editor to load the file. The path to the log file is always listed at the top of Dr. Watson's initial window. The default path is as follows:

```
C:\Documents and Settings\All Users\Application Data\Microsoft\Dr Watson
```

The log file's name is Drwtsn32.log, and you can locate this file after an error occurs (and possibly after a required reboot if the error forces your system to freeze) at the previously listed path.

> If installing a particular software program seems to cause a freeze-up problem, force a system snapshot before you install the program and then let Dr. Watson record another snapshot upon attempting the install. The software's support staff might be able to use the before-and-after Dr. Watson snapshots to determine the problem.

▲   5. Click Dr. Watson's Close button to close the dialog box.

Using the Task Manager

Windows XP includes a new *Task Manager* program that shows you what's happening in your computer and specifies where memory and CPU is being utilized the most. Although the use of the Task Manager is fairly advanced (as are many areas of the Dr. Watson program), the Task Manager does enable you to stop programs that have frozen up and to monitor applications that might be consuming more memory than you want to let them have.

> Previous versions of Windows displayed a window similar to the Task Manager's first dialog box page when users pressed the Ctrl+Alt+Delete sequence to reboot their computers. Ctrl+Alt+Delete displayed a Task Manager-like window that showed all currently running programs and the user could either stop one of the programs or shut down the computer completely. He could also press Ctrl+Alt+Delete a second time to restart the computer. As you will see in the next To Do item, the Windows Task Manager provides far more options.

To Do: Using the Task Manager

1. Press Ctrl+Alt+Delete to display the Task Manager, similar to the one shown in Figure 20.6.

2. The Task Manager's Applications page shows all currently running programs. You can click a program to highlight it and click the End Task button to close any running program. Always attempt to close every program through the program's

menus before resorting to the Task Manager to ensure that all your data is saved properly. Some programs, however, seem to get confused and freeze up, requiring you to resort to the Task Manager to close them.

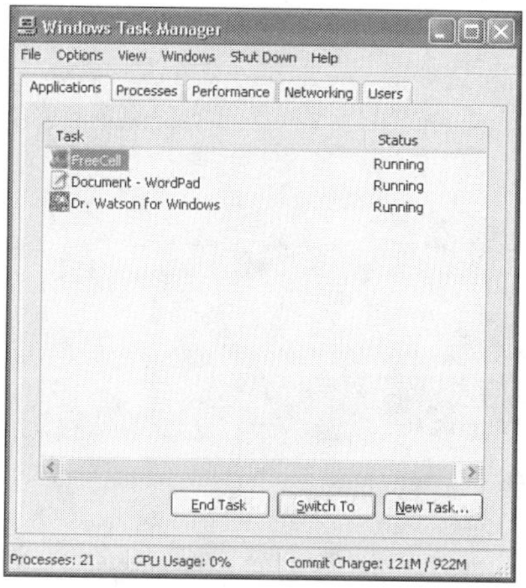

FIGURE 20.6

Use the Task Manager to monitor running programs and resources.

3. When you click the Processes tab, the Task Manager shows all currently loaded *processes*. A process can be an application program, but unlike the Task Manager's Application page, the Processes page shows all operating system tasks that are currently running. That includes all foreground and background processes, the Windows XP processes that control the taskbar, program launching, and everything else that Windows must keep track of. Only in extreme circumstances should a knowledgeable user cancel a running process. Inadvertently stopping a critical operating system process could cause Windows XP to become unstable.

4. Click the Performance tab to display the Performance graphs shown in Figure 20.7.

The Performance page shows you how much CPU time is currently being consumed. If you are running too many programs and your system seems to become too slow, you can check the Task Manager's Performance page to determine if you are overusing CPU cycles. If so, you can then click the Processes tab to determine which process is consuming the most time. If the process comes from a program you've started, and you can do without that program currently, you can switch to that program and close it. Otherwise, if you need the results of the top-heavy program, you might want to close other program windows to devote more CPU time to the important one.

20

▼   The Memory Usage History chart shows how much of your available computer
           memory is used. You can perform a task, such as sorting a large database, and then
           switch to the Task Manager to see if you have ample memory resources. If the
           program consumes too much memory, you run the risk of Windows running out of
           memory and having to shut down. Fortunately, Windows XP manages memory bet-
           ter than previous versions of Windows, and Windows XP will not have the same
           memory constraints that many other Windows versions ran into after running for a
           few hours.

Figure 20.7
*See your CPU and
memory usage
graphically.*

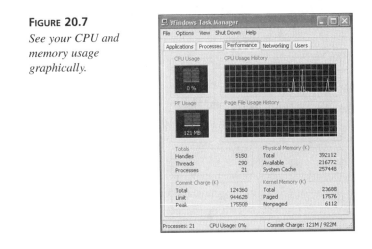

5. Click the Networking and Users tabs to see the remaining two Task Manager
   pages. If you're on a networked system, the Network page shows how many
   resources your network connection is consuming; the Users page shows the status
▲ of each user who might currently be using Windows XP.

Scheduling System Tasks

Throughout this 24-hour tutorial, you've seen numerous tools that enable you to manage
your Windows system and fine-tune its work environment. Hour 18, "Giving Windows
XP a Tune-Up," explains how to update your system to the latest files and download
Windows corrections and upgrades when Microsoft releases them. Hour 19, "Managing
Your Hard Drives," discusses how disk drive tools keep your disk drives running at their
most efficient state. In addition, proper system procedures require that you back up your
operating system settings often, as this hour explains later. Restoring your operating system to its best state in the event of system failure requires recent system backups.

A Windows program called Scheduled Tasks enables you to schedule these system programs as well as any other program to run at preset time periods. You can defragment and back up your hard disk every morning at 4:00 a.m. if you want. You can log into the Internet and retrieve e-mail before work, during lunch, and before you leave work.

> If you use data files, such as word processor documents or database files for scheduled tasks, those data files' parent programs, such as Word or Access, automatically start at the scheduled time and load the data files automatically.

When you designate Scheduled Tasks to run when you start Windows, Scheduled Tasks waits in the background until the time comes to run one of its programs. If you're using your PC when the program runs, you won't be bothered. If, however, a program that you schedule tries to use a data file that you are editing, the Scheduled Tasks program will be unable to function and will display an error or shut down.

> One of Scheduled Tasks' strengths is its scheduling capabilities. You don't have to designate a specific day that a Scheduled Tasks program runs. Instead, you can specify that Scheduled Tasks runs a program (or a group of programs) daily, weekly, monthly, or when certain events take place, such as when you start or shut down your PC.

Scheduling tasks to run is simple. After you set up Scheduled Tasks, you can easily modify the times or dates your scheduled programs run. In addition, you can easily add and remove scheduled programs as the following To Do item demonstrates.

To Do: Using Scheduled Tasks

▼ To Do

1. Select the Start menu's All Programs, Accessories, System Tools, Scheduled Tasks program. Figure 20.8 shows a typical Scheduled Tasks window. If your taskbar shows the Scheduled Tasks icon, you can double-click that icon to more quickly open the Scheduled Tasks program. (Even when you start Scheduled Tasks for the first time, the Scheduled Tasks window might contain some entries.)

2. Double-click the first entry, called Add Scheduled Task. The Scheduled Task Wizard begins, which enables you to set up a scheduled program. Click Next to see the list of programs you can set up with the wizard as shown in Figure 20.9.

   If the program you want to schedule does not appear in the list, click the Browse button to select a program from the folders that appear.

▼

20

FIGURE 20.8

*These programs will
run at preset times.*

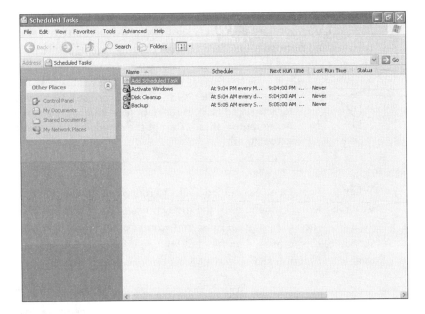

FIGURE 20.9

*The Scheduled Task
Wizard gives you a list
of common programs
to schedule.*

3. Walk through the wizard and set up Disk Cleanup to run weekly. The final wizard dialog box gives you the option of setting up program options available for most programs you schedule. For example, you can set up the scheduled task to stop after running for a certain period of time in some cases. This dialog box appears after you select the check box labeled Open Advanced Properties for This Task When I Click Finish.

4. To change a scheduled task's scheduled time, open that task (by double-clicking it) to display a dialog box that enables you to change the scheduled properties. Click

on the Schedule tab to display the Schedule page shown in Figure 20.10 and make any change you want to make. As you can see, Windows gives you complete control over a task's schedule, even letting you omit weekend days from the schedule. Close the window.

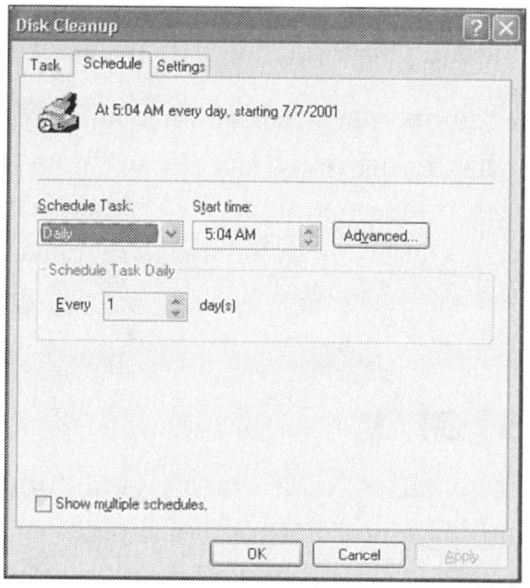

FIGURE 20.10

Change the schedule for a task to suit your requirements for the program.

Click the option labeled Show multiple schedules to see a drop-down list box where you can enter two or more separate schedules for the same task. For example, you might want to run the same program daily before work and at noon.

5. To delete a scheduled task, such as the one you added earlier, select the task and press the Delete key. Scheduled Tasks sends the scheduled task to the Recycle Bin where you can retrieve the task, if you change your mind, until you empty the Recycle Bin.

6. To turn off an individual scheduled task without removing the task, open the task by clicking or double-clicking on the task's entry and uncheck the Enabled option. The task remains idle in the task list until you check Enabled or until you remove the task from the list.

7. You can temporarily turn off all scheduled tasks without having to change each one individually by selecting Advanced, Stop Using Task Scheduler from the menu.

20

▼

If you select Advanced, Pause Task Scheduler, Scheduled Tasks stops until you select Advanced, Continue Task Scheduler or until you subsequently reboot your PC.

▲ 8. Select File, Close to terminate your Scheduled Tasks session.

The Scheduled Tasks program can operate when you are not at your computer. Defragment and back up your disk in the middle of the night so that your system isn't slowed during the day by those routine operations. Schedule certain programs to run when you start or shut down Windows. Scheduled Tasks gives you complete control over your scheduled tasks.

Using System Restore

The System Restore system tool enables you to restore your computer system to a previous state. Perhaps you are installing a new program or a piece of hardware such as a second hard disk. If the installation goes smoothly, you won't need to revert to the original system state. If, however, a problem occurs, the Windows XP's System Restore feature enables you to return to the exact state of the computer before you performed the installation. Even better, you can undo and redo the restore process so that you can go back and forth between previous system states until you locate the one that works best or that enables you to determine the cause of any problems you might be having.

The System Restore program keeps track of all system changes you make as the result of adding hardware or software or when you change settings. When you want to restore a particular computer state, you have three ways to do so:

1. Restore to a particular event, such as the installation of a new hard disk.
2. Restore to a system checkpoint. Windows XP automatically saves system checkpoints throughout the day and keeps a rolling two-weeks' worth at any time. If you are unsure of an event that caused your current system problem, you can keep restoring to previous system checkpoints until your computer begins to behave normally once again.
3. Restore to a particular date.

If you want to restore several iterations at one time, you can do so. System Restore is intelligent enough to know what not to restore, however. System Restore will not change any data files you've saved into the user's My Documents folder, which is a folder often used for data files. In addition, if System Restore runs across a data file that it recognizes, such as a database file, and that file is not inside the My Documents folder, System Restore will leave that data file alone.

> If you want to keep System Restore from changing a particular file but the file is not a registered data file, temporarily move the file to your My Documents folder before starting the System Restore process.

The following To Do item explains how to use the System Restore program.

To Do: Using System Restore

▲ To Do

1. Select the Start menu's All Programs, Accessories, System Tools, System Restore option. Windows opens the System Restore program window as shown in Figure 20.11.

FIGURE 20.11
Use the System Restore program to revert to a previous Windows state.

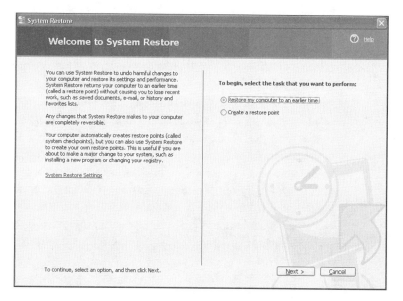

2. Click Next to continue the restore process.
3. System Restore displays a calendar with all possible system restore dates boldfaced. When you click one of the days, the System Restore program displays all the checkpoints performed that day, even those triggered by events such as a hardware change, in the right window.

20

   4. Click on a checkpoint to select it for the restore.

   5. Click Next and Windows XP begins the process. Sometimes a restore can take a few minutes to appear and you might see your computer rebooting one or more times. Eventually, your PC will resume the exact state it was in at the point of the restore's checkpoint. The only exception might be data files you've created between that point and now that will still be intact.

> When you restore, Windows restores your system as it was at the time of the checkpoint. Therefore, if you've scheduled backups, changed your Start menu, and made other system changes, you will lose those changes.

   6. To reverse a system restore, simply start System Restore and click the option labeled Undo My Last Restoration. Windows XP completely reverses the status of the restore you last performed. During the writing of this chapter, I accidentally selected a restore state back to the early days of my Windows XP installation. I lost all my customized system settings, my scheduled tasks, and even Microsoft Word! Frantically hoping the bugs were out of the Undo feature, I clicked the Undo option and waited. A few minutes later, my system was right back where it was supposed to be; Windows XP had restored the restore!

   7. Although Windows XP constantly monitors your computer usage and saves restore points at random intervals and every time you install and remove new hardware and software, you can always specify a restore state yourself. For example, if you're currently satisfied with your system and want to save a restore point now before you change several system settings that would otherwise be difficult to undo, start the System Restore program and select the option labeled Create a Restore Point. Click Next to assign a name for the restore point. When you then click the Create button, the System Restore program will save your system's information so that, in the future, you can return to that point.

Summary

This hour described several system tools you can run to manage and monitor your disk, memory, and other system resources. You can display statistics about your memory, disk, and system usage. Windows handles resources better than previous versions of Windows, but these tools give you additional ways to monitor the usage.

Dr. Watson gives you a perfect snapshot of your system, either when you request the snapshot or when trouble occurs. The Dr. Watson program records vital system information when system errors cause your system to shut down so that technical support people can diagnose the problem better. Sometimes, Dr. Watson's log files offer suggestions you can try to eliminate the problem.

You don't have to remember to run routine tasks because the Scheduled Tasks program runs them for you. You control all aspects of all automated programs that you schedule so that important system check-up and fine-tuning take place when you're not using your PC.

The System Restore helps cure many ills. If your system is working fine one day but erratically the next, run System Restore and revert your system to a previous time when things ran well.

Q&A

Q Should I use Dr. Watson, the Task Manager, or the System Restore when a certain program keeps causing my PC to freeze up?

A Use all three! If you can duplicate the problem consistently, the Task Manager's graph settings can help you locate resource problems before they get out of hand. You might be running out of memory right before you attempt to start a program that pushes your memory limits over the edge. Dr. Watson is the program that helps you trace problems that have already occurred. When your system freezes, you can be assured that Dr. Watson recorded all your system's information right before the crash so that you or a technical support representative can eliminate the problem. If you cannot correct the problem, you might need to restore your system to a previously working state with System Restore.

Q Does my PC have to be turned on for scheduled programs to run?

A Yes, but you can keep your monitor turned off to save on your electric bill. The monitor consumes the majority of power in a typical PC system, so you can turn off your monitor when you're not using the PC but leave your PC running so that you won't have to restart your PC the next time you need to use the computer. If you have a laser printer, you should turn it off as well because laser printers also consume a lot of power.

20

Workshop

The quiz and exercise questions are designed to test your knowledge of the material covered in this hour. The answers are in Appendix C, "Answers to Quizzes."

Quiz

1. Which program graphically shows you memory and CPU usage?
2. How might you use the Task Manager to determine if your PC needs more memory?
3. Why does Dr. Watson provide the option of taking a system snapshot?
4. Which system program enables you to revert your computer to a previous time?
5. What is the difference between Dr. Watson and System Restore?

Exercises

1. Run Task Manager and click the Performance tab to display the resource graphs. Click the window's Minimize button to minimize the window. After you work on your computer for a few hours, click the Task Manager's taskbar button to see how your computer resources are holding up. If resources approach 80%, you should close your open programs and restart Windows XP. Doing so will help prevent your system from freezing up as it can do when resources run low.

2. The next time you want to install a program, first use System Restore. Install the program and then run System Restore to revert your PC to its pre-install state. You should see no traces of the program except, perhaps, a data folder. System Restore is better than an uninstallation routine because System Restore not only uninstalls software but also ensures that Windows XP is untouched by any of the software's stray programs that sometimes stick around long after you've attempted to uninstall the program.

PART VI
Having Fun at Nighttime

Hour

HOUR 21

Using Media Player

One of the most interesting aspects of Windows XP is also the most fun. That is, Windows XP's support for multimedia. You can play audio and video files, audio CDs, and download films from the Internet. If what you want involves graphics and sound, Windows XP comes to your aid. In this hour, you'll learn about Windows Media Player, an advanced multimedia playing device that plays just about any multimedia content you wish.

In this hour, you will

- Watch how AutoPlay eliminates any CD-ROM startup commands on your part
- Master the Windows Media Player program
- Learn why Windows keeps tabs on the Windows Media Manager

Introducing the Windows Media Player

With Windows XP, a Windows multimedia system takes charge of virtually every aspect of your computer's sound and video. Consider just some of the multimedia-based capabilities of the Windows Media Player:

- Plays audio CDs
- Copies audio CDs
- Organizes your entire library of audio and video files
- Generates *playlists*, lists of your favorite songs no matter their source
- Plays Internet-based video and sound, including the *de facto* standard format of digital audio, MP3
- Supports *streaming video* and *streaming audio*, the process of playing video and sound clips from the Internet as they download to your computer from the Internet instead of having to wait for the entire clip to download before playing
- Downloads music on your computer to a portable music player, such as an MP3 player
- Plays high-quality DVD movies on your DVD-ROM drive if your computer has one
- Automatically self-upgrades the Windows Media Player when an update is available on the Internet

Throughout the following sections, the Windows Media Player takes center stage. Instead of a comprehensive study of every aspect of the Windows Media Player, this hour focuses on the primary tasks that users generally want to perform with the Windows Media Player. The Windows Media Player is only a means to an end; the program is much less important than the content, the *media*, such as your music and videos.

Using AutoPlay

AutoPlay is one of the Windows multimedia capabilities. If you've ever played a game or an audio CD in your computer's CD-ROM drive, you'll appreciate AutoPlay very much indeed. AutoPlay automatically inspects your audio CD or CD-ROM as soon as you place it in the computer's CD-ROM drive. AutoPlay then does one of four things:

- Starts the installation on your CD-ROM if you've yet to install the program that resides on the CD-ROM
- Begins the CD's program if the program is already installed
- Begins playing the DVD if you've inserted a DVD into a DVD-ROM drive
- Starts the audio CD player if it's an audio CD

Microsoft knows that putting a CD or DVD into your CD-ROM drive almost always means that you want to do something with that CD. Of course, you might be inserting the CD into the drive for later use, but that's rare; most of the time when you insert a CD, you're ready to do something with it right away.

If you insert a CD but want to bypass the AutoPlay feature you can do so. Perhaps you want to access the CD later but insert the disc now so that it's ready. To bypass AutoPlay, press Shift as you insert the CD. Keep holding Shift until the drive's light goes out. Windows will not start AutoPlay.

To Do: Using AutoPlay to Play Music from an Audio CD

1. Find an audio CD that contains music you want to hear.

2. Place the CD into the CD-ROM drive and close the door or push the CD-ROM drive's Insert button to close the CD-ROM drive.

3. Windows immediately recognizes that you've inserted an audio CD into the CD-ROM drive and begins playing the music. Figure 21.1 shows the Windows Media Player when the first song begins.

FIGURE 21.1

The Windows Media Player plays the CD and displays the CD's information.

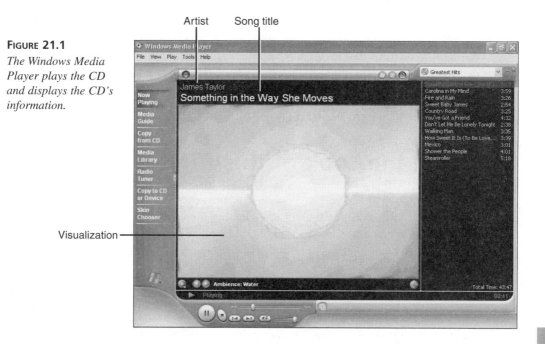

4. Windows Media Player immediately loads and, if you have Internet access, goes to the Internet to look for the CD's artist, title, and song list. If you are not currently connected to the Internet, you can retrieve such information later. Windows Media Player scans your CD, looks for unique identifying information, and searches the

21

▼   Internet where song lists are stored for the majority of CDs published in the world. This magnificent database of audio tracks puts the song list on your computer so that you can later store the CD, or individual selections from the CD, to your hard disk, and you never have to enter the track or artist information. Some CDs will download with art that might appear in the center of the Windows Media Player as the CD plays.

> After Windows XP downloads an audio CD's track information, Windows Media Player never has to search the Internet a second time for that CD. The information stays on your computer for subsequent reference and quicker access if you play the CD again.

The Windows Media Player acts like a physical CD player that you can control by clicking the buttons. It displays Play, Pause, Stop, Eject, Previous, and Next Track buttons, Previous and Forward time buttons, and volume and mute controls. Move the cursor over the buttons on the Windows Media Player's window to see a pop-up help box that describes each button.

5. Click the Pause button. Click the Play button. Double-click another song to play a different track on the CD.

▲   6. Select Play, Eject to stop the play and eject the CD.

Changing the Look of the Windows Media Player

You have full control over the look of the Windows Media Player's window. You can shrink the window to a smaller size and click Maximize to once again restore the player to its full-screen mode. Select from the View, Now Playing Tools to select options such as the equalizer shown in Figure 21.2.

You can drag the equalizer controls to change the tones of the music. In addition, double-click over any song to play that song in the playlist.

Besides changing the size of the Windows Media Player, you can change the entire look of the Windows Media Player's screen. *Skin* is the name for a Windows Media Player theme; you can select a skin to match your musical playlist's mood.

FIGURE 21.2

The Windows Media Player provides you with an equalizer so you can control the sound.

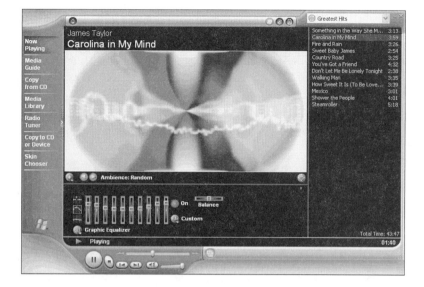

To Do: Changing the Windows Media Player's Skin

1. Restore your Media Player to full-screen if it's not presently maximized.

2. Click the Skin Chooser button to display the list of player skins that you can choose. As you click each skin's title, a preview of that skin appears in the window, as shown in Figure 21.3.

FIGURE 21.3

The Windows Media Player skins can dramatically change the player's appearance.

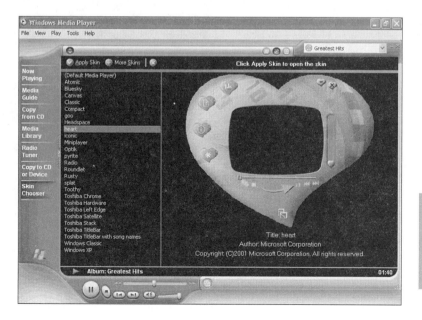

21

3. Double-click any skin for your Windows Media Player to take on the look of that skin. All the Windows Media Player controls appear on the new skin, but the player takes on the theme of the skin.

> The skins never appear when you've maximized your Media Player window. You can download additional skins from the Internet at the Windows Media Player's site available when you click the More Skins button above the skin list.

The Media Guide

The Windows Media Player offers online access to a special Internet site devoted to the Windows Media Player and the types of multimedia that it can play.

Figure 21.4 shows the Windows Media Player's Media Guide. A screen such as this appears, assuming that you have Internet access, when you click the Media Guide button. Microsoft calls the Media Guide a daily online multimedia newspaper that contains news, gossip, and media that relate to the Windows Media Player.

FIGURE 21.4
Check out the Media Player window daily for multimedia news.

CD Audio Extras

When you select View, Now Playing Tools, a list of options appear from which you can select. Depending on the support of the CD's publisher, you can see original album art as shown in Figure 21.5 when you select Media Information. Some publishers provide song lyrics that you can see as the music plays when you select the Lyrics option. At any point, if you click the More button in the Media Information window, Internet Explorer opens to a Web site that details album information about the CD you're currently playing and gives you the opportunity to order other CDs by the same artist.

FIGURE 21.5

The CD Audio window gives you more information, often in a multimedia format, including the original CD case's cover art.

You can even record tracks and the entire CD from the CD Audio window, as you'll see in the following To Do item.

To Do: Recording CD Tracks

1. Click the Copy from CD button on the left side of the Windows Media Player.

2. Click to check every track you want to record. Uncheck those tracks you don't want to record.

3. Click Copy Music and the tracks you've selected will record, along with the track information such as title and artist. The music plays and is recorded to your folder named My Music located in the My Documents folder. To organize your files, Windows Media Player creates a folder for the artist, with all albums you've

21

recorded for that artist in their own subfolders, and individual files inside those folders named with the actual track names. Windows Media Player stores the track files in the default Windows Media Player format with the .WMA filename extension.

> You can change options related to the Windows Media Player, such as the default folder for storing the recorded music, in the Tools, Options menu.

4. After selecting File, Open from the Windows Media Player menu, you can open any music you've stored and select as many songs as you want by holding Ctrl while clicking on the tracks.

> If you see a dialog box such as the one in Figure 21.6, Windows Media Player has determined to employ copy protection so that the music you record can only be played on the computer to which you're currently recording the music. If you check the option labeled Do Not Protect Content, Windows Media Player will make the recording available to any computer to which you copy the file. By copying music for which you own the rights to, you are generally not violating any fair use laws. If, however, you record music and copy that music to multiple computers, you might be in violation of copyright laws.

FIGURE 21.6
Windows Media Player offers to protect your content.

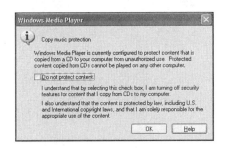

The Media Library and Playlists

To make access to your media files easier, click the Media Library button on the Windows Media Player. The Media Library button produces a tree-structured hierarchy of all your multimedia files, sorted by title, artist, album, or genre. The Media Manager, a database of multimedia content, keeps tabs on your Media Library of files. That way, when you perform a Start, Search, Files or Folders in Media Manager, you'll quickly locate a multimedia file because the Media Manager won't waste time looking where multimedia files are not located.

If you click the New Playlist button, you can name a new playlist, a list of tracks from one or more albums in your music library on your disk. Perhaps you want to create a playlist of your party favorites. Even though the Windows Media Player tracks your recorded CDs by artist, album, and track, your playlists can contain any track from any album on your disk.

A Radio in Your PC

You don't have a radio inside your PC, even though the Windows Media Player includes a button called Radio Tuner. Instead of a radio inside your PC, you have something better: a radio for the entire world.

When you click the Radio Tuner, the Windows Media Player logs onto the Internet and connects you with Microsoft's Radio Tuner Web information, and displays that information inside Media Player as shown in Figure 21.7, and offers you numerous online broadcasts that begin playing in a streaming audio format as soon as you select them. Unlike a real radio, you can listen to what you want when you want. Over time, more stations will be added to your list as the Microsoft Media Player Web site collects more information from stations around the world and makes those stations available to your Media Player's search lists.

FIGURE 21.7

Listen to radio content from around the world.

Downloading to a Portable Player

When you click the Portable Device, the Windows Media Player screen changes to the two-pane Music to Copy and Music on Device screen shown in Figure 21.8. Connect your portable music device to your computer. The device must be able to be plugged dig itally into your computer and cannot be an analog music device, such as a cassette player that has no digital computer connection. Select songs from the drop-down list under Music to Copy, and either drag the songs to the right window or double-click them to send them to the right window, which represents your target portable music device. The space left on your portable device as you copy music updates to let you know how much room is left.

FIGURE 21.8

Select the music you want to download to your portable player.

What About Video?

So far, most of this hour has focused on audio playback and recording. Yet, your computer richly supports the playback of video, as you well know by now. What about video files?

It turns out that little changes between the way you manage video and the way you manage audio files. Use the File, Open option to open a video file as opposed to an audio file, and the Windows Media Player plays the file.

Windows Media Player supports the most common video formats, including those listed in Table 21.1. You won't run across a common video format that Windows Media Player does not support. When you click on a video file on the Web, the Windows Media Player starts automatically and plays that video clip.

> Other types of media players can interfere with Windows Media Player's capability to start automatically. For example, if you have the RealNetworks RealPlayer software installed, RealPlayer might take over the playback of Internet video.

TABLE 21.1   Media Types Supported by Windows Media Player

File Format	Extension
CD Audio	`.cda`
Intel Video	`.ivf`
Mac AIFF	`.aif, .aifc, .aiff`
Microsoft media files	`.asf, .asx, .avi, .wav, .wax, .wma, .wmv, .wvx`
MPEG	`.mpeg, .mp3, .m1v, .mp2, .mp3, .mpa, .mpe, .mpv2, .mp2v, .m3u, .pls`
MIDI	`.mid, .midi, .rmi`
Unix	`.au, .snd`

Playing DVD Movies

When you insert a DVD into your DVD drive, Windows Media Player doesn't miss a beat. Media Player detects the DVD, starts playing the introductory tracks, and you can sit back and watch your movie, controlling the movie just as you would control a regular DVD player sitting atop your TV.

Summary

This hour described how Windows contains integrated multimedia in its windowed multitasking environment. The multimedia capabilities of Windows are advanced and provide smooth video and sound. The Windows Media Player takes charge of your computer's multimedia content and plays, records, and manages your multimedia files and physical CDs.

21

Audio is only part of the multimedia glitz. Full-motion video capabilities enable viewing of video clips by using the Windows Media Player. Depending on the speed of your computer hardware, the video is smooth and provides playback of digital files on your disk as well as digital video you download from the Internet and DVD-ROM movies you watch.

Q&A

Q **What's the purpose of the speaker icon on my taskbar?**

A The speaker icon provides a volume control that's available at all times during your Windows operation. When you double-click the speaker, a multilevel volume control panel opens from which you can adjust the volume of several different types of sound, including your PC's microphone recording level.

Q **Why are there so many kinds of sounds (CD, Wave, FM synthesis, and MIDI)?**

A The different sounds produce different qualities of audio. Your hardware and software determine the kinds of sound that come out of your computer's speakers. Luckily, you probably won't have to worry about the different sounds because Windows recognizes most sound sources and selects the proper playing software accordingly.

Workshop

The quiz and exercise questions are designed to test your knowledge of the material covered in this hour. The answers are in Appendix C, "Answers to Quizzes."

Quiz

1. How can you insert an audio CD into your computer and keep the CD from playing automatically?

2. Where does the Windows Media Player get artist and track information for the CDs you insert?

3. What is a skin?

4. What is a playlist?

5. What do you use to play video clips?

Exercises

1. Log onto the Internet. Locate one of your most obscure CDs, perhaps one you bought at a second-hand shop that contains the best of the early 1950s Frank Sinatra titles. Almost surely, the online database of CD titles will locate that CD and download all the track information to your computer. The database is vast. Although you won't find every CD, and although the CD's information does not always match your expectations, the database is quite accurate.

2. Search the Windows Media Player's radio section and play some stations. You have your choice of all kinds of music or talk 24 hours a day.

21

Hour **22**

Picturing Windows XP Graphics

Windows XP supports digital pictures better than any operating system that has come before it. You can capture, manipulate, and store digital versions of any picture. Although many graphics-related applications let you capture scanned and digital pictures, you no longer have to start your scanner's scanning application to store digital copies of your scanned images. Just make Windows XP do the work after you walk through a simple capture wizard that Windows XP produces.

In addition to capturing and storing images from a digital camera or scanner, you can grab images from Web pages as you surf using Internet Explorer's simple-to-use image toolbar.

In this hour, you will

- Learn why digital images are so popular
- Find uses for the My Pictures window
- Capture digital images from your scanner or digital camera
- Store images to your writeable CD drive

- Send digital images over the Internet to be turned into printed photos
- Use Internet Explorer's image toolbar to work with Web graphics

Reasons for Using Digital Images

Although the picture quality of non-digital film-based photographs called *analog photography* is still superior, digital cameras and scanners are gaining quality all the time and increasing in the *resolution* which is the number of dots per inch that work together to form a picture to make digital pictures sharper than before. Soon, a trained eye will not be able to tell the difference between a digital picture and a picture produced the traditional way.

Given that the quality of digital pictures is still inferior to regular photographed prints, and given that digital cameras are still higher-priced than their film-based counterparts, why is digital photography so important and in such widespread use today?

Several reasons exist for the popularity of digital photography and scanning equipment. More digital cameras are being sold every year, and their popularity has only just started. Here are just a few of the advantages of digital cameras:

- No film is required; just storage chips, such as *memory sticks* or *flash memory*, that you can reuse.
- You can look at a picture through the digital camera's viewfinder right after you snap the picture. Not only can you see the most recent picture you've taken, but you can see *all* the pictures you've taken and stored on the camera's memory chip.
- You can carry several memory chips with you so when you fill up one with pictures, you can replace the full one with an empty one.
- You can copy the memory chip's pictures to your computer, print the photos, or send them to others through e-mail and then erase the memory chip and use it again.
- If you don't like a picture you just took, you can delete it and that space on your storage chip is freed up instantly.
- Unlike film, you have no development costs because you have no film to process. You can pay to have the images on your digital camera's memory chip processed as prints, but you don't have to buy a new chip (unlike film) when you develop the pictures—just reuse the memory chip.
- Web site pictures are easier with digital pictures because you can transfer the pictures directly from your camera to the Web. Put up-to-the-minute pictures on your family's Web page or sell your old memorabilia in an eBay auction that shows pictures of the goods you're selling. With regular prints, you would first have to scan the picture and then upload the scanned image to the Web site.

The key to digital cameras is found in the term *digital*. When you digitize data, such as a picture, you convert that picture into computer-ready data. With a digital camera, the photos are instantly digitized. With a scanner, you can create digital photos of non-digital pictures and other items such as magazine covers that you can scan. Therefore, no discussion on digital photography would be complete without including a little about scanners.

Windows XP is the first operating system from Microsoft to integrate digital image support directly into the operating system.

Not only does Windows XP support digital cameras, but it also supports digital scanners. You can take an old picture produced the traditional way on film and scan it into a digital computer file using a scanner.

The Scanner's TWAIN Compliance

Scanners have adhered to a standard, named the *TWAIN* standard, since 1992. The early and mid 1990s were generally *not* the years that hardware manufacturers adopted standards well among the industry, but the scanner folks got this one right. Most scanners since the earliest ones utilized the TWAIN method of digital capture, making the support of scanners in software much easier and more widespread.

The name *TWAIN* simply comes from Rudyard's Kipling's *The Ballad of East and West*, from the line, " . . . and never the twain shall meet." (The rumor that *TWAIN* stands for *Technology Without an Interesting Name* is false!)

Both PCs and Macs support the TWAIN standard. The bottom line of years of the same standard means that users have more options at lower costs than would be the case if manufacturers did not adopt the same method of scanning.

The Scanners and Cameras Window

The Control Panel has an option named Scanners and Cameras. You'll find the option inside the Printers and Other Hardware category if you have not switched to the Classic view of the Control Panel. If you've installed a scanner or a digital camera or both, an icon will appear that represents your scanner or digital camera hardware as Figure 22.1 shows.

The following To Do item explains how to capture images from your installed digital camera or scanner directly from the Scanners and Cameras window.

FIGURE 22.1

Control your digital picture devices from the Scanners and Cameras window.

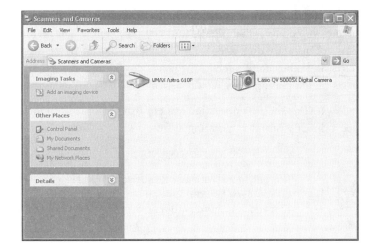

To Do: Capturing Digital Pictures

1. Open the Control Panel's Scanners and Cameras window.

2. Click on the device, scanner, or camera from which you want to capture an image. A wizard begins that walks you through the capturing of an image.

3. Click Next to continue following the wizard's instructions. Figure 22.2 shows a scanning preferences screen from which you control how you want to capture an image. You can request a color scan, a *grayscale* scan (colors appear as shades of gray), a black-and-white scan, or a customized scan where you specify individual color and capture settings.

FIGURE 22.2

Capture from your scanner or digital camera directly from Windows XP.

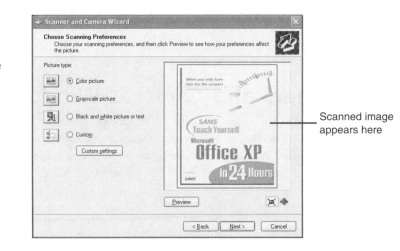

Scanned image appears here

> Click the Preview button to run a quick pass over your scanned image to see approximately how the image will appear after a full scan.

4. Click Next to specify the filename, disk location, and file format such as JPEG or BMP.

5. If you want to put the picture on the Internet, either sent through e-mail or placed on a Web page, click the Yes option next to the question Also Copy These Pictures to the Internet? The wizard will format the picture best for Internet viewing and, on the next screen if you select this option, the wizard asks how to publish to the Internet and connects through the proper Internet service.

6. Click Next and the wizard begins capturing the picture. The wizard saves the picture, unless you changed the location earlier in the wizard, to the My Documents\My Pictures\Picture folder location and displays the folder, with your image enlarged, as shown in Figure 22.3. In the figure, only one item currently exists in the My Documents\My Pictures\Picture folder.

Enlarged version of picture you just captured

FIGURE 22.3
You can now tell Windows XP what you want done with the digital image.

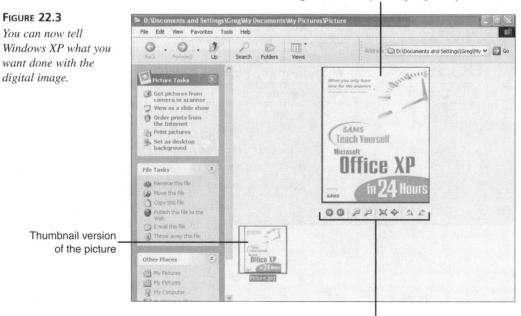

Thumbnail version of the picture

Controls the enlarged image

This example uses a scanned picture to capture the image, but the steps are similar if you use a digital camera instead. The next section explains some of the ways you can use the My Pictures window to manage your digital images.

Working Inside My Pictures

Although your captured image will appear, by default, in the My Pictures window, and the My Pictures window appears right after you capture an image, you can always return to the My Pictures window from your Windows XP Start menu by selecting My Pictures. All of your pictures appear in the window as *thumbnail* (miniaturized) pictures, and any image you click to select appears in the enlarged area so you can work with that image.

The following To Do item explains how to work with a picture inside the My Pictures window.

To Do: Working with the My Pictures Window

1. Open the My Pictures window.
2. Select a folder, such as the Pictures folder, and click on an image to select it and to enlarge the image in the preview area.
3. Table 22.1 explains what each control under the enlarged image does. You can practice zooming into an image, for example, by clicking one of the Zoom buttons.

TABLE 22.1   Controls Within the My Pictures Window

Control	Description
Previous Image	Selects the thumbnail image to the left of the currently selected one for display in the preview area
Next Image	Selects the thumbnail image to the right of the currently selected one for display in the preview area
Zoom In	Enlarges the image so you can see more detail
Zoom Out	Shrinks the image so you can see more of the image at once
Best Fit	Resizes the enlarged image so you can see the image's entire area (unless you zoom out) at one time
Actual Size	Enlarges or shrinks the selected image so it appears onscreen at its actual size
Rotate clockwise	Turns the image one-half turn clockwise
Rotate counterclockwise	Turns the image one-half turn counterclockwise.

4. To capture additional pictures, you can request the capture wizard once again, directly from the My Pictures window, by selecting the option labeled Get Pictures from Scanner or Camera.

5. You can set up selected pictures from the My Pictures window to appear as a slide show, one displaying after another, by selecting the option labeled View as a Slide Show. When you select this option, your screen will go blank, the first image will appear, and the image's size will consume your entire screen. A set of mouse controls appears in the upper-right corner of the screen that you can click to pause the slide show, return to previously viewed images, and close the slide show.

6. When you select the option labeled Order Prints from the Internet, a wizard begins prompting you through screens, such as the one in Figure 22.4. These screens ask which online processing service you want to order from and then that service's own wizard downloads to collect information from you about the order options, payment, and so on. Microsoft plans to add to the initial group of companies and, with an Internet connection, you'll always see the latest services.

FIGURE 22.4

Order prints from your digital images from the Internet services available.

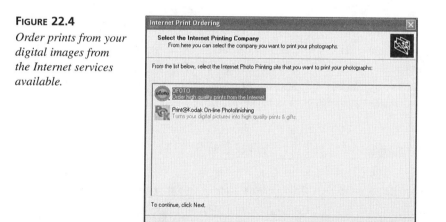

7. The Print Pictures option does more than the typical File, Print command inside other Windows XP windows and applications. A wizard begins when you select Print Pictures that helps you format and print your digital images the way you want them to appear. The wizard walks you through the selection of printers and paper. You then can select the kind of layout you want your images to take on, as shown in Figure 22.5.

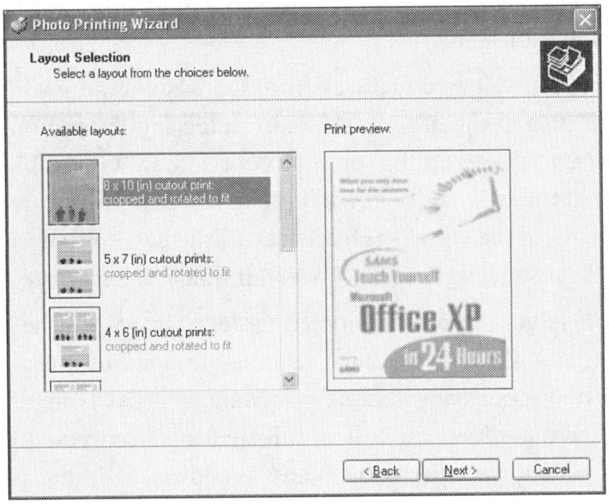

Figure 22.5

Specify exactly how you want your printed images to appear.

As you select layouts, the image preview adjusts to show you how the printed picture will look with that selected layout. When you click Next, the image prints.

8. The option labeled Set as Desktop Background enables you to select an image and use it for your Windows XP wallpaper. After selecting this option, when you close all your open windows, you'll see the image in the background where your original Windows XP desktop wallpaper used to be.

You Can Store Digital Images on CDs

If you have a writeable CD drive, such as a CD-RW drive, you can store images on a CD for others to view from their CD-ROM drives. The following To Do item explains how to do that.

To Do: Storing Digital Images on a CD

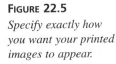

1. Capture all the pictures you want to store on the CD and save them to your disk in the My Pictures folder. Since you can store many pictures on a CD, you might want to wait until you have several to store before you save them. Using a CD for only 10 or 20 pictures seems like a waste when a CD can hold a hundred or more.

2. Insert a blank, writeable CD into your writeable CD drive.

3. Open the My Computer window.

4. Open the My Pictures folder that you want to copy to the CD so all the thumbnail images appear.

▼ 5. If you want to copy every image to the CD, press Ctrl+A to select every image. Otherwise, hold down the Ctrl key while you click over each image that is to appear on the CD.

   6. Select the option labeled Copy the Selected Items. Figure 22.6's Copy Items window opens.

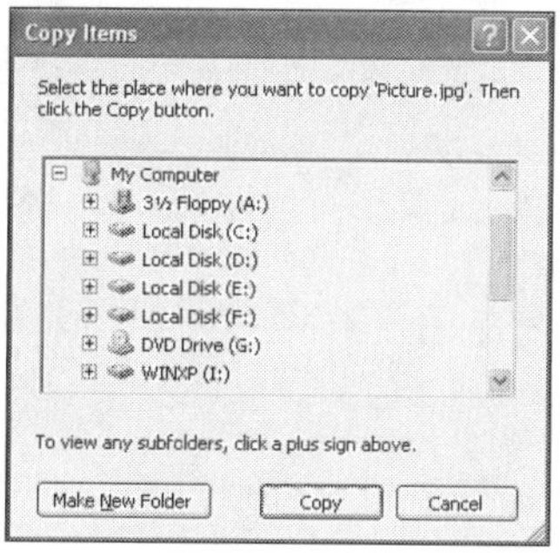

FIGURE 22.6

Select the CD drive on which you want to write the digital images.

Copy Items

Select the place where you want to copy 'Picture.jpg'. Then click the Copy button.

- My Computer
  - 3½ Floppy (A:)
  - Local Disk (C:)
  - Local Disk (D:)
  - Local Disk (E:)
  - Local Disk (F:)
  - DVD Drive (G:)
  - WINXP (I:)

To view any subfolders, click a plus sign above.

[Make New Folder]   [Copy]   [Cancel]

   7. Select your writeable CD drive and click Copy to close the window.

   8. Select your CD drive again inside your My Computer window. Windows verifies the files you want to copy.

▲ 9. Look in the section labeled Files to Add to the CD. If the files are correct, click the option labeled Write to CD. Windows XP opens a short, CD wizard that walks you through the rest of the process. You can continue working in other windows and Windows XP will inform you, with a pop-up message in your taskbar's notification area, that the CD is complete.

> Unlike previous versions of Windows, Windows XP allows you to copy files directly to a writeable CD as this To Do item demonstrates. Before Windows XP, you needed special application software to store files this easily on a CD.

Internet Explorer's Image Toolbar

As Figure 22.7 shows, Internet Explorer pops up an *image toolbar* when you point to a Web page image with your mouse pointer. The toolbar enables you to perform common operations with the image. With the image toolbar showing, you can do the following:

- Save the image to your My Pictures folder or any other folder you select
- Print the image

- Send the image as an attachment to an e-mail message; your default e-mail program, such as Outlook Express, automatically opens and a new message window appears with the image saved as an attachment to the window

- Open the My Pictures folder

FIGURE 22.7

The image toolbar pops up when you point to an image on a Web page.

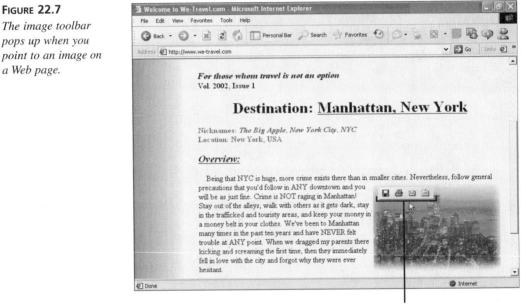

The image toolbar

The image toolbar is just one more way that Windows XP puts tools you need where you might want them.

Summary

This hour explained how to manage your digital image files. The My Pictures window is the central repository of graphics in Windows XP, but you're certainly not limited to the My Pictures window. You can store digital images in any folder and even place them on a writeable CD directly from within the Windows XP My Computer window.

This hour focused on Windows XP's digital picture abilities. Hour 23, "Making Movies with Windows XP," takes you to the next level: digital, multimedia-based video.

Q&A

Q What is the difference between a digital picture and an analog image?

A A digital picture is comprised of dots that are small enough and close enough to work together to form a picture. An analog picture is one that uses film to store pictures in gradients. Computers can manipulate and store digital images much more efficiently than analog images. As a matter of fact, to store an analog image such as a picture you have, you must first scan that picture into a digital image before you can store the picture on your PC.

Q Should I have a scanner or a digital camera?

A The best answer is to get both. A digital camera enables you to take pictures when you're away from your computer. A scanner does a better job at taking pictures (*scanning*) documents and flat items such as magazine articles and book covers. Windows XP works equally well with both.

Workshop

The quiz and exercise questions are designed to test your knowledge of the material covered in this hour. The answers are in Appendix C, "Answers to Quizzes."

Quiz

1. What is meant by *resolution*?
2. What is meant by TWAIN-compliant?
3. *True or false*: You can view a slide show of your digital pictures.
4. From what window can you copy digital images to a writeable CD?
5. When would you want to use Internet Explorer's image toolbar?

Exercises

1. Capture several pictures and store them in a My Pictures folder. Manipulate some of them by rotating them, copying them to a writeable CD, and zooming in and out.
2. Start the wizard that sends digital images over the Internet to be turned into prints. Even if you don't want to use one of the services right now, go ahead and read through the wizard screens up to the point where you actually place the order. You'll learn about their current pricing plans and the time it takes to receive the prints.

HOUR 23

Making Movies with Windows XP

It's time to step up the previous hour's discussion of still digital pictures and explain how to work with full video in Windows XP. Besides playing video clips on your computer to produce full-motion video with sound, you can also play DVD movies.

Windows XP doesn't stop there; not only can you play videos, you can also make your own movies. Windows XP's Movie Maker is an application with which you can edit, build, preview video clips, and even make your own movies!

In this hour, you will

- Learn the terminology behind movie making with Windows Movie Maker
- Manage video clips
- Put together your video clips into a full-length movie
- Adjust the speed and size of your video clips
- Record content directly from within Movie Maker

Starting Movie Maker

When you select More Programs, Accessories, Windows Movie Maker, the Movie Maker application starts. Figure 23.1 shows the opening screen. After you use Movie Maker once to make or edit a movie, the most recent movie you worked on will appear automatically. You can work further on that movie, begin a new movie, or edit a different movie.

FIGURE **23.1**

Movie Maker enables you to capture and edit full-motion video.

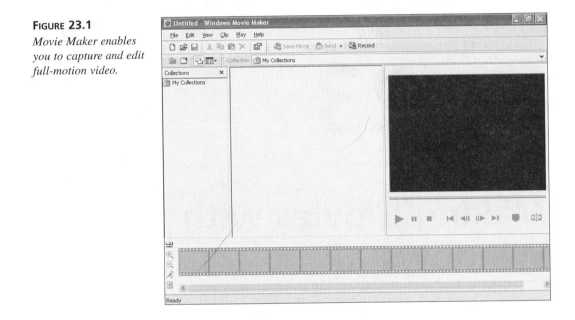

Movie Maker Video Sources

You can transfer video from just about any video source. Here are just a few of the ways to get a video into Movie Maker:

- Load video from a digital video camera.
- Load video from an analog video camcorder. (You must have a video capture card that converts analog video to digital video, such as the ATI All-In-Wonder card.)
- Import video clips found on the Internet.
- Use video clips already on your computer that you or someone else stored there in the past.

Movie Maker is not limited to a single source. You can, for example, transfer a video from your camcorder to Movie Maker and add video clips from the Internet to your video.

After you use Movie Maker to create your video production, you can share your video with others. You control the quality of your video. The higher the quality, the more disk space the video will take and the longer it will take to save and load.

Some of the ways to output your videos include the following:

- Send videos to others as e-mail attachments
- Store video clips on a Web page for all to see
- Save your videos to your disk for future reference
- Send videos to tape, either analog or digital, assuming your video card has the proper video-out jacks for the transfer

Videos consume a lot of disk storage. The combination of sound and color moving images requires huge amounts of disk space. If you're running low on disk space and you find yourself running Disk Cleanup often to recover more space, don't try to use Movie Maker for videos until you get more disk space. The largest file you can store on a FAT32 system is 4 gigabytes. If, when you installed Windows XP or if you upgraded from Windows 2000, your disk drive might be formatted as an NTFS disk that does not have a size limit for files.

Some Movie Maker Terminology

Movie Maker uses special video terms to refer to parts of a video production. You need to understand Movie Maker's terminology to use Movie Maker properly. Fortunately, the terms are fairly common and most people will know most of them already.

A video is a set of *frames*, or single pictures, linked together to produce, when viewed frame-after-frame, a movie. A *still image* is a single frame; a digital camera shoots still images just as your regular 35mm camera does. Movie Maker enables you to place still images in your videos to stop the action temporarily. In addition, you can save still images from single frames where you stop a video's playback.

A fundamental building block of a Movie Maker movie is a *clip*, or a short section of a video. The more you break your video into separate, small clips, the more manageable your video will be. The trade-off for having several clips is that you must keep track of more items. Like a book with many chapters, the separate clips help break down the video's content, letting you rearrange and edit specific parts of the video more easily

> Movie Maker can automatically break videos into separate clips. When you load a video into Movie Maker from your camcorder or another source such as an MPEG video disk file, Movie Maker attempts to break your video into several clips. Often, Movie Maker makes correct assumptions about where to divide a video into a new clip, but sometimes Movie Maker can inadvertently divide a clip into two or more parts that you don't want broken into separate clips. You can merge these separate clips into a larger, single clip.

You'll assign names to clips so you can more easily reference the clips later. For example, if you've stored a video of a backyard barbeque on your computer, you can name one of the clips *Dad In Apron*. If you assign good, descriptive names, you won't have to play a clip to remember what it contains. After you've broken a video into clips, you can store those clips in other videos, produce stand-alone videos of the clip, and modify individual clips. A set of clips is called a *collection*. You can save a collection after you add or modify clips in the collection. Later, you can load a collection and work more on your video.

When you want to add sound to your videos, you add *narration*. You can also add *background music* from MP3 files stored on your computer, from MP3 files you download from the Internet, or from audio CDs you play.

Movie Maker enables you to make a *slideshow* (also called an *illustrated video*) of still images and add narration and background music to the slideshow. The images appear at time intervals you select, and the narration and background music appear on cue when you want them to. Unlike the My Picture's slideshow feature, Movie Maker gives you full control over the video's timing and sound because the pictures show one-by-one.

Throughout the next few sections, you'll see how you can use a *storyboard approach* to lay out what you want to appear in your video and then create the video using your storyboard as a guide. You'll adjust the way that clips *transition* from one clip to the next; for example, one clip might fade into another which is a process called *cross-fading*, whereas another clip might quickly slide from the left into the one previously showing in the video.

A video's *timeline* is always present, both for individual clips under the pre-view area and for your full video above the storyboard area. The storyboard area is also called the *workspace*. A timeline allows you to adjust clips for time. The timeline updates as you play the current video clip or as you modify the storyboard. The timeline enables you to align narration and background music properly to the video they go with.

23

Movie Maker Supports Many File Types

When you load an existing video clip into Movie Maker, you *import* the video (unless the video is already in Movie Maker's standard Windows Media format with the .wmv extension) into Movie Maker's editing area. Movie Maker can import just about any popular video format and work with that file. Most video file formats are recognized by their filename extension. Table 23.1 lists the many file types with which Movie Maker can import and work.

TABLE 23.1   File Types Supported by Movie Maker

File Type	Extensions
Video files	.asf, .avi, .wmv
Movie files (MPEG)	.mpeg, .mpg, .m1v, .mp2, .mpa, .mpe
Audio files	.wav, .snd, .au, .aif, .aifc, .aiff, .wma, .mp3
Windows Media files	.asf, .wm, .wma, .wmv
Still images	.bmp, .jpg, .jpeg, .jpe, .jfif, .gif, .dib

You can import videos, still images, and audio files into Movie Maker (as long as the format is listed in Table 23.1), and combine them into the same Movie Maker movie. The video you save from Movie Maker will be in Movie Maker's default .wmv Windows Media format.

An Overview of Movie Maker's Use

Windows Movie Maker is actually not as jam-packed full of features as other video-editing software that you can get, but as you've already seen in this hour, Movie Maker can do quite a lot. Movie Maker is an excellent introduction to digital video production and management.

Although making video productions with Movie Maker could consume an entire 24-hour tutorial itself, the following To Do items walk you through some common tasks you'll perform with Movie Maker.

To Do: Loading an Existing Clip into Movie Maker

1. Suppose you have a video clip already on your computer and you want to load that clip into Movie Maker and work with it. Start Movie Maker.

2. Select File, Import and select the file. If you want Movie Maker to break the file into clips automatically, leave the option labeled Create Clips for Video Files checked.

> If you're unsure whether to let Movie Maker attempt to create reasonable clips, go ahead and import the video with the option checked. If you don't like where Movie Maker breaks the video into clips, close the file and import it once again, this time with the clip option turned off. You can break the file into your own clips after Movie Maker imports the video.

After the video imports, your screen will show the video, broken into clips, such as the one in Figure 23.2.

FIGURE 23.2
Movie Maker automatically breaks your video into clips.

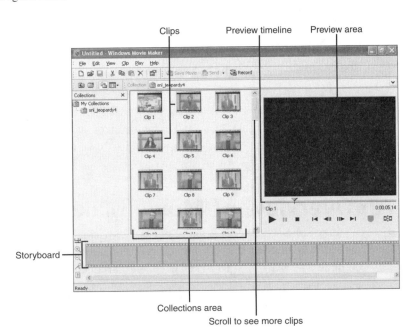

You cannot immediately save your video as a Movie Maker movie because Movie Maker assumes you need to edit the movie first. Otherwise, why would you have imported it? Therefore, you must now learn to work with clips as the next To Do item explains.

To Do: Working with Movie Maker Clips

To Do ▼

1. You can play an individual clip by double-clicking it. The clip appears in the preview area where you can replay the clip.

2. Click the Full Screen button under the preview to donate your entire screen to the playback of the clip.

3. Press Esc to return to the Movie Maker screen.

4. Click the Next Frame and Previous Frame buttons to step through your video one frame at a time.

5. If you want to divide a single clip into additional clips, locate the exact spot where you want to divide the original clip. Pause the clip at the approximate location where you want to split the clip and click Next Frame or Previous Frame until you locate the exact spot of the division.

6. Click the Split Clip button under the preview area to split the clip at the current location. You can further divide the clip if you want.

7. To name a clip, click it to select it and press F2. You might not want to name all the clips, but you can name pivotal clips that you might later need to return to for further editing.

8. One way to name a clip and add other information to it is to select the clip and then choose Properties from the clip's right-click menu. Doing so displays the clip's Properties window shown in Figure 23.3. You can click on any value and set or change that value. Click the window's Close button to save your changes.

23

FIGURE 23.3

See and modify the clip's properties.

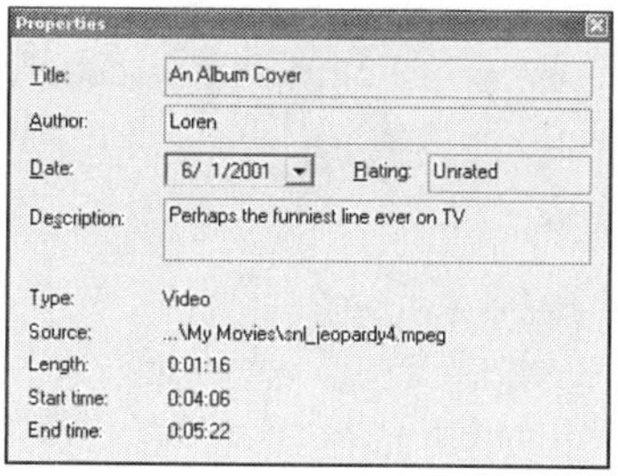

Properties		☒
Title:	An Album Cover	
Author:	Loren	
Date:	6/ 1/2001 ▼	Rating: Unrated
Description:	Perhaps the funniest line ever on TV	
Type:	Video	
Source:	...\My Movies\snl_jeopardy4.mpeg	
Length:	0:01:16	
Start time:	0:04:06	
End time:	0:05:22	

▼

9. Generally, Movie Maker errs on the side of generating too many clips when you import a video. You can easily combine multiple clips by selecting the clips to combine. Hold down the Ctrl key while clicking to select all the clips that you want to combine into one clip. Right-click your selection and choose Combine from the pop-up menu to combine the clips.

10. To see more detail about your clips, select View, Details to change the collections area from a list of thumbnail images of each clips' first frame to a list of clips that includes the clip size, date modified, and other information. Figure 23.4 shows this detailed view of the clips.

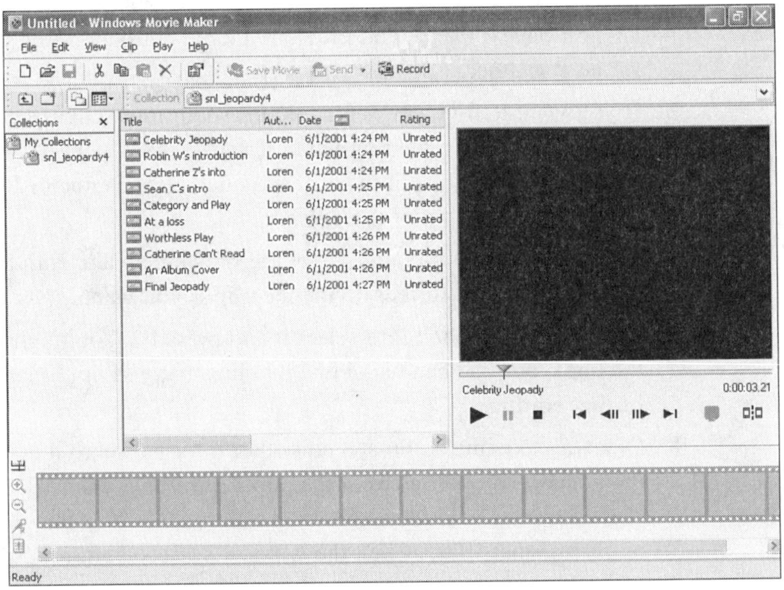

FIGURE 23.4

A detailed collections area might help you more than thumbnails at times.

After you've broken a video into appropriate clips and named them, you're ready to combine the clips into a final movie. You'll work from the storyboard as the following To Do item explains.

To Do: Using the Storyboard

1. The storyboard is where you place clips in the order you want them to appear in your final movie. Select a clip and drag the clip to the first, leftmost cell of the storyboard. Select another clip and drag it to the second storyboard cell. Continue adding clips in whatever order you want them to appear.

2. Select View, Timeline to view the storyboard's timeline. The timeline appears above the storyboard. As Figure 23.5 shows, the clips' opening frames do not all

▼

fully appear in the storyboard. The width of each clip shows, relatively, how long the clip is in relation to the other clips. The clips that are longer than a regular storyboard cell display with part of their title to the right to fill the time width. As you add clips, the storyboard's timeline updates to show you how much time is being consumed by the movie.

FIGURE 23.5

Your storyboard shows your movie's clip order and each clip's relative time.

23

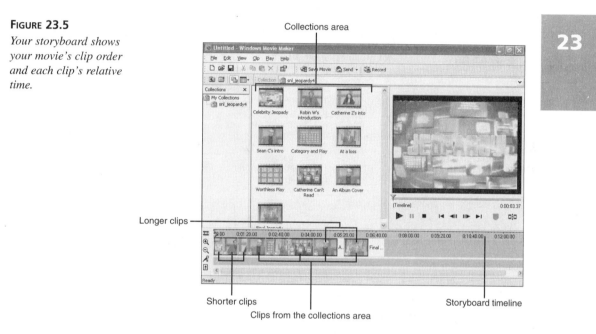

Collections area

Longer clips

Shorter clips

Clips from the collections area

Storyboard timeline

3. You can rearrange clips inside the storyboard, but before you do, turn off the display of the storyboard's timeline. Without the timeline, the clips all display with the same width and are much easier to arrange. Anytime you select a clip in the storyboard, the clip's opening frame appears in the preview area so you can review the clip.

4. After you place several clips in the storyboard, you can play your entire storyboard movie by right-clicking anywhere on the storyboard and selecting the option labeled Play Entire Storyboard/Timeline. As your movie plays, a hairline passes along the storyboard's timeline showing you exactly where the movie's current play point is.

5. When you are satisfied with your movie, select File, Save Movie to display Figure 23.6's Save Movie dialog box. Before you click OK to save the movie, take a moment to analyze and adjust the fields, if necessary. The dialog box's most important element is the Setting value you select. You can select from the drop-down list box to specify exactly how much quality the saved movie is to consume.

▼

The better the quality, the more disk space the movie will occupy and the slower the download speeds will be if you send the movie to a Web page or to someone via e-mail. The file size and the estimated download times change as you select a different quality setting. Use the estimated download times to determine just how much quality your video warrants. You want to save the movie with the highest quality possible while, at the same time, maintaining a fair trade-off of download speeds and file size.

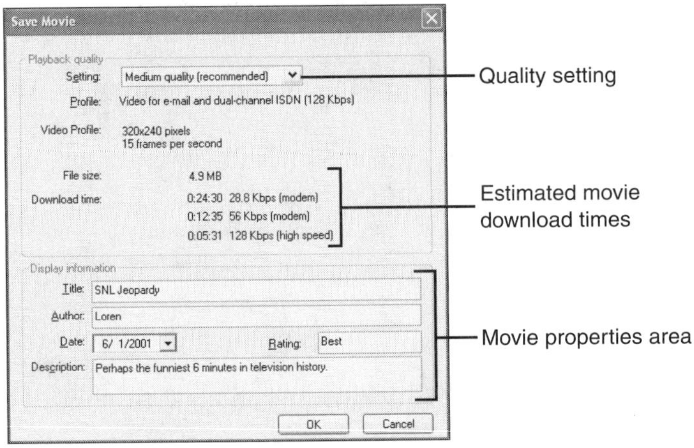

FIGURE 23.6

Adjust the video's quality and enter title information before saving the movie.

When you adjust your movie's quality setting, the Save Movie window's View Profile area changes to show you your selected video setting's playback resolution (width and height in *pixels*, the small dots that comprise your video) and the *frame rate* (the number of frames per second shown during playback).

Preserve your clips after you've saved them to disk. You might need to shorten some of the clips to meet your goals for your movie. Instead of changing a clip, you can *trim* the clip as it resides in the storyboard without changing the clip in the collections area. The following To Do item explains how to trim the clips in your storyboard without changing the original clip file.

To Do: Trimming Clips in the Storyboard

1. After you've moved clips to your storyboard, click to select the clip in the storyboard area. Start and stop trim point arrows appear on either side of the clip in the storyboard area.

2. Click Play to begin playing the clip.

▼   3. When the clip gets to the point where you want to begin trimming, press
         Ctrl+Shift+Left Arrow to set the leftmost trim point. If you don't set a left trim
         point, Movie Maker assumes you want the clip to begin at its normal starting posi-
         tion.

      4. When the clip gets to the point where you want to end trimming, press
         Ctrl+Shift+Right Arrow to set the rightmost trim point. If you don't set a right trim
         point, Movie Maker assumes you want the clip to end at its normal stopping posi-
         tion. As you set trim points, Movie Maker changes the clip's width inside the sto-
         ryboard and displays the trim points on the storyboard's clip when you select the
         clip. Trimming the storyboard clip does not change the clip.

23

> You can remove a clip's trim points by selecting that clip inside the story-
> board and then selecting Clear Trim Points from the Clip menu.

      5. If your storyboard clips get too thin to manage easily, click the Zoom In button to
         the left of the storyboard. Your storyboard clip's width expands because the time-
         line on the storyboard grows. The top figure in Figure 23.7 shows a storyboard
         before the zoom, and the bottom figure in Figure 23.7 shows a storyboard after
         zooming in. Although you'll have to scroll the storyboard left and right more for
▲   long movies, zoomed-in storyboards are often easier to adjust.

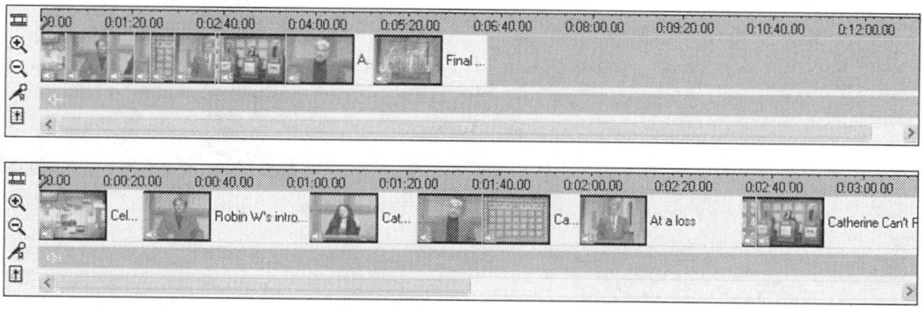

FIGURE 23.7

*Top: A storyboard
gets cramped before
zooming.
Bottom: The zoomed-in
storyboard is easier to
manage.*

Inside the storyboard, any and all clips that contain audio show a speaker icon in the
clip's lower-left corner. You can add additional audio and you can place a soundtrack
such as narration over a movie that doesn't currently have sound. You'll add audio clips
to your movies using virtually the same method you use when you add video clips. The
following To Do explains how to add such narration.

To Do: Adding Sound to the Storyboard

1. Choose File, Import to load an audio clip into your collections area.

2. Drag the audio clip to the storyboard. The storyboard area's audio bar shows the audio track.

3. You can overlap audio clips within a video clip. Drag the rightmost audio clip to the left on the storyboard's audio bar to overlap the clip with a previous one or simply to start the audio earlier in the movie. As with video clips, you can trim an audio clip after you've selected it.

▲

If you want to use Movie Maker to record video clips instead of recording the clips outside of Movie Maker and then importing them, you can collect video and audio recordings directly from within Movie Maker's application as the following To Do item explains.

To Do: Recording Directly Within Movie Maker

1. Click the toolbar's Record button. Figure 23.8's Record dialog box opens. Depending on your graphics card, you might see more options available to those who can capture video directly.

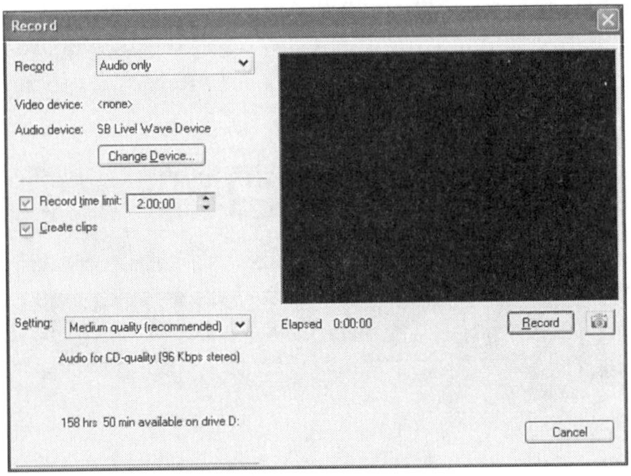

FIGURE 23.8

Set your record options from the Record dialog box.

Record	
Record:	Audio only
Video device:	<none>
Audio device:	SB Live! Wave Device
	Change Device...
☑ Record time limit:	2:00:00
☑ Create clips	
Setting:	Medium quality (recommended)
	Audio for CD-quality (96 Kbps stereo)
	158 hrs 50 min available on drive D:

Elapsed 0:00:00   Record

Cancel

2. Select the recording device, either an audio device or video device depending on what kind of clip you want to record.

3. Adjust the recording time limit and click the Create Clips option if you want Movie Maker to request that Movie Maker divide the video into separate clips.

4. Adjust the quality and click Record. If you are recording video, the video appears in the Record window's Preview area.

> Click the camera button to the right of the Record window if you have a
> digital camera or scanner attached to your computer and you want Movie
> Maker to record still images for a video slideshow.

5. Click Stop when you want to stop the recording. Movie Maker opens the Save
   Windows Media File window where you can name your clip file and select a storage location. The recorded clip appears in your collections area where you can then
   transfer the clip to its appropriate place in the storyboard.

23

Summary

This hour showed you how to record and manage full-motion videos using Movie Maker.
You can put together some rather complex movies. Although more powerful video-
editing programs exist, Movie Maker is a super, introductory program that enables you to
create movies quickly and easily.

As Internet bandwidth gets faster, and as more people adopt the faster bandwidth, online
videos will become more commonplace than they are today with the majority of users
owning and using dial-up modems. Movie Maker is a first step toward putting together a
video library.

Q&A

**Q Would I use Movie Maker or my scanner to save color images on my hard
disk?**

A You can use either, but if you plan to use those images in a video, as you might do
for a slideshow with audio, you will probably want to use Movie Maker to record
the pictures.

Workshop

The quiz and exercise questions are designed to test your knowledge of the material covered in this hour. The answers are in Appendix C, "Answers to Quizzes."

Quiz

1. *True or false:* Movie Maker's clips must come from the same source and be the
   same file type.
2. What is a frame?

3. What is a disadvantage to saving your videos in a high-quality format?

4. What can you trim: a clip in the collections area, a clip in the storyboard, or both?

5. How can zooming improve your use of the storyboard?

Exercises

1. Make a movie! A video named `Windows Movie Maker Sample file.wmv` appears in your My Documents folder. Load the video and adjust the clips. Put the clips in a different order to create some comedic action.

2. Make a slide show using still images that you grab from your favorite Web page. Right-click over any Web page's image and select Save Picture As from the pop-up menu. After saving several images, put them together in a slide show and add narration over them if you have attached a microphone to your computer.

HOUR **24**

Advanced Windows XP Tips

You've worked hard to master Windows XP. You've already mastered the basics, so now you're ready to move up to the level of Windows XP Guru. This hour teaches several practical tips that you are ready for now that you understand the ins and outs of Windows.

Because of the nature of tips, you won't find step-by-step tasks in this hour. Instead, this hour presents its Windows tips in several categories. For example, if you are comfortable with Windows's interface, you can now turn to this hour's first section for some advanced tips that will help you manage the desktop.

In this hour, you will

- Learn desktop tips that help you more quickly manage Windows
- Create a startup disk for safety
- Use Internet Explorer shortcuts that save you online time
- Learn where to look for Outlook Express shortcuts
- Improve your computing efficiency when on the road with a laptop

Windows Desktop Tips

When you master this section's desktop tips, you'll more quickly select programs and manage your desktop. You will learn how to rearrange your Start menu and modify the Start menu so that it behaves the way you want it to.

Rearrange Start Menu Items

If you don't like the location of a menu item on one of your Start menus, drag the item to another location. When you've opened one of the Start menus, such as the More Programs, Accessories menu, you can click and drag any menu item to another menu.

Sometimes you will move a menu item from the Start menu's top level to one of the other menus further into the Start menu's structure. Windows XP warns you with Figure 24.1's message window that this move will affect all users of the system. Other users might be confused if they expect to find the menu item on the Start menu's top level and it's not there because you moved the item further down into the menu structure.

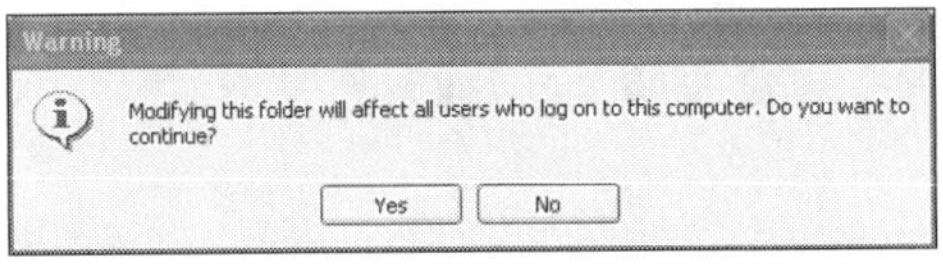

FIGURE 24.1

Some menu restructuring will hide menu items from the top level of the Start menu.

> **Warning**
>
> Modifying this folder will affect all users who log on to this computer. Do you want to continue?
>
> [Yes]   [No]

If you use a program frequently, place that program at the top of the Start menu. Suppose that you use WordPad a lot to edit text files and want to place the WordPad program at the top of your Start menu so that you don't have to traverse all the way over to the Accessories menu. Open the Accessories menu and drag the WordPad option to your Start menu. You'll notice that you cannot drop the item onto the lower section of the Start menu (the section with the Settings and Programs options). The cursor turns into the international Don't symbol if you attempt to place the WordPad item over a part of the Start menu that cannot accept menu items, such as the My Computer icon.

When you release your mouse button, the menu option appears on the Start menu.

> The menu item does not move. Instead, the item appears in both places. If you want to move a menu option instead of copying the option, you must delete the menu item from its original menu location.

Deleting Menu Items

To remove a menu item, click the taskbar's Show Desktop icon to minimize all open windows. Right-click over the menu item and select Delete. (If you remove a menu item from the left side of the Start menu, as opposed to removing the item from the More Programs portion of the menu, right-click the menu and select the option labeled Remove from This List.

If you want to rearrange more than one or two items from your Start menu, the following To Do item shows you one way to accomplish this without having to move each item individually as described above.

To Do: Rearranging Start Menu Items

1. Right-click the Start button and select Properties from the pop-up menu.
2. Click the Start Menu tab.
3. Select Classic View and click Customize to display the Customize Classic Start Menu dialog box shown in Figure 24.2.

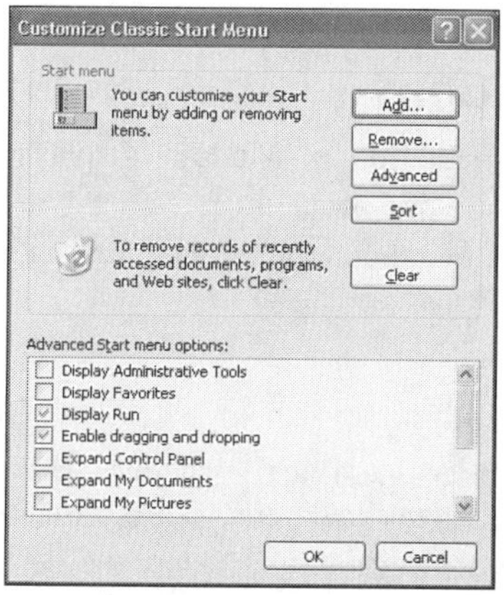

FIGURE 24.2

The Start Menu Explorer window enables you to perform advanced menu editing.

4. Click the Advanced button to display a window that displays your Start menu in an Explorer-like hierarchy of options.
5. Open the menu hierarchy by clicking plus signs next to any menu items you want to change.
6. Drag the items (including menu folders if you want) to any other location.
7. Close the window and click OK to return to the Taskbar and Start Menu Properties window.

▼   8. Select the option labeled Start Menu to leave the Classic style and return to the Windows XP Start menu style. (The Classic style is helpful when you want to rearrange menu items as done here, but most Windows XP users prefer the new look of the Start menu to the older, Classic version.)

9. Click OK to close the window.

▲   10. Click your Start button to check the results.

> You can move some menu options from the Start menu's Explorer-like view and send other options to the Recycle Bin that you want to delete. In deleting menu options, you do not delete the programs themselves. The Start menu contains *shortcuts* to programs. A shortcut is just a pointer to a program, not the actual program. When you drag a shortcut from one location to another, the pointer moves but not the file.
>
> You can drag a menu item to your desktop. Then, if you want to launch that program, you need only click open the desktop's icon. You won't have to use the Start menu every time you start the program.

Right-Click Menu Options

When you right-click over a Start menu option, Windows displays a pop-up menu. You can delete or rename menu items with the pop-up menu as well as view the item's properties. The Properties option describes the menu option and its underlying file information.

Don't Wait for a Disaster!

Most people back up regularly . . . after they've had a disaster! Don't wait. Get a backup program and back up your system. For a complete backup program, go to your local software dealer and search through the many inexpensive programs on the shelves for one that looks as though it will suit your needs and hardware the best. Many of today's backup programs include other system utilities that help keep your system in its tip-top shape. Your disk drives are mechanical and will break down over time. Don't wait to make your first backup or you'll regret the first time your disk has a problem.

> Software is available that not only makes a backup of every file on your system, but also actually makes a disk drive image of your hard disk. From that saved image, you can restore your computer to its exact configuration if you ever have a disk breakdown. Look for products such as DriveImage (their Web site is www.powerquest.com for more information) if you want to make an image of your disk for backup storage.

Make sure that the backup program you buy is compatible with Windows XP. Anytime you use system-related software, that software must be certified for your specific operating system or you could have problems with compatibility. Finding out after a disaster occurs that your backup was not made properly can be more than frustrating.

Make Yourself More Comfortable

What's the most important component in your PC system? It's not your system unit, your CPU, the speed with which Windows performs, your hard disk, or your printer. Your most important component is the very chair you sit in. Smart PC users spend more money on their chair than on their operating systems.

If you spend an hour or more a day at your PC, run, don't walk, to your local office furniture store and check out their desk chair selection. If you've never paid much attention, you'll be shocked at how many kinds of chairs that you find. Your back, arms, shoulders, and wrists (not to mention the body part on which you sit), deserve far better than the average chair most people place in front of their computers. You'll be more productive, work more accurately, and you'll take care of your body.

24

The better desk chairs provide separate controls for the arm rests, back and lumbar support, and height. Make sure that you can adjust these components easily *while sitting in the chair*. Look for a chair on wheels that rolls easily so that you can move between your PC and other work areas.

Start Windows Explorer Quickly

If your keyboard is a Windows keyboard—that is, your keyboard has a key with the flying Windows logo that displays the Start menu when you press it—you can press the Windows key along with the letter E to start Windows Explorer. (This is not Internet Explorer but the Windows Explorer program you use to manage disks, folders, and files.)

Adjust the Toolbar in Any Window

You can right-click over any Windows XP window's toolbar to display a menu of toolbar options, as shown in Figure 24.3, which determine how the toolbar appears.

FIGURE 24.3

The pop-up menus give you control over a menu option.

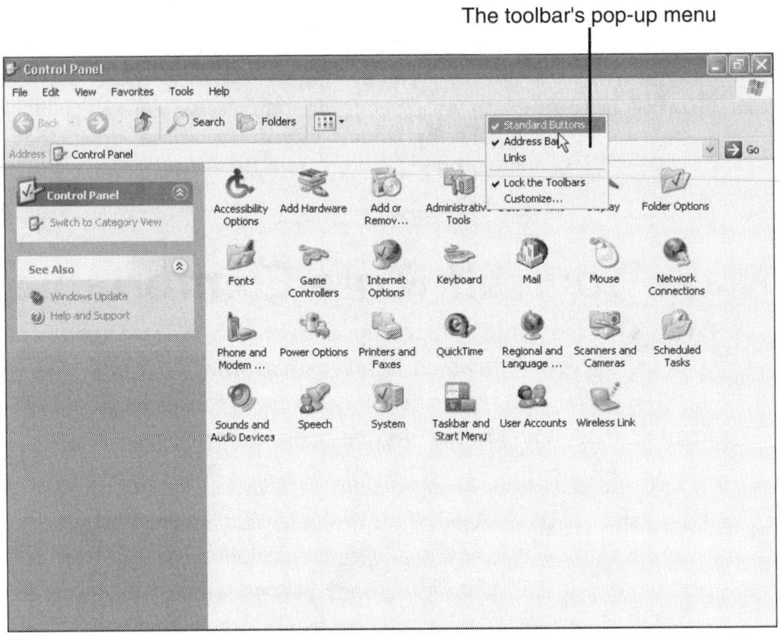

The toolbar's pop-up menu

You can display or hide any of the following on your toolbar:

- Standard Buttons: Displays the toolbar buttons using the icon-based standard.
- Address Bar: Displays the Web Address text box in which you can type a Web URL or any pathname to a folder in which you want to work.
- Links: Displays hyperlink buttons (they appear next to the address bar if you display the address bar) that quickly point the window to a Web or folder location. You can drag other shortcuts to the links to add your own buttons, and you can also right-click over a link button to change its property or rename the button.
- Lock the Toolbars: Fixes the toolbar's settings so you cannot inadvertently change or move it until you unlock the toolbar.
- Customize: Enables you to add or remove buttons on the toolbar.

Internet Explorer Tips

Internet Explorer will probably become such an important part of the Windows interface that you find yourself using it more and more when you upgrade to Windows. Therefore, the more shortcuts you learn about Internet Explorer, the more efficient and effective you will be with the Internet Explorer program interface.

Learn the Web As You Use It

After you start Internet Explorer, point your browser to this Web address to start an interactive Web tutorial that teaches you about the Web: `www.Microsoft.com/insider/internet`. Figure 24.4 shows the start of the online tutorial.

FIGURE 24.4

Take an Internet Explorer tour to learn more about the Internet.

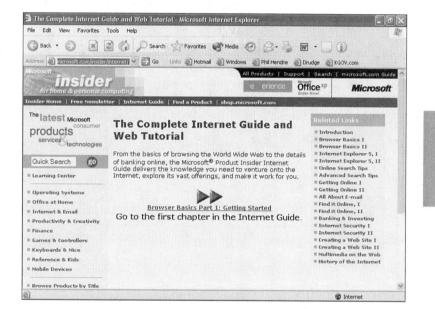

Quickly Enter Web Addresses

If you often type URLs in Internet Explorer's Address text box, you'll find yourself having to click the Address box first to place your text cursor there to type an address.

Internet Explorer maps a shortcut key to the Address text box. When you press F4, the text cursor instantly moves to the Address text box so that you can enter a new address there.

Speaking of the Address text box, all addresses that appear there have a small icon to the left. You can drag that icon to your desktop, e-mail message, or anywhere else you want to place that address for later reference. If, for example, you visit a Web page that you want to remember, you can drag its icon to the toolbar's link buttons to create a new link button (assuming that you've turned on the toolbar links, as previously described in the section "Adjust the Toolbar in Any Window").

Set Up Internet Explorer Security

When you select Tools, Internet Options, Internet Explorer displays a dialog box that enables you to adjust Internet settings. Click the Security tab to display the dialog box shown in Figure 24.5. Click the Custom Level button to change to the Security Settings dialog box. Four options appear in the drop-down list labeled Reset Custom Settings. The four options determine how secure you want to be with your Web browsing.

FIGURE 24.5

You can customize many of Internet Explorer's security options.

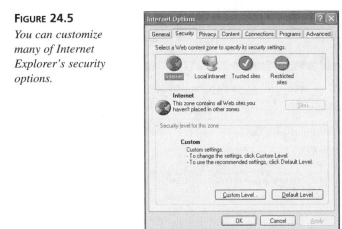

A high security level protects your PC from incoming information that could possibly contain virus-laden files. A virus is a computer file that destroys other files. The problem with this high security level, however, is that you often access secure sites and want to purchase something or give other information, and Internet Explorer will not let you send that information. You can always lower your security level when you know that a site is secure.

Keep More History for Faster Access

The General tab of the Tools, Internet Options dialog box enables you to enter a value that determines the number of history days to keep track of. As you traverse the Web, Internet Explorer saves each Web page that you visit in a history area. By adjusting the value in the option labeled Days to Keep Pages in History, you can make Internet Explorer keep more pages in case you return to recently visited pages.

The more days of history you keep, the less disk space you will have. Some Web pages consume a lot of disk space. Click the Clear History button to remove all the saved Web pages from your disk if you need to free some space.

Take a Look at Advanced Internet Explorer Options

Select Internet Explorer's Tools, Internet Options menu and click the Advanced tab to display the customization list shown in Figure 24.6. Each item in the list describes a different aspect of Internet Explorer that you can control, from browsing tasks to toolbar information.

It pays to return to this dialog box every month or two. As you use the Internet in different ways, and as you develop procedures you routinely follow, set options that help Internet Explorer work the way you do.

Change Your Home Page

If you begin traversing to a particular site as soon as you sign into the Web, you might want to make that page your home page so your browser automatically displays that page when you start Internet Explorer. Instead of using the Edit menu to change your start page, drag the Address text box icon to Internet Explorer's Home button on the toolbar to change your browser's home (start) page. The next time you start your browser, the page will appear as soon as you sign into the Internet.

Disconnect Quickly

To disconnect your Internet dial-up connection, double-click the taskbar's Web icon next to the clock to display a small connection dialog box window. (The Web icon might show two PCs connected by a wire or a different symbol, depending on your Internet connection.) Select Disconnect and Windows immediately signs off from your Internet provider. (Always on connections, such as T-1 connections, might not show an Internet connection icon.)

Outlook Express Tips

You'll often work in Outlook Express because of the prevalence of e-mail in today's online world. You can make Outlook Express more enjoyable by utilizing some of the following tips.

Compress Files

If you store many sent and retrieved e-mail messages or subscribe to a lot of newsgroups, your disk space can fill up quickly. To help, you can reduce the amount of space consumed by messages and newsgroup files by selecting Tools, Options, and clicking the Maintenance tab. When you click the Compact button, Outlook Express compresses your message and file space.

If you click Remove Messages instead of Compact, Outlook Express removes the message bodies but retains all message headers (descriptions) so that you'll know which messages you've already read. (Outlook Express places a read icon next to your read messages as long as you've saved the headers.)

If you click Delete, you save the most space because Outlook Express removes all newsgroup messages and files from your disk; but you have to download those newsgroup messages and files if you ever need them again. Reset performs a cleanup that deletes both message headers and bodies.

Clean Up Your Deleted Folder

Like files that you delete to the Recycle Bin from within Windows Explorer, e-mail messages that you delete from your Inbox and Outbox don't really go away; they move to your Deleted Items folder. If you want to free space completely of unwanted, old e-mail messages, routinely open your Deleted Items folder and delete the messages from there. You have to confirm the delete because Outlook Express knows that the files are truly gone when you delete them from the Deleted Items folder.

If you decide not to delete one or more messages from the Deleted Items folder, you can drag messages from the Deleted Items folder to any other folder at the left of the Outlook Express screen. Feel free to create new folders from the File menu or by right-clicking over the list of folders if you want to create an organized set of folders. You can create a folder for your business correspondence and one for your personal correspondence. You then can keep your Inbox, Outbox, and Deleted Items folders free from messages that should appear in other folders.

Create a Personal Signature

You cannot sign your e-mail with your handwriting, but Outlook Express's signature feature is the next-best thing. An e-mail signature is text that appears at the end of your e-mail. Your signature might be just your name, or you might want to close all correspondence with your name, address, and phone number.

You can choose not to enclose your signature with certain e-mail messages.

Outlook Express enables you to add a signature to your e-mail messages, your newsgroup postings, or both. To create the signature, select Tools, Options and click the Signatures tab. You can select a default font to use for the message as well as a signature if you click the Signatures button to display the dialog box shown in Figure 24.7.

24

FIGURE 24.7

Create a signature for the bottom of your messages and postings.

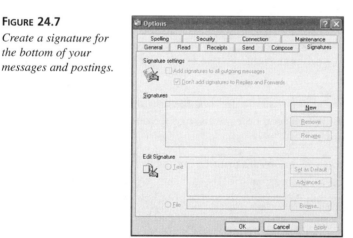

Your signature can come from text you type at the Text option or from a text file on disk that you select at the File option.

Check E-mail Often

If you receive much e-mail throughout the day, select Tools, Options and decrease the time that Outlook Express waits before checking for new e-mail. If you read your e-mail only once or twice a day, you might want to check for new e-mail less often than the 30-minute default so that your system runs more efficiently when you don't want e-mail. You must have Outlook Express running before it can check for new e-mail.

Outlook Express emits a sound when new e-mail arrives. When you hear the sound, it's time to check the Outlook Express Inbox for new messages. Check or uncheck the option on the Options General page labeled Play Sound When New Messages Arrive to request or cancel the new message sound. (Open the Control Panel's Sounds icon to change the sound that plays when you get a new message.)

Printing Tips

Windows adds advanced printer support that enables you to manage the documents you send to the printer. As you probably know, you can begin printing a second (or more) document even before the first one finishes printing. Windows stores the output in memory and on disk until all the documents are printed. Have you ever sent two or three long documents to the printer and then wished you could cancel the first one? You can, as the next tip shows.

Manage Printer Jobs

As soon as you select Print, Windows sends the output to the print queue. The *print queue* is a temporary file that resides partially in memory and partially on disk. The print queue holds the document or documents that you've sent to the printer but have not finished printing yet.

From the time you issue a print command to the time the document is completely printed, Windows displays a printer icon on your taskbar. If you double-click that icon, the printer window appears.

The printer window tells you which jobs are printing and what their status is, including the number of pages printed for the current job. If you change your mind and want to cancel a job that's started or one that has yet to start, right-click over the job's name and select Cancel printing.

Rearrange print jobs when you want to move a more important job up in the queue. Drag a job up or down to change its priority and printing order.

Cancel All Print Jobs Easily

Sometimes you might want to cancel all your print jobs. No problem. Just select the printer window's Printer, Purge Print Documents option to remove all jobs from the print queue.

Multiple Users Should Print Separator Pages

If you share a networked printer with others in an office setting, make sure that you've specified a separator page for your networked printer. A separator page prints before or after every print job. If several people print at the same time, the separator pages help you determine where one print job begins and ends.

The separator page can contain text, but if you select a large graphic image (the image must end in the graphics file extension .wmf), you can more easily locate the separator page when sorting through a list of printed output.

Miscellaneous Tips

Although Windows offers hundreds of shortcuts and tips that you'll run across as you use Windows, your 24 hours is almost over. The following sections round out the final Windows tips offered here.

Save the Scraps

Suppose that you work within a word processor and want to copy a paragraph or two from the word processor to several different programs over the next few days. The Windows Clipboard will hold data only as long as you don't replace the Clipboard with additional contents or until you shut down Windows.

You can create a *scrap,* a portion of a data file, by dragging selected text and data from an application to your desktop. When you release the data, a scrap icon appears on the desktop. Keep in mind that a scrap is not a complete document but only text you've selected and copied to the desktop.

The scrap stays on your desktop until you delete it. Therefore, as long as the scrap remains on your desktop, you can copy it to any file.

Stop a Copy or Move

Sometimes you begin a copy or move operation with your mouse by dragging something from one location to another, and you realize that you want to cancel the copy or move. Press Esc to cancel the current copy or move in process.

Laptop Security

If you use a laptop, you can help get your laptop back if you lose it. Right now, before you forget, tape your business card to the bottom of your laptop. If you leave the laptop in an airport or hotel, the finder of your PC will be able to contact you to return the laptop. Sure, if a thief steals your laptop with a business card, he will know whom to thank!

Delay On-the-Road Printing

Without a laptop printer, you cannot get a hardcopy (a printout) of your data. You can, however, print all your data to an offline printer. When you print to an offline printer, you appear to print but your laptop stores the printing for later.

To convert your laptop to offline printing, open your Control Panel's Printers and Faxes folder and select File, Use Printer Offline to request the offline printing option. All subsequent printing goes to the disk. You can print as much as you want, and Windows XP stores the output for when you eventually connect a printer to your laptop. When you get back to the office, plug a printer into your laptop, choose File, Use Printer Online, and the laptop will print every file you sent to the printer while on the road.

Print to a Hotel Fax

When you create something with your laptop while you're on the road, you probably won't have your printer with you. Although you can back up your files to a disk, you might feel better if you print your data. You'll then have the printed hardcopy in case something happens to your disk. If you don't have a printer, fax your document to the hotel fax machine. You will, in a few seconds, have a printout of your document.

 If you want to back up your files and you have a laptop modem, e-mail the files to yourself! When you get home, you can download the mail or ignore it if your laptop files made it home safely.

Purchase a Desktop Infrared Transmitter

If you transfer files between your desktop and laptop more than once a week, you'll soon tire of the cable connection that you have to make. If you use a network, plug the network cable into your laptop's PC card slot, perhaps also removing your PC card hard disk or modem first and inserting the network PC card. If you use a Direct Cable Connection or network, you might have to unplug your desktop's printer or modem before you can cable the desktop to your laptop.

An infrared device frees you from the cables. People who use an infrared transmitter to transfer files between their laptop and desktop are more likely to keep their files up to date than users who must use cables.

Purchase a Digital Camera Interface

If you have a digital camera with a USB port that connects directly to your computer, you can transfer pictures from your camera directly to your PC. Over time, however, connecting your camera directly to your PC causes extra wear on your camera's motor.

Most digital camera makers produce a desktop device that attaches to one of your USB ports into which you can insert your camera's memory chip. For example, Sony cameras use a *memory stick* to store photos internally in the camera. You can eject the memory stick and insert the memory stick into Sony's *Memory Stick Reader*, a small box that sits on your desktop. The reading device enables you to transfer pictures from the stick to your computer without using your camera.

Summary

This hour wrapped up your 24-hour tutorial with some tips that help you streamline your work. As you work more with Windows, you'll find many other tips that lighten your workload. Windows is there to help you, not to hinder you. As you've learned throughout this 24-hour tutorial, Windows often provides several ways to accomplish the same purpose.

> Because of the nature of this hour's material, questions and answers aren't necessary.

24

PART VII
Appendixes

APPENDIX **A**

Differences Between the Windows Home and Professional Edition

Although this book's focus is toward users of the Windows XP Home Edition, a quick comparison of the extra features found in the Professional edition will help you decide if you need to upgrade to the Professional Edition.

General Impressions

If you are familiar with either edition of Windows XP, you will have no trouble adapting to the other version. For example, you will be able to use Windows XP Home Edition at home and the Windows XP Professional Edition at work, without problems, because the interface of both editions is similar.

Upgrade Path

Generally, those users happy with Windows 98 or Windows Me should upgrade to the Windows XP Home Edition. For those users already using Windows 2000 or Windows NT Workstation, the Professional Edition is needed.

> You cannot upgrade from Windows 2000 or Windows NT Workstation to Windows Home Edition. In addition, you cannot upgrade from Windows 95 to Windows XP Home Edition. If you use Windows 95, you must obtain a full version of Windows XP Home or Professional Edition.

Other versions of Windows XP are available to those who need a server edition. Specifically, the Windows XP Server Edition and the Windows XP Advanced Server Edition provide the editions needed by server-based installations. In addition, a special Windows XP Datacenter Server is available for those who need a special datacenter edition.

System Requirements

Although both the Home Edition and the Professional Edition run on the same, minimum hardware, if you want parallel processing, you'll have to use the Windows XP Professional versions or one of the Server editions.

General Differences

Although the Professional Edition includes the entire repertoire of Windows XP Home Edition utilities, the Professional Edition includes additional utilities with which you can support a server-based, networked system. To give you an idea of some differences so you can know whether to look deeper into the Professional Edition to see if you need the extra power, here are a few features you can expect in the Professional Edition that you won't find in the Home Edition:

- Active Directory Enhancements: Windows XP Professional supports the Active Directory concept that enables server-based computers to retrieve uniform and familiar data across several types of systems.

- Remote installations: Windows XP Professional Edition enables you to install software from a server to all or some computers on your network. The software can install at the time the remote user logs onto the computer.

- Terminal Services: All of the remote network administrative tools are encapsulated inside the Terminal Services area of Windows XP Professional Edition. These services enable you to manage servers and client computers over a network from a central location. In addition, you can test network operations and remove system resources. Advanced users can use a Telnet interface to manage servers.

- Resultant Set of Policies (RSoP): Enable you to more easily manage all logon policies of your users, giving specific access to those users who need access.

- Server-based IIS capacity-planning: Enables Web server users to determine where the online user load impacts your server's Web sites the most.

- Enterprise backup and Recovery: Enables networked backup programs to take system snapshots at any moment in time to recover system functionality across the network if a problem arises later.

- Automated System Recovery (ASR): Allows System Administrators to recover application settings if a restoration is required.

A

GLOSSARY

10BaseT wiring A common, flexible network cable used in Ethernet networks.

accelerator key A key found on a menu (usually a function key used in conjunction with the Alt key, such as Alt+F4) that enables you initiate a menu command from the keyboard without first having to display the menu.

account Each Windows XP user has an account that keeps track of that user's desktop settings and Windows XP preferences.

active desktop The Web-based desktop you can create for Windows XP that contains active content from the Internet.

Address Book A Windows repository of data, often created from Microsoft Outlook's contacts database, that contains information such as e-mail addresses and phone numbers of your contacts.

alias file The name of a link to an existing file.

analog photography The traditional approach to photography that uses film.

anchor position The starting coordinate pair of lines and other geometric shapes. You'll use the pair of coordinate values to determine how far down and across the screen that a drawing is about to begin.

animated cursors   Cursors that display movement during the cursor's display, such as a cursor showing a picture of a running horse or a playing piano.

applets   Small programs that give life to Web pages by making the pages interactive. Usually, applets are written in the Java programming language.

AutoPlay   The Windows XP feature that starts the loading and execution of CDs as soon as you place the CD into your computer's CD-ROM drive.

background program   An active but not currently viewable program. You can run one or more programs in the background and they can continue to process while you interact with another program in the foreground.

bandwidth   The speed and transfer flow consistency of an Internet connection. The better your bandwidth, the faster your Internet connection will be.

binary data   Compressed, non-textual data, such as programs and graphics, as opposed to text files.

BIOS   Basic Input Output System. The system unit's ROM-based code that handles I/O devices.

Briefcase   The Windows application that synchronizes the document files from two computers so that you can always have the most up-to-date files.

browser   Software that searches for, loads, and displays Web pages. Browsers display the text, graphics, sound, and even video that appear on modern Web pages. Internet Explorer is the name of the Web browser that comes with Windows XP.

buffer   An area of memory that temporarily holds data.

burn-in   The damage resulting from a monitor that has been turned on for too long, characterized by outlines being "burned in" to the monitor even when the monitor is turned off.

category view   The Windows XP Control Panel's default look that organizes the Control Panel entries into related categories.

central processing unit   The chip inside your computer that processes data. Also known as a *CPU*.

check box   A Windows XP control, which appears next to each item in a list, that you use to select one or more items from the list.

Classic view   A view of the Control Panel that changes the Windows XP Control Panel's category view to look and behave like the one in previous versions of Windows.

clip   A file that holds audio or video data.

Close button   A button in the upper-right corner of a window that, when clicked, closes that window.

collection   A set of clips in Windows Movie Maker.

command button   A Windows XP control that appears and acts like a push button on the screen.

Compatibility mode   A special Windows XP feature that makes legacy applications run that might not otherwise run in a multi-tasking, windowed, operating system such as Windows XP.

contacts   Friends, family, and associates you keep track of inside a contact management program such as Outlook Express.

context-sensitive   Describes the process Windows XP uses to respond to what you're doing. When you right-click over an item on your screen, Windows XP displays a context-sensitive menu that relates to whatever item you clicked.

context-sensitive menu   See *pop-up menu.*

Control Panel   A folder within the My Computer window that enables you to change your computer's system settings such as your screen resolution, default printer, and mouse movement speed.

controls   Elements within dialog boxes and program windows, such as check boxes and command buttons, with which you indicate preferences and select features.

coordinate   A point position on the screen defined by a coordinate pair.

coordinate pair   A pair of numbers in which the first represents the number of drawing points from the left edge of the drawing area of an image, and the second represents the number of drawing points from the top edge of the drawing area. In Paint, the coordinates appear on the status bar.

CPU   See *central processing unit.*

crackers   Users who break into other computers, through a networked or online connection, and cause harm to those computers or access unauthorized information. (Also see *hackers.*)

cursor   A pointing device, such as the arrow that represents the mouse pointer location and the insert bar that represents the Windows XP text location. The cursor moves across the screen as you type or move the mouse. Another cursor, a vertical line also known as a *text cursor*, shows where the next character typed will appear on the screen.

data   Raw facts and figures that computer programs process.

deferred printing   Printing to a file that you will send to a printer at a delayed time.

desktop   The Windows XP screen and background that you see when you first start Windows XP and sign into your account.

desktop themes   See *themes*.

dialog box   A window containing text and one or more screen controls that you use to issue instructions to Windows XP.

differential backup   See *incremental backup*.

digital   A representation of data that uses discrete computer signals to represent data.

direct cable connection   The connection between two computers with a cable attached to both parallel or serial ports.

directory   See *folder*.

DirectParallel cable   A cable that plugs into the parallel port of two computers so the computers can share a direct cable connection.

Disk Cleanup   A program that removes unneeded files from your disk.

disk operating system   The program inside memory that controls all the hardware and software interactions.

docking station   A device into which you can insert some laptop computers, which instantly connects the laptop to a full-size screen, keyboard, mouse, and printer.

documents   A common name for data files.

Dr. Watson   A system program that records system information when your PC freezes up. You can use the information saved by Dr. Watson to locate the cause of the problem.

drivers   Software files that often accompany hardware to tell the computer how to control the hardware when you install it.

DriveSpace   The Windows utility program that condenses the disk space so that more data fits on a disk drive.

drop-down list box   A list of choices that opens when you click the down arrow to the right of a list box.

e-mail   Electronic mail service that enables you to transfer files and messages to others who have an online account.

emoticon   A popular combination of punctuation that represents emotions onscreen. Two of the most popular emoticons are happy faces and sad faces, :) and : (respectively.

Energy Star   A name applied to monitors that comply with environmental guidelines that limit the use of continuous power applied to your monitor.

Ethernet   A high-speed network connection and the most common network connection in use today.

Explorer   A powerful file-listing application that gives you both high-level and detailed descriptions of your computer system and the files on the system.

export   The process of saving a file in a format that differs from the application's native, default format.

Fast User Switching   A Windows XP feature that enables one user to switch quickly from another user's account. If more than one person shares a home computer, each person in the family can have their own account on the computer. When a person signs into his or her account, Windows XP changes its settings such as colors and wallpaper to that user's preferences.

field   A data entry text box located in dialog boxes and program windows.

firewall   A software program or hardware that shields online users' computers from unauthorized access from the Internet.

FireWire   A high-speed port into which you can plug external devices, such as digital cameras, into your computer. Also known as *IEEE 1394*.

flash memory   A storage device for some kinds of digital cameras where the pictures are stored.

focus   The highlighted command button or control in a dialog box that Windows XP automatically selects when you press Enter.

folder   Shown as a special Windows XP icon, a folder is a separate, named location on a disk drive that holds files (also known as a *directory*).

font   A specific typestyle. Fonts have names that distinguish them from one another, such as Times New Roman and Courier. Some fonts are fancy, and others are plain.

font family   A set of fonts from the same typeface. For example Arial and Arial Black are from the same font family.

foreground program   The active and currently viewable program. On the Windows XP taskbar, the foreground program's taskbar button will be the one highlighted. You can click any button on the taskbar to bring that program into the foreground.

fragments   Small pieces of files that get scattered over a disk drive and result in your processor being slower. You can fix those fragments and improve your file access speed by running Disk Defragmenter.

frame   An individual image that comprises a movie.

frame rate   The speed at which frames in a movie appear.

graphical user interface   See *GUI*.

grayscale   Colors printed on a black-and-white printer with the various colors appearing as shades of gray.

guest   The computer that uses files and printer resources, accessed by cable, in the Direct Cable Connection Wizard.

GUI   *Graphical user interface*. It represents the icons and other graphics elements that comprise the Windows XP interface.

hackers   Users who know advanced ways to interact and connect to networked computer systems. (Also see *crackers*.)

hardcopy   Another name for printed output.

header   The Inbox's one-line display that shows an incoming message's sender, subject, and date received.

Help and Support Center   An area within Windows XP that provides answers to common user questions and shows users how to perform routine Windows tasks. Also known as the *HSC*.

hibernate mode   A mode that utilizes the least amount of laptop power possible while still maintaining your current memory contents.

Home Networking Wizard   A Windows XP wizard that walks the user through a network's setup.

home page   A Web site's foundational page from which all other pages connect. Often, your browser's starting page will be the home page of a Web site such as Microsoft.

host   The computer that supplies the file and printer resources shared by guest computers in using the Direct Cable Connection.

hot links   See *links*.

hot spot   See *links*.

hotkey   The combination of an Alt keypress combined with another key that selects command buttons. The key you press with Alt is displayed with an underlined letter.

HSC   See *Help and Support Center*.

HTML   See *Hypertext Markup Language*.

hyperlink   See *links*.

Hypertext Markup Language   Also called *HTML*, the language behind all Web pages that formats the page to look and respond the way it does.

ICF   See *Internet Connection Firewall*.

icons   Small pictures that represent commands and programs in Windows XP.

IEEE 1394   See *FireWire*.

illustrated video   See *slideshow*.

image toolbar   A pop-up toolbar that appears when you point to a graphics image inside Internet Explorer.

import   The process of loading a file into an application when the file was not originally stored in the application's native, default format.

Inbox   The Outlook Express folder that holds your incoming e-mail messages.

incremental backup   A backup you make that only backs up the files that have changed since your previous backup. Also called *differential backup*.

infrared   Invisible light that works well for transmitting between digital devices, such as television remote controls and infrared peripherals.

installation routine   The steps needed to add programs to your PC so that they interact properly with the Windows XP environment.

instant messaging   See *MSN Messenger*.

Internet   A collection of networked computer systems that you can dial in to by using a modem; the Internet contains a limitless assortment of information.

Internet Connection Firewall   A simple Windows XP firewall system that helps protect users from unauthorized, outside access. Also known as *ICF*.

Internet Explorer   The Web-browsing software that Microsoft provides with Windows.

ISP   Stands for *Internet service provider*; the company that you use to connect to the Internet. Examples of ISPs include America Online, Earthlink, and MSN.

Java   A language that programmers use to create Web page applets.

legacy applications   Programs written for previous editions of Windows.

legacy hardware   Older hardware that was designed before engineers invented the plug-and-play specification.

links   Web page items with descriptions that you can click to display other Web pages. Often, a Web page will contain several links to other sites that contain related information. Also called *links*, *hot spots*, *hyperlinks*, and *hypertext links*.

logging on   The process that enables you to gain access to a networked computer. Also known as *signing on*.

maximize   The process of enlarging a window to the full size of the screen.

media   The types of storage on which you store and back up data. Examples of media are disk, tape, and paper.

memory recall   The Windows XP calculator's ability to recall a value from memory that you've stored there.

memory stick   A storage device for some kinds of digital cameras.

Messenger   See *MSN Messenger*.

Microsoft Network   The name of Microsoft's online Internet service.

Microsoft Outlook   A program that comes with Microsoft Office that keeps track of contacts, to-do lists, phone calls, messages, faxes, and your appointment calendar.

Microsoft Passport   An online repository of information that an Internet user can securely store on the Internet to enable quicker access to certain Web features.

minimize   The process of shrinking a window to its taskbar button without closing the window completely.

modem   A device that enables your computer to communicate with other computers over the telephone.

mouse cursor   See *mouse pointer*.

mouse pointer   The arrow cursor that moves on the screen when you move your mouse (also called the *mouse cursor*).

MP3   See *MPEG-3*.

MPEG-3   A common file format that compresses video and audio files to relatively small sizes. Most of today's online music is stored in the MPEG-3 format. Also known as *MP3*.

MSN   See *Microsoft Network*.

MSN Messenger   A program that enables users to send instant messages to each other from across Internet and network connections. Also known as *Messenger*.

multitasking   The process of a computer that is running more than one program at the same time.

My Computer   A window that enables you to see and manage your computer's devices.

narration   The voice that plays during a video clip.

net2phone   An Internet service that enables you to place calls to telephones.

network   One or more computers that share files or hardware resources by means of a cable or wireless connection.

Network Administrator   A person in charge of monitoring network usage and controlling access to the network.

network hub   A device that connects multiple computers together to form a network.

network interface card   An adapter card that you place inside a computer to connect that computer to a network. Also known as a *NIC*, pronounced "nick."

network server   The networked computer that supplies programs and data to other computers on the network.

newsgroups   Areas of the Internet, organized by topic, that contain files and messages you can read and send.

NIC   See *network interface card*.

notification area   The bottom-right side of the Windows taskbar where icons appear.

null modem cable   A cable that plugs into the serial port of two computers so the computers can share a direct cable connection.

offline format   A Web page stored on your disk that is viewable without an Internet connection.

offline printing   The process of printing to a disk file when no printer is attached to your PC.

online   The mode in which a printer is ready to print. Also refers to communicating with another computer or the Internet remotely.

opening a window   The process of starting a program in a window or double-clicking an icon to display a window.

option buttons   A Windows XP control that appears next to each item in a list that you use to select one item from the list.

orientation   The direction, horizontal or vertical, that a printer uses to print output on a page.

Outbox   The Outlook Express folder that holds your outgoing e-mail that has yet to be sent. After Outlook Express sends the message, the Sent Items folder holds a copy of the message.

Outlook Express   A Windows-integrated address book and e-mail system that handles e-mail messages and gives you access to Internet newsgroups.

Paint   The graphics drawing program that comes with Windows XP.

pathname   The disk and folder location of a file.

PC cards   See *PCMCIA Cards*.

PCMCIA Cards   Also called *PC cards*. Small credit card-sized I/O cards that add functionality, such as modems and memory, to laptops and to some desktops.

peer-to-peer network   A network system in which each computer can share files, programs, and resources—such as printers—with other computers on the network.

permissions   The determination of how much access to Windows XP's system that a user can access. A user might have file-reading permission, file-writing permission, or both.

Personal bar   An area at the left of some Internet Explorer screens that contains common Web pages and other online information the user prefers to see.

pixel   Stands for *picture element*. A pixel is the smallest addressable dot on your screen.

playlists   A grouping of songs, categorized by favorite artist or by type of music.

Plug and Play   The feature that detects and automatically configures the operating system to match new hardware that you install on your computer system.

point   A measurement of 1/72 of an inch (72 points equals one inch). Most computer onscreen and printed text measures from 9 to 12 points in size.

pop-up help   A help window that appears when you click the What's This button on a dialog box (a button that contains a question mark) and then click over a control inside the dialog box. Also known as *roving help*.

pop-up menu   A menu that appears when you right-click your mouse button. Also known as a *context-sensitive menu* because the menu's choices relate to whatever item on the screen you right-clicked over.

print queue   A combination of memory and disk space that temporarily holds printed output until the printing completes.

process   An active program or routine currently loaded into memory.

property sheet   A name given to an individual tabbed page inside a multi-page dialog box.

queue   See *print queue*.

Readme file   A file with last-minute changes, notes, tips, and warnings about the software you're about to install. Often a software vendor puts notes in the Readme file that didn't make it into the printed owner's manual.

reboot   The process of restarting your computer through the keyboard (by pressing Ctrl+Alt+Delete).

Recycle Bin   A location that holds files you delete from within Windows XP; as long as you do not delete the files from the Recycle Bin, you can restore the files to their original location.

registered   A file is registered when you've associated an application with that file's extension.

Registry   A central repository of all possible information for your hardware.

remote assistance   The ability of one user from a networked location or from across the Internet to temporarily take control of another's computer for help and support.

resolution   The number of dots per inch used to form a digital picture.

Rich Text Format   A common file format that retains special character formatting. Also known as *RTF* after the filename extension, .rtf, used for the format.

root directory   The top-level folder on a disk drive.

roving help   See *pop-up help*.

RTF   See *Rich Text Format*.

running total   The calculator maintains a constant display. For example, if the display contains the value 87 and you press the plus sign and then press 5, the calculator adds the 5 to the 87 and produces the sum of 92.

scalable   A font that can be printed in multiple sizes.

scientific calculator   A Windows calculator that supports trigonometric, scientific, and number-conversion operations.

scrap   A part of a data document you place on the Windows desktop.

screensaver   A program that waits in the background and executes only if you stop using your computer for a while. The screensaver either blanks your screen or displays moving text and graphics. Screen savers can help eliminate burn-in problems. Many computer users use screen savers to put fancy designs and pictures on their monitors when they are not using their computers.

ScreenTips   See *ToolTips*.

scrollbars   Windows XP controlling tools that enable you to view a window's contents more fully.

Search Companion   A comic character that helps you search for data.

search engine   A Web-based program that looks for Internet information for you.

Sent Items folder   The Outlook Express folder that holds all messages that you have sent over the Internet.

separator page   A page that contains text or graphics that prints between print jobs.

shortcut   A link (the shortcut) to a file item that takes the place of a copy and saves disk storage.

signature   An optional text message that follows the e-mail and newsgroup postings you send. Some users place their address and phone number in their e-mail signature so that they do not have to type the information each time they send e-mail.

signing on   See *logging on*.

site   The location of a Web page or set of related Web pages.

skin   A specific look, or theme, or Media Player.

slideshow   The showing of images, one at a time, with optional background music and narration, in Windows Movie Maker. Also known as *illustrated video*.

snapshot   A saved image of your computer's memory at one point in time.

sneakernet A slang term used to describe the transferring of files from one computer to another using a disk.

spooling The process of Windows controlling a printer's output.

standard calculator A Windows calculator that performs common mathematical operations.

Start button The button at the left of the taskbar that displays the Windows XP cascading menu of choices. When you click the Start button, the Windows XP Start menu appears.

Start menu A Windows XP system and program menu that appears when you click the taskbar's Start button.

status bar A message area at the bottom of a window that updates to show you what is happening at any given moment.

still image A single frame of a movie or a picture.

storyboard The laying out of scenes that help in the planning of a movie.

streaming The process of sending audio or video data to a media player as the player plays the clip, as opposed to the entire audio or video clip being sent before beginning to play.

synchronize The updating of a Web page with its contents currently appearing on the Internet.

T1 connection A high-speed constant Internet connection available to people who work in companies that install T1 lines.

Task Manager A program that enables you to stop programs that are currently running or that have stopped running but still consume memory. Also, you can use the Task Manager to view memory consumed by each currently running program.

taskbar The bar at the bottom of a Windows XP screen where running program icons appear along with the system clock.

taskbar properties menu The menu that appears when you click the right mouse button over an empty spot on the taskbar. You can control the performance and appearance of the taskbar and Windows XP through the taskbar properties menu.

text cursor See *cursor*.

themes A collection of colors and window elements found in the Control Panel that you can apply to your computer to make its appearance more to your liking.

thread   A set of postings that go together, such as a question and the answer replies.

thumbnail sketch   A small representation that shows the overall layout without showing much detail.

tiling   The effect of placing all open windows on the screen so that the body of each window appears next to, above, or below the other windows.

timeline   A row showing the length of video elements in a movie.

toolbar   A strip of buttons across a window that offers one-button access to common commands and tasks.

toolbox   Paint's collection of drawing, coloring, and painting tools.

ToolTips   Pop-up messages that describe buttons under the mouse cursor. Also known as *ScreenTips*.

transition   The way one clip or image changes to the next in a slideshow or video.

trim   The process of shortening a video clip.

TrueType   A Windows type of font that renders well in the Windows environment.

tunneling   The process of connecting to a networked or stand-alone computer from a remote location.

TWAIN   A format for digital cameras and scanners that makes the devices compatible with computers.

typeface   The look of a font; fonts with similar typefaces look similar to each other, such as Courier and Courier Modern.

uninstallation   The process of removing installed programs from the Windows XP environment.

URL   The address of an Internet Web site. URL is an acronym for *uniform resource locator*.

USB   A port you use to plug external devices into your computer. Also known as *Universal Serial Bus*.

utility program   A program that helps you interact with Windows XP more efficiently or effectively, as opposed to application programs that you run to do your work.

virus program   A program that destroys other files, often coming as an attachment to e-mail or embedded in software that you download from the Internet.

wallpaper   The background graphics that appear on the Windows XP desktop.

Web   A system for formatting Internet information into readable and manageable pages of text, graphics, video, and sound, short for *World Wide Web*.

wildcard character   A character that represents one or more characters in file and folder names.

Windows Clipboard   An area of memory that temporarily holds data you send to it until you replace the contents with other data or until you restart Windows XP.

Windows Movie Maker   The Windows application that enables you to edit and create movies.

Windows Media Player   The Windows application that plays audio and video clips.

Windows Update   A program that automatically checks your Windows system files against an online database to ensure that they match the latest release.

wizard   A step-by-step process that leads you through the execution of a Windows XP task. Many Windows XP programs, such as Microsoft Word for Windows, include specific wizards.

WordPad   The simple word processing program that comes with Windows XP.

WWW   World Wide Web. See *Web*.

APPENDIX C

Answers to Quizzes

Answers for Hour 1

Quiz Answers

1. The Windows desktop often mimics the way your own desktop might appear, with overlapping items with which you work.

2. True. Microsoft provides a Home edition and several Professional editions of Windows XP.

3. When you move your mouse, the mouse pointer (also called the mouse cursor) moves; but when you drag, you point to an object on the screen, click, and hold your mouse, and then move the mouse which, in turn, drags the object along with the mouse pointer.

4. The artwork on your desktop is called wallpaper.

5. A ScreenTip is a pop-up message box that appears when you right-click over something on your screen.

Answers for Hour 2

Quiz Answers

1. An administrator account has more access to files and system utilities than a guest account has.

2. You can lose some data.

3. When you close a window, it goes away completely from the desktop; when you minimize a window, the window disappears from the screen but the window contents, such as a program or a data window such as My Computer, remains open and ready for use.

4. False. The taskbar displays a button for each active window, minimized and maximized. Only when you close a window does its button go away.

5. A window menu contains commands from which you can select; a toolbar holds buttons you click to perform tasks.

Answers for Hour 3

Quiz Answers

1. The Auto Hide taskbar option keeps the taskbar out of site until you point to the edge of the screen that holds it.

2. The taskbar's Properties menu appears from which you can change the taskbar's look and actions.

3. Double-click the time on the taskbar or right-click the taskbar and select Adjust Date/Time to display the Date/Time Properties dialog box.

4. Tiling windows refers to the way you organize several open windows on your screen.

5. You can drag to increase the size of your taskbar or move your taskbar to a different location on your screen.

Answers for Hour 4

Quiz Answers

1. The My Computer window enables you to manage many hardware and software settings, as well as networking and dial-up networking options.

2. Depending on the window's contents, you might need to see the items differently. For example, you might want to see a detailed view to learn the date and time that you created a file, or you might prefer to use icons to locate types of files with which you want to work.

3. A shared folder's icon appears with a hand holding the folder.

4. The Control Panel contains a Mouse icon with which you can specify your mouse's behavior.

5. True. If the program's icon appears on your desktop, double-click the icon to start the program.

Answers for Hour 5

Quiz Answers

1. The thumbnail view shows not only the filenames and icons, but also a small version of the first page of the actual file contents for graphics and Web files.

2. False. Use Windows Explorer to manage disk elements.

3. The extensions show up in all of Windows file listings when you display the extensions in Windows Explorer.

4. Use your mouse to drag any Start menu item to a new location on the menu.

5. The shortcut's icon includes a small arrow that indicates the shortcut.

Answers for Hour 6

Quiz Answers

1. You can obtain online help from the HSC if you have an Internet connection.

2. You can move back and forth between topics, displayed as Web pages, inside the help system by clicking the Back and Next buttons.

3. You can send an invitation by e-mail, by MSN Messenger, or save the invitation for your remote user to retrieve later.

4. Display the help system and click Index to locate specific topics.

5. True. You can see the What's This help for an item that you right-click on to learn more about that item.

C

Answers for Hour 7

Quiz Answers

1. HTML files appear on the Internet.
2. False. Today's screens do not have the burn-in problems of older monitors.
3. Energy Star monitors the screen and helps you save money on electricity by turning off your screen after a period of non-use.
4. By protecting your screensaver with a password, you can leave your computer for a while. After the screensaver begins, your password is required to shut down the screensaver and use the computer.
5. Use the Appearance page of your Display window to change the colors of Windows items.

Answers for Hour 8

Quiz Answers

1. The Add/Remove Programs option helps you install and uninstall applications.
2. The application's installation routine usually begins automatically. If it does not, go to the Install/Uninstall tab and click Install to begin the process.
3. You can change the installed options of Windows from the Windows Setup page on the Add/Remove Programs dialog box.
4. You can use the Add/Remove Programs dialog box and select the uninstall option on the application's menu if such an option exists. You can also purchase uninstallation utility programs that help you uninstall some applications. Finally, you can manually delete files related to the program as a last resort.
5. Actually, you will want to uninstall Windows XP but only when you replace Windows XP with a new version of the operating system. Until then, you might want to change Windows XP options from the Windows Setup page of the Add/Remove programs dialog box.

Answers for Hour 9

Quiz Answers

1. Windows XP looks for data on your computer, on computers networked to yours, and on the Internet.

2. A wildcard character is a character that stands for zero, one, or more characters. The wildcard acts as a placeholder in searches.

3. The * can substitute for multiple characters in the search target but the ? can substitute only for single characters.

4. True. A common way to execute programs buried somewhere on your disk is to make Search locate the program on one of your PC's hard disks and then execute the program from the search window.

5. A search engine is an Internet-based program that locates information over the Internet. Each search engine has its own personality and traits. You might try two or three search engines for some searches looking for a particular piece of information.

Answers for Hour 10

Quiz Answers

1. The Windows XP calculator contains a standard and a scientific calculator.

2. WordPad offers more powerful text-editing features than Notepad but does not contain the same rich assortment of features you find in Word, such as an outliner or spell checker.

3. Pica is 1/6th of an inch. A pica is 12 points, and 72 points are an inch high.

4. The WordPad toolbar offers buttons with which you can center text. You can also use the Format, Paragraph menu.

5. Hold the Shift key while you draw a rectangle, and Paint will keep the four-sided figure a perfect square.

Answers for Hour 11

Quiz Answers

1. No central Internet computer exists; the Internet is the composition of all computers networked using Web protocols.

2. The URL is the uniform resource locator. It specifies the exact location of a Web page or series of Web pages that comprise a Web site.

3. The Internet service provider gives you access to the Internet.

4. Hypertext links, also called hyperlinks or just links, enable you to jump back and forth between Web pages.

5. Internet Explorer uses a similar search interface to Windows XP.

Answers for Hour 12

Quiz Answers

1. The Explorer bar can contain a media player, a search pane, a history of sites you've recently visited, your favorite site list, and folders you traverse.

2. True. When you click on an audio clip, Windows Media controls appear on the Explorer bar.

3. Microsoft Passport is a personal data-storage area on the Web. MSN Messenger is a real-time instant messaging system. Microsoft Hotmail.com is a free Internet-based e-mail service.

4. An emoticon is a combination of punctuation symbols that look like familiar symbols such as happy and sad faces.

5. It is more critical that you limit the world's side of the Internet to keep unauthorized users out of your system when you're connected.

Answers for Hour 13

Quiz Answers

1. A network is a group of locally wired computers that share files and printers. The Internet is a loosely connected set of computers worldwide that share files and access of a limited nature.

2. A wireless networking connection is by far the easiest to install.

3. The Ethernet connection provides the fastest speed of the typical network connections.

4. True. Windows XP's Internet Connection Sharing system makes sharing a single PC's Internet connection simple.

5. Tunneling refers to the access of your network or an online PC from a remote location.

Answers for Hour 14

Quiz Answers

1. False. You can set up multiple e-mail accounts in Outlook Express.

2. If you enter e-mail addresses into the Bcc field, Outlook Express sends a copy of the e-mail to everyone in the Bcc field, and the other recipients of your e-mail will not know about the copy sent to the Bcc entries.

3. Choose Insert, Attachment, or click the Attachment tool on the Outlook Express toolbar to send an attached file (or files) along with your e-mail.

4. Your incoming mail goes to the Inbox folder.

5. A newsgroup is a collection of recent messages sent by users interested in the newsgroup topic.

Answers for Hour 15

Quiz Answers

1. A legacy device is a pre–plug-and-play hardware device that you must install.

2. When you power-off your computer and install a plug-and-play device, your computer often recognizes that device and installs it automatically or with minimum intervention on your part.

3. You do not need to power-off your computer to install a USB device.

4. A PC or PCMCIA card is a wallet-sized circuit board that contains extra memory, a network card, a modem, a disk, or a combination of external devices.

5. The Direct Cable Connection feature operates with either a serial or parallel cable.

Answers for Hour 16

Quiz Answers

1. Windows sends all printed output to the printer subsystem's spool file before the output is actually printed.

2. Use the Add Printer Wizard to install printers unrecognized by Plug and Play.

3. Select the target printer from the Print dialog box.

4. True. Use the Print Queue to rearrange documents lined up to print.

5. TrueType fonts are considered to be the best Windows fonts.

Answers for Hour 17

Quiz Answers

1. The docking station enables the laptop user to utilize full-size peripherals, such as a monitor and keyboard.

2. Laptop users often update their systems with PC cards.

3. The My Briefcase application keeps your computer files in sync.

4. True. You can use either your floppy disks or a network connection to route files from a briefcase to their target disks.

5. False on both counts. Infrared signals are invisible and transmit only a few feet.

Answers for Hour 18

Quiz Answers

1. Assuming that you've turned on the automatic System Update option, Windows checks the Update Internet site every time you log onto the Internet, even if you are going to a completely different site. Windows Update checks in the background.

2. You can turn off the automatic update, but you should manually check for updates regularly. People who have slow modem connections to the Internet often prefer to look for the updates manually when they can devote the entire connection time to the update download instead of sharing the connection with another Internet process.

3. Use the File and Settings Transfer Wizard to transfer Windows XP settings from one computer to another.

4. True. The Files and Transfer Wizard eliminates the need for you to copy data files yourself from an old computer to a new one.

5. Run the System Information program to see your hardware and software details.

Answers for Hour 19

Quiz Answers

1. Disk Defragmenter collects fragments on your disk and gives you larger and contiguous chunks of free space, whereas Disk Cleanup removes files you no longer need.

2. False. Disk Defragmenter does not remove unwanted files.

3. False. Disk Cleanup does not defragment your drive.

4. When you regularly use Disk Defragmenter, your hard disk has fewer gaps between data within the same file. Your PC can read and write that file much faster because the PC doesn't have to skip the holes.

5. A full backup is a backup of your entire system. An incremental backup backs up only the files that have changed since the most recent backup.

Answers for Hour 20

Quiz Answers

1. The Task Manager can show you current memory and CPU usage.

2. If the Task Manager shows few memory resources are left as you run several common programs that you often run, you'll want to get more memory.

3. If a system error occurs, Dr. Watson can compare the current state of the computer to the snapshot's and help you determine problems that might arise.

4. The System Restore program enables you to restore your computer files to a previous state.

5. Dr. Watson makes suggestions about problem sources, whereas System Restore completely restores your system to a previous state.

Answers for Hour 21

Quiz Answers

1. Hold the Shift key while your CD drive door shuts and spins up.

2. The Windows Media Player gets its data from the Internet in most cases, although you can manually enter the information if you don't have Internet access or if you own a CD that doesn't happen to be found in the online database.

3. A skin is a theme that controls the look of the Windows Media Player.

4. A playlist is a list of tracks that you collect and name.

5. Use the Windows Media Player to play video clips.

C

Answers for Hour 22

Quiz Answers

1. Resolution refers to the number of dots that comprise images on your screen or printer.

2. TWAIN-compliant means that your scanner or digital camera meets industry compatibility standards.

3. True. Use the My Pictures slide show feature to see your pictures one at a time.

4. Use the Windows Explorer or My Pictures window to copy images to a writeable CD.

5. Use Internet Explorer's image toolbar when you want to copy graphics images from a Web page to your computer.

Answers for Hour 23

Quiz Answers

1. False. Movie Maker imports video clips from several different sources.

2. A frame is a single image that comprises a video.

3. High-quality videos consume more disk space than low-quality videos consume.

4. You trim clips in the storyboard area so the clips in the collections area remains unchanged.

5. You can more easily adjust frame and clip detail when you zoom into your storyboard.

INDEX

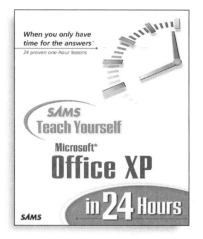